Architectural Knowledge

The Idea
of a
Profession

The Idea
of a
Profession

Architectural
Knowledge

Francis Duffy

with

Les Hutton

E & FN SPON
An Imprint of Routledge

London and New York

First published 1998
by E & FN Spon, an imprint of Routledge
11 New Fetter Lane, London EC4P 4EE

Simultaneously published in the USA and Canada
by Routledge
29 West 35th Street, New York, NY 10001

© 1998 Francis Duffy and Les Hutton

Typeset in 11/13 Sabon by Studio Hh

Printed in Great Britain by
TJ International Ltd, Padstow, Cornwall

British Library Cataloguing in Publication Data
A catalogue record for this book is available from the British Library

Library of Congress Cataloguing in Publication Data
has been applied for

ISBN 0 419 21000 8

Contents

Preface

To the social historian the record of the professions in the twentieth century has been one of continuous and indeed accelerating success. My own experience as president of the Royal Institute of British Architects for two years in the mid-1990s felt very different. From this particular perspective, whatever collective successes the architectural profession may or may not have achieved over the last few decades seemed totally unimportant to individual members. Why was this? Could it be because, as so many architects made a point of telling me, they felt bitter personal disappointment that the expectations stimulated by a long and arduous training had never been fulfilled? How can this contradiction be explained? Is the sense of individual failure and alleged collective success peculiar to architects? Are the criteria for individual and professional success inherently different? Is there, indeed, any relation between the two?

The difficulties so many individual architects face have made them demand that their professional institute should be doing much more for them – generating new work, advertising architectural services to an ever-widening public, making a compact with the government, neutralizing or, even better, annihilating the competition. Underlying this question are deeper and more general ones: what should a professional body be trying to do for its members? What is a profession actually for?

As we approach what promises to be a golden age of professionalism – an information-rich period in which access to specialized knowledge will be valued more highly than ever before – answers to these questions are critically important, and not just for architects. The papers in this collection were written hurriedly over three decades and to mark many occasions. Despite this scattered provenance, the contribution they make to this debate is oddly consistent. This is the argument, repeated and developed in many ways, that it is not so much the possession of knowledge that justifies the existence of the professions but rather the degree of success with which professionals have found better ways to develop their own particular kinds of knowledge. Professionalism flourishes to the extent that professionals work openly together in the context of action to augment and develop the bodies of knowledge peculiar to their own disciplines. Conversely, if professionals squirrel knowledge away for themselves or fail to share what they know, in order to gain some temporary and illusory advantage for themselves as individuals or as groups, then professionalism decays. Free access to knowledge, transparency in its application, sharing, developing and handing on knowledge in an open-ended way – these are the essential means of making professionalism work. It is these qualities, only fully comprehensible in the course of continuously having to exercise fine judgement in generally quite stressful circumstances, that keep professionals straight, intellectually as well as ethically. And for the architect – as I combatively argued in the pages of *Building Design* in 1992 – that knowledge is based on design and unites, in the context of action "past and future, science and art, demand and supply, decision making and reflection. Consequently the husbanding of that body of knowledge, its continual improvement, and its passing on through education to future generations are the essential functions of the architectural profession – our *raison d'etre,* our responsibility, our collective destiny."

The classical hallmarks of professionalism – restricted entry, standardized and visible qualifications, fixed fees, the publishing and policing of codes of conduct – are more concerned with keeping things as they are than with developing an intellectual programme. It is, unfortunately, still true that many, if not most, professionals continue to define professionalism defensively, in terms of "keeping standards up", usually through procedures that tend to promote exclusivity and encourage boundary maintenance. The consumers of professional services tend to see things in a reciprocal but very different way – and, certainly, without the same warm self-regard. Clients stand outside the professional barricades looking in. How they interpret professional behaviour and professional institutions is less as a struggle against the forces of evil than a conspiracy against the public interest.

BACKWARD GLANCE

The papers collected in the three parts of this book are a record of the growth of an idea about the nature of professionalism and also a record of major shifts in British society that fundamentally changed the position of the professions within that society. The realization of the development of knowledge as both the basis and guarantee of professionalism came to me gradually – which justifies, I hope, the perhaps over-emphasis on my own professional field in this selection of essays, and legitimizes the reprinting in part of three pieces previously collected in a 1992 work of mine, *The Changing Workplace*, looking at the impact of ideas on the design of the workplace. The gradual unfolding of this idea of professionalism is reflected both in the tripartite structure of this book and in the selection of entries – which, with a single exception, record my witness to events chronologically and contemporaneously: this is what I felt and saw at the time.

The first set of papers describe the development in the 1960s and 1970s of my own professional knowledge base: learning how to use office design for the benefit of international corporations and their employees. What is striking, in retrospect, is how quick those commercial corporations were to exploit for their own purposes research and programming methods, many which had been originally developed in the planned economy of the British Welfare State, where user research, brief writing, planning and design were, in theory at least, highly integrated for the benefit of all. This was the period in which I and my colleagues at DEGW were learning not only how to conduct design-based research in the context of practice but also, more importantly, discovering that research-based design was certain to become increasingly important to knowledge-based enterprises. The essays reflect a residual belief in the importance of design to a society based on centralized planning. For architects, this belief was not only ideological but financial, since at the beginning of the 1970s over half of the profession was employed directly or indirectly by government. Although at that time I was largely working for international corporate organizations, there is little of what I wrote that would not have been equally applicable had I been working for the state. Indeed, the underlying assumptions in DEGW's work were formed in that era of centralist planning: all architectural problems can be solved by better user research and better programming.

The essays in Part Two reflect the violent swing in the 1980s towards a totally different basis for government policy – that planning was unnecessary because market forces could always be relied upon, if not to pick up the pieces, at least to make sure that the fittest survived. While this new policy was fundamentally against the interests of all professions – no group should have a special place in society – architects were particularly vulnerable. Unlike doctors, they had not negotiated in the 1940s a politically unbreakable contract with the government. Unlike lawyers, they were not smart enough to make vast amounts of money both from victims and survivors of the new policy. Unlike accountants, they were not able to take advantage of the globalization of business. Instead, architects were numbered among the chief victims and did not have the collective wit to understand that many things they had idealistically taken for granted as the basis of their professional self-esteem were being washed away. The most successful architects in this period – and there was plenty of talent – began to rely increasingly on their own individual design skill rather than on collective action as members of a united profession. A handful of supremely talented, and spectacularly unclubbable, individuals became part of the growing star system. Others in the commercial sector were too busy to look over their shoulder until the mid-1980s property boom began to collapse in 1989, revealing the full weakness of their individual positions. Many, including the unhappy people I referred to earlier, simply could not understand why no one seemed willing to use their hard-won skills any more.

This group of papers shows a growing confidence in making generalizations on the practice of architecture based on the experience gained as DEGW developed, in the Thatcherite 1980s, into a large, specialized firm with a network of European offices. By this stage, DEGW's very particular and original attitude to the relationship between consulting and design had matured. We had wide experience of the changing nature of architectural practice in several countries. It did not seem likely to us that sophisticated clients would tolerate for much longer the individualistic, craft-based and unreflective kind of service that most of our fellow professionals at that time seemed increasingly content to deliver. Something altogether more imaginative, responsive and predictive was required.

The papers from the 1980s record what sometimes seemed at the time to be a deeply unfashionable position. It was obvious that the old regime of centralized planning would never return. The over-simplifications, even scientism, that had propped up the modern movement in architecture had been exposed. Nevertheless, it was clear to us in DEGW that architecture needed a more sophisticated intellectual basis, one that would not deny the importance of design invention – far from it – nor of cultural relativism but which would be robust enough to allow the majority of non-star architects to resist what was so clearly destroying their work: severe short-term pressure from under-informed clients to build ever more cheaply. Research about what design was for, and what value design could add, seemed to be the obvious answer. The course we in DEGW chose, as will be apparent from these papers, was to affirm the relation of design to user research, including user feedback, so that the benefits of design invention could be demonstrated to clients and users, in the hope of eventually allowing architects to regain the influence so many of them had lost on the processes of procuring and constructing buildings.

The final papers – Part Three, written in the 1990s – are very much the product of my presidential period at the RIBA. To come to terms with a scale of problem that I had not been able to comprehend before, I was driven to think not just about how architectural services could be reconstituted to meet the needs of the changing clients whom I had learned to understand but to explain in the most practical and fundamental terms how the whole range of professional architectural services could be justified throughout the whole of the society that had been irreversibly, if not totally, shaped by Margaret Thatcher's government. The task faced was no less than to help practising architects discover, define and overcome the limits of the efficacy of the market economy.

These papers develop the theme of design value but with two differences: because of my presidency, I now had the task of developing the argument about the centrality of architectural knowledge to comprehend the entire architectural profession and, more importantly perhaps, it turned out that I was doing so in a period that was beginning, by the end of my presidency, to show signs of becoming markedly more favourable to architecture. For the first time for decades, or so it seemed at the time, we architects, whenever we spoke with conviction about quality and adding value, were starting to get a more favourable response and even to attract allies. The high tide of Thatcherism was over. Environmental issues were attracting much more general attention. The international success of the best British architects was becoming much more apparent. Influential fellow professionals, such as the engineer Sir Alan Muir Wood, with whom I wrote a paper, had begun to speak of the "intelligent market", in which it was becoming possible to defend informed design decisions on the grounds of longer-term benefits transcending initially-higher capital costs. Sir Michael Latham, in his critically important report on increasing the productivity of the British construction industry, was quickly convinced not just of the importance of the role of architects in achieving higher design standards but also of the need for better briefing and better relations with ever more demanding clients.

A BELEAGUERED PROFESSION

The impact of free market politics was as evident to British architects in the early 1990s as the Welfare State had been all-pervasive in the careers of an earlier generation of architects in the 1950s. Competition was everywhere – to the extent that state-protected colleagues in the Architects' Council of Europe could not believe that architectural values could be sustained in such a hostile climate.

The political position of the Royal Institute of British Architects at the time that I became president in July 1993 was perhaps as bad as it had ever been. In addition to experiencing what seemed to be the co-ordinated public vilification of even the most talented architects' work, and the continuing bad effects of the longest and deepest recession for half a century, architects were suffering direct governmental attack on no less than three fronts. First, it seemed to be taken for granted by government that unfettered fee competition was always and everywhere in the public interest. Price preceded quality. Clients in the public sector especially were encouraged to believe that the only audit-proof way to procure professional services was on the basis of the lowest price. Sadly, many hard-pressed architects were prepared to respond to this pressure in a most unprofessional and, I might add, highly uncommercial manner by bidding too low in order to secure work at any price. A rapid deterioration in the quality of service was the immediate result. The second line of attack was on the architectural profession's traditionally long and therefore relatively expensive educational programme. Surely, reasoned the Government, to abbreviate the five-year course to four years would save 20 per cent of annual costs – an obvious good, easily justified by those who had no experience of the process and practicalities of design education.

The third assault was the most radical. The Government proposed to deregulate the architectural profession, stripping away the title of "architect" – British architects have never enjoyed protection of function – that had been protected by the first Architects' Registration Act of 1931. It was argued that to remove this distinction was self-evidently in the public interest, since there was nothing similar elsewhere in the construction industry and for architects to be singled out was unfair to their competitors.

The unfolding, the deflection and the ultimate defeat of these attacks forms the *mise-en-scène* of Part Three of this book. Despite this relatively successful outcome, however, the experience hurt. My excursion into the micro-politics of professional life taught me never to expect any government, any statutory instrument, any departmental financial arrangement to do the work that architects have to do for themselves. Surely, whatever tactical benefits may temporarily accrue, no profession can be ultimately defended by such Maginot-like devices. Architecture is too important to be left to the protection of instruments that are rigid and restrictive yet in time of crisis turn out to be flimsy, jettisonable and easily manipulated by those who are no friends of architects or architecture.

The only defence is attack: for architects to develop their own discipline faster and more perfectly than anyone else. Architects, under attack, used many tools to defend their profession. However, defensive arguments based on architects' self interest turned out, in the course of our struggle with government in 1993–5, to be far less effective than much tougher and more open-ended demonstrations of what architecture does, of what architecture means and of what changing architecture should continue to achieve and represent in a constantly-changing society.

TOWARDS A DEFINITION OF ARCHITECTURAL KNOWLEDGE

Westminster and Brussels can't be trusted to protect architectural values because they cannot be expected, on their own, to understand architecture even as it is today – let alone the directions in which it is developing. To address this issue, it seems to me to be absolutely necessary for architects to be very explicit themselves about the special features of their professional discipline. This means defining architectural knowledge in a way that is verifiable, open to scrutiny and sufficiently robust to distinguish it from other kinds of knowledge.

Architecture is a very practical and site-specific discipline and "knowledge" is not a word with which most architects instinctively feel very comfortable as a way of describing the essence of their discipline. Things have got to be done, decisions have to be made, brick has to be laid on brick. To architects generally, "knowledge" sounds as if it has more to do with books and libraries than with creativity at the drawing board, being good with clients or business-like precision at the project team meeting. Similarly, "research" is rarely given the same reverence by architects as in other professions. For an architect to be relegated to "research" is sometimes a code for failure as a designer, detailer or project manager.

There are historical reasons for this. The pedagogy of architecture had developed up to the end of the nineteenth century independently of the universities. Since then the five-year, design-dominated architectural course has never been assimilated fully into the university system but has co-existed – uncomfortably at times – with more conventionally-academic disciplines. Teaching people how to design – that is, helping young potential architects to decide what ought to be built, never with adequate information, to satisfy present and future users for an unspecifiable future, at a level of quality that is likely to be publicly debated for decades to come on practical grounds as well as in relation to subtle cultural issues – is very different from educating historians, mathematicians or sociologists. Moreover, to an unusual extent, the teaching of architecture touches many other disciplines – economics and history, information technology, mechanical, structural and industrial engineering, art, all the social sciences from psychology to anthropology, business studies as well as the science of materials – in a vast, sometimes superficial, sometimes profound, way, interconnecting everything in the service of design.

Architecture, in effect, is an inherently idea-hungry, project-based, solution-orientated discipline, open-ended and systemic, capable of connecting anything with anything, in any order, as long as new solutions can be formulated for as yet hardly-articulated requirements, both practical and cultural. In all these respects, architecture resembles the new information-based disciplines of Silicon Valley and the media industry of Los Angeles and New York more than it does traditional academic subjects.

In what we expect to be an increasingly knowledge-based society, it is probable that the open-ended and problem-solving characteristics of architecture will increasingly be seen as normal rather than eccentric, an advantage rather than a cause for apology, while the intellectual limitations of conventional, tightly-bounded, introverted disciplines will become more apparent. But in order to take advantage of this entrancing perspective, not only individual architects but the entire architectural profession will have to overcome the habit of aversion to intellectual matters, described above, that has been encouraged in architecture by the combination of the stubborn persistence of the anti-intellectual materialism of the arts and crafts tradition and the inferiority complex engendered by proximity, in British universities at least, to what may be obsolescent models of academic structure and funding. There is, to summarize, an urgent need for architects to reaffirm the intellectual basis of their profession, to align it with other rapidly-developing disciplines to make sure that the design of the built environment takes its proper place in a society based increasingly upon the development and transmission of all kinds of knowledge.

THE PRACTICAL IMPLICATIONS OF ARCHITECTURAL KNOWLEDGE

Architectural knowledge is concerned with buildings, the ways they are made and the people who inhabit them. Architectural knowledge has two special characteristics. The first is that it is unusually combinatory and complex – linking understanding of user requirements with the capacity of buildings to accommodate those requirements: linking, because of the vast extent and longevity of the existing building stock, what has been done well in the past with predictions of what ought to be done better in the future; linking practicality with artistic judgement; linking many disparate elements because buildings are such large, complex and value-laden objects.

The second characteristic is that architectural knowledge is unusually concerned with the deontic rather than the descriptive – things as they ought to be, rather than things as they are. The primacy of judgement that consequently forms such a large part of architectural knowledge does not mean that the observation, quantification and systematic measurement that are so important in engineering have no place in architecture. Not at all: absolute measurement ought indeed to be given much more importance by architects than it is – but it is liable to have to take second place to over-riding, relative and qualitative considerations such as taste, originality, fitting in, striking out, achieving the appropriate sense of place, saying what has to be said, echoing historical precedents, expressing the appropriate cultural message. For today, what is vital is that architectural judgements are not seen as autonomous: they only make sense within a common architectural culture, the development of which depends upon two kinds of ongoing discourse – between architects themselves and between architects and their audience: the people who inhabit buildings and enjoy the spaces between them.

The conditions that favour the development of both levels of discourse are, of course, exactly the same conditions that are needed for the development of architectural knowledge.

Here we have the real basis for justifying professionalism in architecture and, indeed, for the existence of a professional institute such as the RIBA – not exclusivism to promote narrow self interest, nor a statutory registration to ensure a minimum level of public accountability, but voluntary membership of an open, independent, self-questioning, intellectual and artistic body, capable of conducting a continuous discourse between architects themselves and their public, committed to building up and sharing knowledge about what has been and what ought to be done, dedicated to developing the highest possible standards of architectural performance. I am speaking about nothing new. Nor am I dreaming up a fantasy constitution for an idealized RIBA – the Institute certainly had in my presidency as many faults as virtues. I am talking only about what the Institute's eloquent charter of 1837 insists are practical objectives.

> ...forming an Institution for the general advancement of Civil Architecture, and for promoting and facilitating the acquirement of the knowledge of the various arts and sciences connected therewith; it being an art esteemed and encouraged in all enlightened nations, as tending greatly to promote the domestic convenience of citizens, and the public improvement and embellishment of towns and cities
>
> (RIBA Charter 1837)

The aim is the most rapid development possible of architectural culture through sharing knowledge for the common good by means of an ongoing discourse, involving both architects and their clients. In achieving this the universities have a vital part to play; clients and users are, of course, essential; intelligent critics are a marvellous stimulus; research institutes invaluable. However, what matters most – and is hardest to achieve – is access to practice, to the context of action, because only here are to be found the data, the challenge and the achievement that are the matter of the discourse. It is possible that a better means may be found of developing architectural excellence. Certainly RIBA members have not always lived up to the nobility of their charter. However, it is the continuing potential of direct access to the accumulating experience of practice, together with the benefit of informed criticism, that makes practice-based bodies like the RIBA so hard to replace. With the ability to harness much greater amounts of data to more effect through the shared networks of information technology, that potential is rapidly increasing rather than diminishing.

It remains to be seen whether architects will succeed in reforming their professional structures fast enough to take advantage of this shift in opinion, only made possible by huge advances in information technology. They will have to overhaul their educational programmes, including CPD for architects in practice. They will have to rethink their research practices, especially user feedback and client focus groups. They will have to develop new forms of practice, interdisciplinary working with other professionals in the construction industry, taking the initiative in making the construction industry more productive. However, whatever the outcome, it may be that we have succeeded in doing something rather wider in its implications for the next century. By virtue of being a relatively weak profession forced to think very hard in a time of crisis about our very survival, we may just have been able to do what other, more protected and economically more favoured professions have not done so far – articulate the fundamental justification not so much for any special status for the professions but for their continuing existence in modern society. This is nothing less than the capacity to develop specialized, judgemental and action-based knowledge better and faster than any feasible alternative.

Come to think of it, that is not so much a justification as a measure and a test of all professions.

Francis Duffy

Part I   1945 – 1979

THE

DISCIPLINE

OF

ARCHITECTURE

Simon Head

In a world more planned than ever before, architects understandably sought to exploit the security – shoring up their banks of knowledge as well as building empires based on the possession of that knowledge. The fact of planning led to the need for data and the obligation, moral and practical, to undertake research. In the built environment there was a great deal of information about the aesthetics and procurement of structures, woefully little about the uses to which structures were put, and almost none about the key use of the second half of the twentieth century – the organizational use of space: the office. If design was the specific type of architectural knowledge, this was the contemporary form.

Ideology and Methodology in a Planned Economy

The key societal shift in the Britain of the three decades after the Second World War was the reluctant shedding of a collectivism that had seemed not only necessary but in the wake of Europe-wide depredation a moral obligation. There were, of course, dissenters. But while Von Hayek and the Mont Pelerinites waited in the wings for their apotheosis, the Platonic guardians of communitarianism held sway. This centralized planned economics was tolerated as the price of survival and renaissance at the same time as a largely unexamined assumption of individual self-determination thrived – the reward for the same survival. From the start, architects were caught up in the web of paradox created by this period of liberal and at times libertarian collectivism.

The post-war period began with Britain in dire need and with few resources – impoverished by the war effort and to a certain extent vitiated culturally. There was, however, great political will for the social and physical regeneration of the state. Planning was in the air everyone breathed. In 1944 the Butler Education Act guaranteed secondary education for all. The Beveridge Report proposed an extensive programme of social benefits. After the Blitz of 1940 had devastated the City of London, the docks and the East End, Abercrombie had proposed a plan for reconstruction of London, that among other recommendations suggested the idea of new towns. In 1945 the Labour landslide provided the mandate to carry out this programme of popular social engineering and the 1946 New Towns Acts and the 1947 Town and Country Planning Act provided the machinery.

Such large-scale social planning demanded public architecture and got it. There was a rise in numbers of public service architects (Alex Gordon, Hugh Wilson, Richard Llewelyn-Davies, Henry Swain, Bernard Adams) and an era of public office presidents of the RIBA (William Holford, Robert Matthew, Donald Gibson, Lionel Brett), drawn from the LCC, the Ministry of Education and the Ministry of Town and Country Planning.

Architects matured and strengthened in this era of overt need, optimism and control. Architecture is an applied art, and after the war it was fittingly applied to the tasks of reconstruction and revitalization: rebuilding houses and the industrial base that had been destroyed or redeployed by the war effort; building the ten new towns modelled on Letchworth Garden City; and building the new schools to accommodate the children of the Butler Act: 2500 schools within a decade. On the other hand, architecture *is* an art. The public works made architects highly visible, highly accountable – but not responsible: they were in danger of being seen as tools of the state. The answers were already known: all architects had to do was to provide the means – a debased form of craft and inimical to art. The result was a monolithic and at times almost moribund profession made up of thousands of state employees – people educated as designers and then employed, ultimately, as decorators.

Those architects who were aware of their untenable position evolved a number of stratagems to resolve this dilemma. The most popular was solecism: I am an architect, therefore what I do is architecture. The next was the smug medical imperative: what I am doing is so self-evidently useful that I won't brook any criticism of how or why I am doing it. I really must go – I have children to house. Stylistic schisms were a useful evasion: neo-Georgian, contemporary, people's detailing, decayed modernism, humanized modernism, new humanism, brutalism, indeterminate plan, clip-on and non-plan.

Some of these evasions were laudable and some were contemptible but all skirted the issue, which was intractable as long as the central paradox in political life remained unresolved: a liberal Welfare State was a contradiction in terms, a humane dishonesty. Architecture was at the heart of this inconsistency. So was a very incomplete attitude to the whole notion of planning. A series of reports addressed the issue of architecture's place in the social fabric and specifically the profession's concern as to what it was educating its members to be. In 1939 the RIBA set up a special committee on architectural education. This reported in 1946 and came out firmly against social or economic research. After the 1952 Ad Hoc Report, the 1955 MacMorran Report advised the profession to close the gap between education and practice and to extend the debate on pupillage. The 1958 Oxford Conference marked the shift from an aesthetic to a scientific basis for architectural education (a consolidation of this drift, not a revolution) and in 1962 two documents commissioned by the RIBA were published: *The Architect and his Office* and Elizabeth Layton's *Report on the Practical Training of Architects*. Both marked a shift towards the managerial. Layton advocated a two-year practical training, in line with the MacMorran recommendations, and concentrated on the need for building experience and management training. *The Architect and his Office* asked, direct, "How can the efficiency of the architect be raised through better management of the office and the job?" and foresaw the rise of the "architechnologist" – a term that didn't catch on. "Architectural education should be diversified in order to bring technical design skills back into the profession. Architects who choose to specialize in the application of these skills ("architechnologists") should not be debarred from membership of the RIBA."

None of these tactical and procedural reports, of course, could resolve that fundamental and strategic paradox: they were attempting to unravel something that was knotted at both ends. Until the brutally unimaginative, over-achieving Thatcherites had slashed free at least one end of the tangle, architects, like everyone else, could only pretend to plait and replait the material of their craft, interpret the meaning of their art, between two fixed points. An illusion, if convincingly performed. A delusion, if believed by the performer.

For much of those three decades, architectural performance was delusional: in a key area of economic activity it presumed a knowledge base that simply didn't exist, and relied on collective self-interest or self-deluding ignorance – neither of them flattering to notions of professionalism – to disguise what was in effect a sleight of hand. Maintaining the illusion in the eye of the beholder (or shareholder), it began to believe its own publicity.

While the ideological storm raged – or, more conspicuously in the first part of this period, failed to rage – one methodological deficit essential to planning was quietly being made good in several quite disparate corners of architecture. People can go to hell their own way in a market economy. A planned economy – a planned anything – requires structure. This is what architecture should have been concerning itself with in this contentious period and what a few, a very few architects were concerned with – research: an intellectual framework to stand fast against whatever was brewing up on the political surface.

Andrew Saint in *Towards a Social Architecture* charts the way in which the natural distaste in Britain for a planned society was overcome in the 1930s by economic depression and the concomitant unavoidability of the need to plan for the distribution of resources – supercharged by the lowering prospect of war and the need to plan the country into the same league as Germany, even at the cost of using the unpalatable means of Soviet social coercion to do it. He documents the connection between the Architectural Association and the Mass Observation study, the link from the Modern Architecture Research

Group (MARS) into the Building Research Station (BRS – later the BRE). By the outbreak of war, in the provision of public buildings a clear line of development can be traced from the morality of planning to the ethical need for research – and after the war, boosted by organization methods such as operational research, despised "official" architects proudly rebadged themselves as public sector architects, to win the peace.

This line of organizational rigour initially quite bypassed the private sector – the commercial world of office buildings in which, post-war, most people were to work and have their being. The promiscuous technology came through, its progress uneven but across a wide front: the failure of the heavyweight panel system, the success of the school building lightweight system, CLASP, the take-up of the construction, engineering and servicing innovations that made possible, or inevitable, the new generation of corporate HQs from the Lever House and the Seagram building to, decades later, Bruce Graham's Hancock building, courtesy of Fazlur Khan. The technology crossed over – but not the sociology, the occasionally flaky sociology of the planning era that permitted a concentration of intellectual and research effort in the public sector and denied it to the private sector.

Why did the sociology fail to make the transition? After all, these were expensive buildings, essential to the country's economic well-being, and they housed an increasingly sophisticated workforce. Were the clients – the procurers of these workplaces for the second half of the twentieth century – less sophisticated than their employees, the eventual users? Or than their municipal equivalents?

It could be that they retained such a paternalistic control over their employees – or the illusion of such control – that they saw the iterative process, the slow, dragging, accountable grind of democratic public institutions, as irrelevant to their simpler, plain man's world of commerce. They organized for their work, their workers – not for types of work, categories of worker. The quality of the workspace would depend on their ability to brief; how deep was the pocket, how wide the imagination, how high the aspiration: not on taxonomies of use.

Or it could be that until there was a healthy tradition of speculative commercial office building – effectively, forward trading in property – there was no market in such information: there was no premium attached to getting it right, no penalty for getting it wrong.

Or perhaps it was simply that the best architects went into the public sector and with them the bulk of the intellectual curiosity about how people related to the built environment: architecture has never been a unitary discipline.

But it was a time of unexamined righteousness in many small and large ways. Offices and organizations were far country for architects still hypnotized by the idea that public was good and private was bad (and yet for whom dystopias were public, fantasies of achievement were private). There was no synthesis of design input and organizational output and, because of the low criticality of design, no one much noticed. If it ain't broke, don't fix it.

But it was broke. And the need to fix it had roots, just like public works, in social usefulness. The office was becoming a vital focus for post-war economic resurgence – particularly the office as part of the infrastructure of large-scale international and multinational business: the organization. Most people work in offices. Most people work in organizations. Why should the relationship between the design of one and the theory of the other be permitted to be a mystery? Slowly, the profession began to make amends for the guesswork that had kept it penned, ineffectual, in its Beaux-Arts ghetto, or had trapped it, data-free, in an outmoded Modernism. Its success in making good this omission, in shucking the cynicism of self-interest, can be seen as the beginning of the latest and in many ways the most honourable stage of development of an activity that in dealing with harder realities and more intractable contingencies than other professions can claim, through intellectual discipline and rigorous commercial practice, to test the value of professionalism as a mechanism for providing society with certain key services. This is not to say that architects live in the real world while other professionals don't. But the forensic subtlety of a response to a change in sentencing policy, say – though it may be subject to intense peer and journalistic scrutiny – while it may have either the hole-in-the-ground immediacy of construction or the long-term horse-trading of a real estate deal, does not have both: concrete and abstract, process and product. Nor does it have its beginnings in research, typology, methodology and its end scarring the physical face of the city and the lives of its citizens in ways that expose and test the quality of its beginnings.

Les Hutton

1 Architects and the Social Sciences (1968)

Why should architects concern themselves with social conditions in office buildings? This is not a question to be taken lightly. Immediately it lands us in the thick of one of today's most bitterly-fought arguments about design. On the one hand are ranged the architects – good, honest, bluff fellows who motivate themselves by believing that their buildings are making people do more or live better, happier lives. They believe that buildings determine people's behaviour – so if, for example, you design housing on the neighbourhood unit basis, people will become more neighbourly. Every now and then these "architectural determinists", as Broady calls them, find some support among social scientists, but on the whole empiricism is not so important to them as the feeling that they are somehow doing good.

Facing and attacking them are those few social scientists who are sufficiently interested to admit that buildings may influence behaviour but who really regard buildings as something independent of human activity – like music to a film, parallel but not a shaping force. And these social scientists are undoubtedly considerably more in touch with the data.

Which side are you on? This decision, I believe is crucial. If you are an architectural determinist, your attitude to social conditions in office buildings – depending on your viewpoint – must become cheerfully paternalistic at best, or grimly exploitative for the sake of higher productivity at worst. If you adopt the second attitude and regard buildings as neutral in relation to behaviour, then there is no point in troubling yourself further with these worries. Architects are wasting their time if they study social conditions in buildings.

The history of this argument is very interesting and its significance extends well beyond architecture. Architectural determinism or more widely environmental determinism is an old idea, dating back to the work of geographers before World War I. Some industrialists assumed that environmental conditions could increase or decrease an employee's output, just as earlier, pure water and good drainage had been proved to lower the death rate in cities. The famous Hawthorne studies in the 1930s were the first thorough test of this hypothesis. Of course, these studies revealed that there were other factors influencing employees' productivity besides levels of amenity. Raising light levels increased productivity but so also did lowering light levels to a point at which the workers could hardly see their work. The notorious "Hawthorne Effect" had been discovered – the workers' interest in their work was stimulated by the compliment of being observed. After these studies it was no longer possible to conduct environmental research which dealt only with overt stimuli and responses. The consequences were enormous. In industry there was a swing away from human engineering to human relations; among social scientists there was a rapid decline of interest in environmental variables; architects became even more cut off from the stimulus of good empirical work in their own field. The question of the effect of the environment on man was not closed but hidden, swamped, under hundreds of new preoccupations. We are still suffering from the Hawthorne trauma and it is only in recent years that a handful of sociologists, social psychologists and psychologists have begun to interest themselves again in the environment of buildings. What work will they do and what use will it be?

This is why it is crucial today for architects to decide what their attitude is to the social and behavioural sciences. Does behaviour determine design or not; if it does, how far does it shape design? My own answer is direct and all-encompassing. I recommend it as a model for busy architects and inquiring social scientists.

Buildings provide a framework for behaviour. They exist only to allow people to do what they want to do. Often they fail in this task and get in the way of what people want. Signs of this can easily be found in offices – doors left open permanently, departments not able to share the same part of the office floor, nowhere to pin notices or pictures: small stray examples which show that the building is in one way or another failing to give people's wishes and tendencies free play. Other more underground effects of the failure of an office building may be expressed not by abuse of the building but by indices of unpunctuality or absenteeism, deeper symptoms of unhappiness.

I suggest that rather than neglecting the relation between buildings, organization and behaviour, or attempting to use buildings to exploit behaviour patterns, it is sanest to try to design buildings and organizations which permit all possible behaviours to coexist without coming into conflict. I do not mean coexist in a compromised way, however, but real coexistence in their entirety, of apparently conflicting sets of tendencies such as the management's wish to get so much work done and the worker's wish to be able to feel at home in the office.

Perhaps this is an impossible ideal; certainly it is a strong hypothesis. I look forward to refutation. Until that comes, however, I am going to use it as the foundation of my argument. This is the only way I can see of accepting the promise of data from the behavioural sciences, without having to take sides in regulating its use.

JOB, WORKER, BUILDING

My model contains three sets of variables: those which are about the organization of work; those that concern the way people behave at work, and those to do with the physical disposition of the office environment – in short, job, worker and building.

My argument is that given a certain job, say that of a lawyer, there can be isolated a basic organization of work, which together with the predictable behavioural patterns of lawyers, clients and assistants, will lead to typical locations, plans and furnishings for a lawyer's office. Obviously such basic arrangements may be modified or transposed depending on personal whims, and on what resources are available. Nevertheless, they remain basically the same, until, as time passes, organization is improved or customs and behaviour are modified.

Such a model provides a sound basis for architects to design offices because it is based entirely upon real evidence about jobs and workers. It provides the motive for architects to demand useful and appropriate applied research from the organizations and behavioural sciences. Because architects will be accustomed to seek generalities as well as to find peculiar local features, they will appreciate the value of scientific data. The behavioural scientist will understand why the architect wants his research and what relation behaviour has to organization and buildings. The same will be true of the student of organizations.

A change in one of these sets of variables is likely to have repercussions in the others. My preoccupation is to discover what these relations are and how they work, and my aspiration is to design a set of generic building relationships or patterns that may be elicited by appropriate combinations of organizational and behavioural variables. I recognize that essential relationships are likely to be transformed but not destroyed by local circumstances, different resources or individual preferences. It is worth pointing out that this kind of investigation of complex relations is made possible by the techniques of operations research, which allow us for the first time to discover and plot "systems connections" between fields that were previously thought to be, to all intents and purposes, divorced. For example, industrial engineering and social psychology were once quite separate fields and the practitioners in the former tended to know all about machines and nothing about people, and vice versa in the latter case. The "socio-technical" approach embraces both fields and relates them by the same systems language. What I am doing is extending one kind of socio-technical system to include another set of phenomena, making it a socio-technical-environmental system for offices.

Before I go on, I should mention what I mean by "office". I do not mean only prestige office buildings housing large corporations. I mean all places where professional, administrative, recording, accounting activities are carried out, whether in factories, surgeries, shop windows or prestige blocks – any place in which the people who used to be called white-collar workers work. I realize that automation is making some office tasks very like factory work, but since I think a workable distinction between the two can still be made, and since I don't want to be drawn into factory design, this problem will be left alone.

GENERIC RELATIONSHIPS OR "PATTERNS"

The idea in design of generic relationships or "patterns" has been taken furthest by Christopher Alexander at the Center for Environmental Structure in Berkeley. The work that is described in this paper has been carried out under his guidance and reflects his ideas.

A pattern is a building block, or an atom of design. It is the smallest isolable relationship between physical objects which resolves a conflict between the desires or tendencies of the people who inhabit and use the built environment. A door is a version of a pattern. One person wants enclosure, another wants access – a hinged or sliding piece of wall is the answer. This is a very simple-minded example but it serves to show how a pattern is a complete resolution, not merely a compromise based on weighted values – and it demonstrates the generic nature of the solution. Doors can be all shapes and sizes, made of many different materials, but underneath all this bewildering variety is still the essential pattern idea of an operable barrier. Most important, the essential idea of an opening is based on fact, because it can be shown empirically that people do want enclosure in certain circumstances, and that they do want access, and above all that the door does in fact satisfy these real tendencies.

The relevance of patterns to the job/worker/building model should now become clear. The model is an overview of all the relations between organization, behaviour and building form that come together to make the office building. It is a kind of aerial photograph of an important area of architectural concern. The patterns are the elements that fit together to make this photograph. They are the way that each isolable relationship is made possible in physical terms. Patterns are building blocks, resolved problems, great and small, that may be fitted together in an infinite variety of ways, to build the design of an office floor or an office building.

So the argument using the model runs thus: if an architect addresses the organization of, say, a lawyer's office, then certain kinds of behaviour may be predicted and such and such a physical form is appropriate. Such an argument is nothing less than a grouping together of the appropriate cluster or galaxy of patterns.

Such patterns may be stored and retrieved mechanically, given the appropriate cues. Not the least advantage of such a system is that it is far more sensitive to design problems at all levels than any alternative method, and yet it avoids the designer's drudgery of labouring through every design problem from the very beginning.

THE PRESENT STATE OF OFFICE DESIGN

Of all the areas of architectural practice, office design is probably the most poverty stricken in ideas, in innovation, in sensitivity to human needs, in allowance for organizational structures. Schools, hospitals and housing have far more social and organizational thought put into them. I have never understood how good architects, who do not hesitate to discover the minutiae of an individual client's taste for a house, switch off 90 per cent of their normal inquisitive conscience when it comes to the design of office buildings, concentrating on one or two dominant concerns such as structure, and proportion of "rentable" office space. Now, I am prepared to answer attacks on the pattern-language on the grounds that it concentrates too much on the generic and is liable to be unable to cope with whatever is peculiar and local. However, my defence is easy compared to the case that conventional office architects would have to prepare, if the same charge were brought against them. How well do they meet the client's needs? How many types of office building are there? Look at a set of student schemes, or at a book like Joedicke's *Office Buildings,* and you will see the whole conventional range of types – single-banked, double-banked, central core, open layout, air-conditioned or not. There is hardly a word about how to decide when each type is appropriate, hardly a word about the dreary business of what goes on inside.

It's amazing that the client ever gets people to enter such buildings.

Perhaps the problem is easy. I don't think it is, and, in fact, it is generally a coalition of office managers, sensible but unimaginative as they often are, and interior designers, who feel too lowly to emulate the architect's bland unconcern with client needs, which succeeds in making these buildings habitable. This might not be such a bad situation if the over-all decisions made by the architect were sensible, but often they are the opposite – wasteful, inhibiting and inflexible. No wonder people are always telling you how inconvenient their office space is. There is some excuse, of course. Architects often design their buildings for real-estate people, developers who don't know who their tenants are going to be and who want to attract as wide a range of likely tenants as possible. This is not a position that encourages detailed study of client needs. But this can't be the whole answer, for the same simplistic designs recur even in buildings designed directly for the client.

In Germany some interesting innovations have recently improved this dark situation. You have probably heard of bürolandschaft, or, in English, office landscaping, the big open floors where apparently random arrays of desks are screened or partially screened from one another by little portable partitions and tubs of plants. Often office landscaping is dismissed as another version of the hated bullpen, only dressed up a little to make it more palatable. In fact, office landscaping is very much more than that, and deserves very serious attention, particularly in America, because the underlying ideas of management theory that the Organisationsteam Schnelle have the credit of putting into practice were developed here many decades ago. They are using your ideas.

Office landscaping is based first upon a very thorough study of communications in the office; the net of communications is charted and optimized. Secondly, it is based on the concept of an organization as a series of interrelated and interacting groups, quite the opposite of the old hierarchical structure of the organization chart. Thirdly, and only thirdly, after the previous principles had been firmly established, was it decided that the large open floor with portable screens and desks provided the most controllable and flexible milieu for such an organizational structure. The Schnelles are, after all, management consultants, not architects, and it is their organizational flair, their background in management theory and operations research (together with a lot of imagination), that led them willy-nilly to the "architectural" notion of office landscaping. And, of course, it is this very organizational competence that architects are blind to when they grumble about this new idea which irritates them so much.

My criticism is on different grounds. The Schnelles are strong in organization theory and practice (organizational variables) but relatively weak in the study of behaviour (behavioural variables). I must be careful about what I say here because they have introduced some important social improvements into offices, for example, the coffee areas with armchairs to which employees are free to go at any time. However, these improvements tend to be closely related to organizational goals of getting the most out of the worker. Moreover, their assertions about behavioural factors, such as the effect of not having a view, or even of being free to have a rest and a cup of coffee when you feel like it, or of being visible to your boss, tend to be optimistic and not very well supported by solid data. We just don't know the answers to these questions yet. Moreover I suspect also that they may be guilty of playing down the differences between different kinds of organizations, but this may be simply because they have always been consultants to rather similar firms. It would be interesting to see, for example, what they would recommend for outfits as different as a bank or a lawyer's office.

Nevertheless the Schnelle approach is incomparably superior to any rival I have yet come across. I hope that the early experiments with office landscaping in the US will raise many questions about the relations between job, worker and building and will perhaps hasten the empirical studies that I should like to see made.

TESTS TO EVALUATE STUDIES

In the same way as I criticize office landscaping because it fails to take into account behavioural variables, I find it necessary to take issue with a great many of the empirical studies of the office worker because they frequently fail to cope adequately with organizational factors. Frequently one is allowed to think that office work is a shapeless, characterless phenomenon which need not be discussed. The major point that I am making in this paper is that it is meaningless to discuss job and office building without considering the job. This awareness of interacting relationships is so important to me that I have established the trident test as a measure of the validity of empirical studies of the office. Quite simply the three-pronged test demands that all three sets of variables – organizational, behavioural and physical – are accounted for in any experiment. Of course, one set of variables may be held steady – a legitimate and useful scientific device – but "held steady" naturally does not mean "forgotten about" as I am afraid, is often the case. In my review of office experiments I have wielded the trident test rigorously to rake through various entangled relationships.

Another test that I apply is the utility test. My aim is again very simple: I want to ensure that experiments are useful to a designer, that they tell him directly how to improve the design of offices. Perhaps to the social scientist my stress on utility may seem overstated but to me, an architect, starved of hard data all my student and working life, it is a matter of vital necessity. In effect, work in which the building form variable is kept steady is, in consequence, rarely interesting, unless of course a deliberate attempt is being made to chart how wide a range of organizational and behavioural variables the same building form can accommodate.

STUDIES OF JOB, WORKERS AND BUILDINGS

I shall attempt to survey the present state of empirical studies of office work, workers and buildings.

Do buildings matter? is the first question to ask. Unfortunately it is difficult to give a straight answer to this question, although two recent studies have attempted to provide one.

The first is by Dr Langdon (Langdon 1966a) of the British Building Research Station (BRS). Langdon's work is based on a survey of user attitudes to postwar office buildings in central London. When 9300 office workers were asked how important a "comfortable office" was to them compared with such other factors as "responsibility" and "good pay," they gave the answer which one half-expects – not very. On the other hand, they did not judge a "comfortable office" as the least important part of their work experience.

The second survey of this kind, which by contrast is rather thin and unmethodical, is an American study by J. T. Fucigna (Fucigna 1967) and is a before and after study of the effect of some new and well-considered furniture on the work-habits of three consultants. Very little difference was found in the amount of time these people spent at various office activities – reading, writing, phoning – during the two months that were being compared.

I don't think we have enough evidence yet to make up our minds on this question. Fucigna's study – although interesting because he is one of the few people who have studied "executive" habits in detail – suffers from too small a sample, and inadequate indices of productivity. In Langdon's case we encounter the fundamental difficulty that asking people what is important to them does not necessarily bring out the real issues. Noise happened to be a nuisance and was mentioned a lot; comfort was presumably adequate and was therefore paradoxically underrated. Had Langdon chosen the sample of offices that Robinson surveyed in his investigation of the office stock in the City of London – many of which are very old and run-down – perhaps the user reactions might have been quite different.

THE USER AND BUILDING FORM

One cannot fail to be impressed, however, by the body of user-satisfaction data that Langdon has collected in the second part of his study. His sample was enormous; the range of buildings studied, though new, was very wide. Reactions were noted to daylight, artificial light, internal wells, internal acoustics, external noise, heating, ventilation, security and space provision. Users were subdivided by age, sex and grade. Overheating in summer, poor ventilation and external traffic noise emerge as major problems.

Perhaps this may seem rather banal. In fact, there is no comparable body of facts on how well offices serve the people who work in them. The facts do not flatter architects. My reservations are that I am suspicious of user reactions alone without corroboration by other indices of success or failure. People sometimes use buildings to complain about something entirely different. Moreover, Langdon completely ignores all organizational variables and these may well have influenced user reaction. The study therefore fails to pass the trident test. More interesting from a sociological point of view is one of the surveys carried out by the Pilkington Research Unit in the Co-operative Insurance Society headquarters in Manchester. Here people were shown a picture of a typical floor in their building and were asked to choose where they would like to sit. Eighty-one per cent chose the row of desks immediately adjacent to the window. The most common reason given was "natural daylight" which is odd, because, as we shall see later, people are poor at gauging what is natural about daylight.

We have now encountered one of the great mysteries of office design—the importance of the window. I suspect that the people who answered "natural daylight" were simply failing to make distinctions between daylight, view and sunlight, the error that has bedevilled all research in this area. Markus recounts a survey made at the new Robinson building in Bristol and makes some very interesting points about the use of windows in offices. Most people (86 per cent) say they want sunlight at their desks all the year round, but when asked to rank in order of importance good lighting, sunshine, comfortable summer and winter temperature, clean toilets and so on, most people put sunshine near the end of the list. Perhaps the reason is that they all enjoy sun anyway; perhaps rank ordering is not a meaningful device in this context. Similarly with view; view is ranked low in order of importance but nevertheless the majority (51 per cent) of workers would prefer to be near windows. Complex factors are at work here – not just a simple feeling of being deprived of a view, but status and thermal and lighting conditions. The evidence suggests that both excessive brightness and the sensation of cold influence people.

Markus has some interesting data and even more interesting intuitions. Much research, however, remains to be done although Wells has some further data on this subject. A current British design orthodoxy is the alleged necessity of some component of natural light in any artificially-lit office. By comparing actual light measurements of natural and artificial light at various desk positions, to the estimates people make of the percentage of natural light, Wells found that people overestimate natural light the further away they are from the windows. Moreover, being far from windows had nothing to do with belief in the importance of natural light for the eyes, or even with estimates of the importance of being able to see out. You will notice that this result seems to be in conflict with another of Wells' findings – that most people in the deep offices of the CIS were anxious to sit in the window positions. Why should this be so? Many other research questions are suggested by this confusion. One of the most interesting is, when does an internal view become a substitute for a view through the window? Banks, which have always been designed as internal halls with no vision to the outside world, might reveal some answers.

Noise is another aspect of building form which has been shown to affect workers. Langdon (Langdon 1965) has published an exemplary study (which completely satisfies both trident and utility tests) of annoyance caused by noise in automatic data-processing offices. Three types of staff were affected – clerks, card punchers, and machine operators – and it was found that annoyance, caused by the same noise level, varied according to the job. Each job has certain expectations of the environment. But noise interferes with communication, too, and this is clearly more important in one job than another.

SOCIOMETRIC STUDIES

Since Moreno invented the technique of sociometry – measuring the interactions between individuals in various situations – it has been obvious that informal interactions in the office could be charted in this way. The American sociologist Homans conducted what amounts to a sociometric study of office girls and one of his students, Gullahorn,used a similar technique to show the relation between distance and friendship among a group of 12 invoicing girls ranged in three rows, separated by filing cabinets. He found that there was more contact within a row than outside it, and more contact with the adjacent rather than the further row.

Festinger used sociometry to explain how friendships developed in a housing scheme, in perhaps the most famous of all architectural applications of the technique.

Wells in the wonderful Pilkington Study (Manning and Wells 1965, Wells 1965b) has taken sociometric techniques furthest. In fact all of Wells' work strikes me as being full of elaborate methodological fireworks. He compares the attitudes to the open office of three categories of staff – managers, supervisors and clerks. Managers prefer large open offices (needless to say, not for themselves); supervisors and clerks preferred the smaller offices. However, clerks who had experience in the large open offices are less extreme in their dislikes of others. The sociometric consequences of larger and smaller offices are quite distinct, although age, sex and interpersonal distance all play their part. The people in the larger offices made, on the whole, a greater average number of choices, many of which were widespread beyond sections and even departments. People in the smaller offices tended to reciprocate choices made within their own section. On the other hand, these smaller offices contained more isolates. So you either get on very well with your neighbours in the smaller office or you are ostracized. But whatever happens you don't go further afield for friendship.

Wells tries to argue that there are direct implications for management in these findings. For example, management might be advised to choose smaller office rooms if it wishes to promote small exclusive work groups of high morale and efficiency. Or conversely, the large open floor might lead to a better sense of the whole organization. However, I'm afraid that Wells is stepping into the realms of speculation here. No relationship has yet been found between room size and productivity – a necessary index to give meaning and measure to the words "morale" and "efficiency." I have no doubt that such a link could be found, but until it is we must not anticipate. I think this is my best example of the distorting effect of neglecting organizational variables, because until the organization links have been found, all these sophisticated studies of individual responses to the office environment are practically useless to the designer. He can draw no firm conclusions from them. Perhaps you will understand a little better now why I stress so much the trident and utility tests.

WORK HABITS IN THE OFFICE

There is an astounding lack of evidence about what people actually do hour by hour in any but the most mechanical office occupations. I suspect this is part of a universal white-collar self-defence conspiracy – "My job is so complicated it can't be rationalized." Two unpublished studies make one wonder how solid this defence really is.

Tennant of the Stanford Research Institute (Tennant 1966) has compared the time spent by single researchers in two quite separate research establishments. It had been assumed previously that entirely different habits and customs prevailed in each centre. In fact both groups were found to spend almost exactly the same amount of time on the telephone, talking face-to-face and so on. This is not to say that the individual scientists were not doing creative and original work, only that there are obviously generic types of even the most complex work which can be classified for the benefit of the designer.

Another study of IBM programmers (Bairdain 1966) is equally interesting. An argument is made for privacy from interruption and distraction for computer programmers who often do complicated and difficult work. However it is found that pairs of programmers sharing rooms are subject to interruption and distraction once every 110 seconds, more than once every two minutes. A further survey of 10 companies revealed that, like everyone else, programmers are customarily allocated rooms according to "company policy," not in accordance with their real needs. However, eight of the companies are in practice forced to allow their programmers to use extra rooms and quiet corners to do their work. Perhaps such muddles would be avoided if, in future, the actual needs of office workers were better understood at the beginning by management and designers.

I have described these studies because they are almost the totality of the material I have found directly on this subject. Obviously they are inadequate, and chart only a few of the many possible interrelations between organization, behaviour and building. However they are enough to suggest research techniques that will be invaluable in the future. And certainly there are already some ambitious projects under way. In America, E. T. Hall, the anthropologist, is in the middle of a five-year study of the Deere Headquarters in Moline, Illinois. In

England, David Canter is studying the relation of office size to productivity. Moreover, work parallel but not directly related to office design is being carried on by psychologists like Sommer and Argyle and sociologists like Goffman. Perhaps things really are getting better all the time. If behavioural and social scientists are really becoming more interested in environmental problems, designers should get ready immediately to direct scientific interest towards the problems that are most pressing, in which information is thinnest and where the consequences of design errors are most serious.

What sort of studies are likely to reveal most? I suggest that when an office moves from one building to another – not, after all, such an uncommon happening – an ideal opportunity occurs for the study of the relationship of organizational and behavioural variables to the environment. The building obviously changes; organizational changes may or may not be carried out simultaneously. But whatever happens, significant social changes or non-changes are certain, and it may be possible to trace their courses.

Clearly, the effect of new buildings or different social circumstances on the organization may be measured by such indices as productivity, increased or decreased communications, lengthening or shortening of distances travelled. The effects on behaviour of building or organization variables may be indicated by absenteeism, sociometric change, unpunctuality, rate of depreciation of equipment, neglect of facilities provided or accretion of unwanted objects. There are obviously many more such signs. However, it is only scientific curiosity that will be able to transmute into real signs what would otherwise seem meaningless phenomena, to provide real indices of what is happening underneath the bland surface of photographs of office buildings in architectural magazines. There ought to be a law making such studies compulsory.

Another, easier course of action is simply to observe people at work. Of course, to observe acutely is never "easy" and I am suggesting observation comparable in acuteness to Goffman's studies of behaviour in public places. Again the theoretical framework of organizational, behavioural and environmental variables is fundamental to such research. Recently I have spent a little time comparing the workplaces of bank officers and lawyers, and I have found this a rewarding task, because similar work is carried out in very different physical surroundings. What is it about the banker's work or behaviour that makes a bank official sit in the open, near the public (in California at least), while lawyers generally enjoy a private office? With the passage of time and a few questions one begins to understand some of the complex answers to this question. And one finds, too, that variables which seemed trivial have a disproportionately gross effect on the physical layout, while others which you would think would be dominant are subservient.

I wish more of this work were done as a matter of course and recorded for the general good. In time it may be that such humble deductive observations will provide data that will be the basis for new hypotheses to be tested with sophisticated research techniques.

One of the great drawbacks of architectural research is that buildings are expensive, heavy and, for all practical purposes, eternal. This makes the development of simulation techniques particularly interesting. Test offices have been used in Britain and Sweden. However, it may not be long before entire building environments can be simulated by electronic means. To sum up, designers must demand applied research, that is useful, that is not too difficult or expensive, and that is conducted within the framework of a model of relationships between job, worker and building. We need to know more facts.

I have done more than simply discuss social conditions in office buildings. Had I stuck to my brief, I might have provided one or two sociological explanations, or even given you some scattered clues about how to increase productivity by, for example, painting walls a certain colour. However, I wanted to do more than that: to show the vital necessity for organizational and social research, and to stress that office buildings exist only to accommodate organization and behaviour and to suggest a way of redesigning design to make full use, for the first time, of our knowledge of people at work.

First published as "Architect, developer, user, government, manufacturer and the office building" in *Building Research*, July 1968.

2 Petrified Typologies (1969)

Most office buildings are financed and built by developers who are not certain who will eventually be their tenants. This has greatly discouraged architects from studying office planning. Architects, certainly in the UK, have made far more contributions to the design of schools and hospitals than offices. Although it is clear that office managers and office furnishers have amassed considerable expertise in this field, such knowledge is bound to be inadequate because it is based upon the assumption that certain basic building forms are constant and cannot be changed. The architect who has the power to manipulate these basic building forms in order to accommodate organizations in a better way, at present lacks both the detailed knowledge necessary for radical innovation and the motive to obtain it. The purpose of this paper [written in the Department of Architecture of the College of Environmental Design at Berkeley, California] is to propose to architects a simple method of obtaining detailed knowledge from any client. A method is suggested of displaying this data in such a way that it leads naturally into the design process. It is hoped that such a method will encourage architects to develop a wider range of office forms than the single zone, double zone, triple zone and open layout range of types that even the most competent of architectural authorities considers to be a sufficient typology for office purposes.

Why should a wider range be necessary? What's wrong with what we have now? Langdon has compiled for post-war office building a list of inadequacies in such matters as heating, ventilating and solar control. The more urgent task remains of preparing a similar list of failures of offices to cope with the various technologies, organizations and behaviours which they are expected to accommodate. It is not easy to make such a study because no model exists that expresses the precise relationship of office buildings to office work. To construct this model is a top priority. Nevertheless there is certainly some relationship and some popular feeling that modern offices are not giving organizations all that they might. Moreover, the well-publicized work of the German firm of management consultants, Organisationsteam Schnelle, is a formidable argument that formal innovation is to be expected if office organization directly influences the architect's brief.

The Schnelles are management consultants, not architects, and their major work is the preparation of technical briefs for clients who have decided to build new offices for themselves. Their preparatory surveys of internal communication are so thorough, and their faith in team and group working is so strong, that they have been able to persuade numerous clients and architects to adopt the flexible form of open planning which they invented and called bürolandschaft or "office landscaping". So undeveloped is the study of organizations and methods that not the least novel part of the Schnelles' approach is simply to survey what does go on in an office before designing it.

There is, however, little incentive to spend money on innovation where office buildings are most often built by developers and where there is a very heavy demand for office space, which is of course exactly the situation today in the United States. Unless tenants' demands become more strident or locational analysis shows that specialized kinds of offices can be profitably located in certain districts only, it is likely that improvements will at first be made only within conventional building forms. Nevertheless this paper is based on the assumption that, in the long term, developments in organization and methods (O and M) studies will build up pressures which will eventually force widespread innovations. The analytical method described here is a step in this direction.

Many offices are being designed today and some of these must work tolerably well. Apart from a few elementary rules in textbooks on office management, there seems to be very little published in book form to explain such limited successes. The work of the Organisationsteam Schnelle is very fully described in the various publications of Verlag Schnelle and in contrast to the textbooks appears to be incomparably more rational and advanced. It is hard to believe, however, that the gap between the Schnelles and the rest of the world is really so wide. An undone but necessary research task is to search the journals that deal with office equipment and office management for evidence of the use of planning methods.

CHARTING METHODS

One of the most puzzling phenomena of the study of work is that there are so many different ways to chart what work is done and how it is done. Each concentrates on a different aspect of the problem and no method is complete in itself.

• A process chart breaks down each office worker's job into parts.

- A procedure flow chart breaks down work into steps and shows how part of a task is done by one person and is then handed on to another.
- A flow diagram is a development of the procedure flow chart and distinguishes between the various flows – of information, material and orders – and includes symbols for controls, sources and "sinks".
- An organization chart represents the line of authority and also staff line relationships.
- A movement diagram is a means of charting the frequency of movement between points.
- A communication chart measures not only movement but the frequency of any kind of link between points.
- A sociometric diagram represents reciprocated and non-reciprocated choices of friends within a group.
- Layouts and plans are the means of representing the disposition of objects in space.

The architect wants to decide on the best possible layout for the client. What route should be taken from the process chart to arrive at a plan? Does the architect need all the information offered by the eight charting techniques or not? Is there any further information that is required, not given by these techniques?

If buildings are influenced by technology, organization and communications, then information from all of these fields is required in design. In the past it has been customary to study organization theory apart from technology, and technology apart from communications. More recently the so-called "open socio-technical systems" method of studying work has emphasized the practical advantages of looking at the interrelation of technology and human communications. Other writers have stressed how closely organization theory and technology are related. Once this has been learned it is difficult to forget, because the study of work becomes the investigation of complex relationships and the old separate emphases seem misleading and irrelevant. It is fortunate that systems analysis techniques now provide language common to such diverse fields of study. For architects, the next step is clearly to add their own physical variables to the analysis. In this way a route may be found from the starting point of technology to a decision about the appropriate building form. Technology is the driver. Once the goals have been set, the next most important decision is to choose the technical means that seem appropriate. Decisions about organization and communications follow naturally from an understanding of technology. The network of communications demanded and permitted by technology, and the appropriate structure of authority, are the forces that most directly influence layout and other decisions about building form. The building is the framework that permits technology, organization and communications to coexist.

Architectural data

What does an architect need to know about any work situation?

• Technical variables. Equipment used and in what order. Space the equipment occupies and space needed to operate it. Noise level or other environmental effects the equipment may have.
• Socio-technical variables. The way in which people communicate. Movement. Supervision. Informal activities permitted. Barriers to communication required. Appropriate modes of communication.
• Technical and organizational variables. In what manner authority is delegated. What staff/line relationships there are. Symbols of status considered necessary. Opportunities for group working. What span of control is appropriate. Grade and skill of staff involved.

The problem is to find a way of setting about obtaining these data. The advantage of the overall view described is that it makes it easy to combine separate techniques into a complete and rounded information-gathering and analytical method. Current practice, since it has largely been developed in industry, does not provide ways of obtaining all the information which is vital for the design of offices. Above all, there seems to be no method of noting that bars are required to prevent the transfer of certain kinds of information. Not only must documents be protected but the fact that a conversation is being conducted at all may be a major office secret needing to be hidden from the public eye. Sometimes the question of who initiates a transaction becomes of first importance. The content of messages in offices may influence the manner of their transmission. The mode of transmitting messages – word of mouth, in writing or by signals – needs to be more carefully differentiated than in industrial engineering situations. Any new information-gathering method must be sensitive enough to make all these distinctions.

PROPOSED CHARTING METHOD

The proposed method rationalizes the three data groups into three similar but subtly different parts. – technical variables, mapping interrelationships, and node proximity.

Technical variables

The first part is elementary. It is necessary to collect some basic facts about the essential technical variables. These are:

- numbers of staff in each grade
- job descriptions for each grade
- equipment required for each grade
- space requirements for each grade
- vulnerability to distraction or boredom of each grade.

It is to be expected that most firms will already have a clear standards policy. Failing this the Schnelles provide the example of a range of workplace types claimed to include most grades of traditional office staff. Workplaces for card punchers or ADP or other mechanical office grades are not yet included. Novel measures are required to deal with vulnerability to distraction and boredom of staff. In addition to data on individual workplaces, some overall guides are useful. These are:

- proportion of space devoted to circulation, structure, storage, lavatories and so on in various forms of office and building types
- amount of space per person devoted to lounges and rest areas
- areas of such special service areas as print rooms and computer rooms.

Mapping interrelationships

The second part is more complicated. Given a list of people and equipment, the next task is to map the interrelations between them. Some of the actors in this scheme come from outside the organization. They may be visitors or professional colleagues. Some "equipment" may be machines, the rest simply files or storage. Nevertheless each person and each piece of equipment, however different they may seem, is called a "node", and each relation between any two nodes is called a "link". Mapping of links between nodes is the main task. Such mapping is based on an average through time and depends upon the assumption that the nodes will continue to perform the same function. Of course, they sometimes do not – for example, the bank officer whose role changes after the bank doors are shut at 15.00 hrs. Another possible source of confusion is the distinction between formal and informal activities. Formal activities are directly concerned with getting a job done. Informal activities may, like rest pauses, help to get the job done in the long run, or they may simply be compatible with getting the job done, like gossiping while typing – or they may be directed against getting work done, like smoking in the lavatory or mislaying important papers on purpose. The first two kinds of informal behaviour are acknowledged in this charting method. The third is not.

Each link can be isolated and described with some precision. Each description will then become naturally a kind of performance specification that lays down the physical relation between nodes and the degree of physical protection and openness needed by each.

Socio-technical variables are charted by:

• content, describing nature or purpose of meeting, duration, supervision, work or non-work
• mode – is the contact documentary, telephonic, face-to-face, by signal?
• bars – no restrictions, private, controllable, qualifications which are applicable to each of the various communication modes
• frequency, indicated by relative thickness of lines used for links
• initiation, indicating who began the exchange
• movement, indicating who moved towards another to complete.

Technical and organizational variables indicate authority – status in this transaction. The performance specification for the design is derived from the fact that, in the case of a bank, say, the customer must meet the banker face to face; the customer initiates the transaction and moves towards the officer; a quarter of an hour is spent at business; the bank officer is in a superior but friendly position; what is said and written must remain private but there need be no bars to anyone seeing the transaction. It is clear that the traditional Californian bank, with its open area for officers who are accessible to the public but somewhat apart from each other and whose desks are rather grand, fulfils this performance specification. In making these assessments there must be strict control over the amount of information recorded. The criterion is simply whether or not the information recorded will lead to any effect on the building form.

Node proximity

The third part of the exercise is to draw up rules for locating each node in relation to the others. Since the architect is chiefly interested in spatial relations, telephone links are of subsidiary importance and documentary links are significant only because papers must be carried from one point to another. The really vital links are face-to-face and visual, because the need to provide proximity and access results from them. Such links must be listed separately. The three rules for determining relative proximity of the nodes are simply stated: visual links must always be possible; communications must be kept centralized, so that the whole system is as like a circle as possible; and the cost of separation between any links must be minimized. Movement cost may be measured by such indices as the hours lost in transit or the likely cost to the business, if the contact is not made. Thus it is cheaper to place people who are in constant day-to-day contact next to each other – since it is probable in a bank that business will be lost unless customers are easily able to make contact with the bank officers, bank officers should be easily accessible to the public.

Some difficulties remain to be resolved. The charting method puts such a strong stress on communications, that an individual worker's needs for concentration or vulnerability to distraction, measured here as a technical variable, may possibly be neglected. In many cases some sort of compromise is necessary between an individual's personal requirements and the needs of the organization as a whole. To keep this point in mind it is enough to remember the distinction between two sorts of privacy: that required to enable someone to concentrate, and the more "public" form which is required to prevent communication leaks. Any charting method based on time average has drawbacks and it must never be forgotten that people are capable of moving, and of changing their roles occasionally. Moreover, rules such as those regulating opening hours in banks may have an enormous effect on any communications systems. Such temporal conventions may easily change. Again, there is no easy remedy except to look out for such circumstances and not to forget to draw charts if necessary. A warning is necessary in case the permanence of this kind of analysis is taken for granted. Many social and technical factors are in a state of constant change and any analysis, however thorough, may be assumed to have only a temporary usefulness. Charts may become very crowded with details and it is useful to remember that, as in any other form of draughting, different drawings may display different scales of detail. Sections may be "blown up" to show particularly complex interrelations. Non-work relationships may be distinguished by dashes; telephone links by dots; visual links by circles; supervision by arrows; frequency by thickness.

CASE STUDIES

In order to show the charting method at work, two case studies are discussed here. One is of a bank, the other of a law office. Both were visited and observed several times in the winter quarter of 1968. These particular offices were chosen because they are generally as different in physical layout as can be imagined, one being very open, the other very enclosed, and yet both have some factors in common; confidential business is discussed in both banks and lawyers' offices; bank officers and lawyers both have some sort of standing in the public eye; visitors come in and out of both banks and law offices. What functional reasons account for their different forms and locations? How successful is the new charting method at displaying these functional reasons?

Data were gathered in the course of several conversations with two officers of a large bank and three attorneys in a medium- to-large law firm specializing in business cases. Since questioning was unsystematic, some figures are more impressionistic than accurate. I have little doubt that a larger sample and a better-designed questionnaire would serve only to make more precise the general impression referred to here.

Evaluation of the charting method

A test for the success of the charting method is whether it can detect reasons for the differences between the layout of the bank and the lawyers' office. Common sense alone suggests the following four explanations which are capable of being tested empirically.

1) Banks are anxious for two kinds of business – account handling and loans. Both kinds of work depend upon a considerably greater volume of business than lawyers'. Moreover, the loan section (that is, the bank officers) depends for its success upon being easily adjacent to the account handling section. The bank officer values the informal contact with customers passing by on routine account business.
2) Bank officers want to make rapid, simple decisions. Attorneys are less interested in rapid turnover of customers but more in intensive study of the needs of a limited number of clients. It is not surprising, therefore, to find that bank officers choose open surroundings which make it easier for them to terminate and control conversations, while attorneys pick enclosed rooms which promote prolonged confidences.
3) Bank officers deal with limited areas of jurisdiction and are accustomed to pass on difficult or specialized customers to other, more

competent colleagues. The open office lends itself to this procedure because the officer can see whether his colleagues are occupied or not and can therefore confidently pass a customer up or down the line.

4) No one minds being seen going to talk to a bank officer. Such financial transactions are part of normal life. Lawyers, however, tend to place much more emphasis on the confidentiality of their clients' business, to avoid accidental encounters, to hide names of files.

Charts drawn up from the interviews immediately give a sense of enormous differences in links, although the nodes are disposed in roughly similar positions. Certain links in the bank are visual. For example, the bank officer requires visual links both with customers passing by and with his colleagues while his secretary and his particular customers want to be able to see him. None of the attorney's links is visual. This one observation is enough to take care of explanations 1 and 3. Many links in the bank are heavily trafficked. This suggests that, at the very least, there is reason for easy contact between, say, the general public and the officer and this, of course, is part of explanation 2. The links in the law office are so attenuated that it seems that little time will be saved or opportunities lost if there are even considerable barriers between the nodes. It must be admitted that the charting method does not pick up the rest of this explanation, which is that openness can be used as a device to prevent the nuisance of prolonged pleading, and that enclosed rooms are a way of making clients feel that they can take time to reveal, eventually, their deepest motives. Explanation 4 is picked up by the data on complete bars to face-to-face links in the lawyers' office.

A further advantage of the method is that it brings into focus other important relationships which also have space planning implications. For example, not only is the use of the job file made clear in the lawyers' office but also the powerful effect this has in welding together partner, attorney and their secretaries into something like a work group. There is no equivalent of this relationship in the bank because officers handle their own work and a common file is shared by all.

Certain inadequacies in the method should be noted. The category "authority" conveys insufficient information about relative status even though it may be supported by "technical" data about space standards. The whole question of status in various kinds of work situation is very difficult and it is not yet clear in exactly what way authority should modify the basic communications net. Another weakness is that although there is the potential that distance between any two nodes as they are drawn in the chart could give some indication of whether it is important to locate those nodes near to or far from each other, this potential remains to be exploited. Another irritating deficiency is that no satisfactory symbol has yet been found to represent bars, and since communication bars, and especially face-to-face bars, lead straight into ideas for physical design this is a grave weakness. The difficulty is that it is easy to represent bars for each separate link, but when all the links come together in a chart, it is impossible to show from whom privacy is really required. There is also a danger that too much is shown on the charts. It becomes necessary to ask if there is anything that is redundant. Frequency of traffic and visual links seem to have a dominant effect on physical form and yet equally, in a negative way, so do telephone links. However, data on informal contact and supervision seem less immediately useful, at least in these two examples. It may well be that types of offices exist in which these relations are critical but, even so, it is unsatisfactory to collect information which is not vital for the problem in hand.

ANALYSIS AND DESIGN

The charting method is intended to help architects to design buildings. So far, the data on each separate link can be considered as a performance specification which tells the designer which nodes must be in contact, how long they will talk, how they communicate, what bars they need to their conversation, how often they do it, who begins the exchange and who is in charge. The chart summarizes all these separate specifications into a map of the most convenient and cheapest arrangement for exchanging information. The next step is to convert these specifications into plans and layouts with the aid of the technical data. One can almost imagine an electronic machine assembling building variables in response to this unified method of presenting the socio-technical and organizational brief.

The two questions that remain are – how can building variables be made to relate to this kind of brief, and in what form should they be assembled? One argument is that each situation is unique. Designers should respond, their minds *tabula rasa*, capable of responding to the demands of that situation. Of course, to some extent this is good policy and an antidote to the grossly inadequate office building types which we discussed at the beginning of this paper. There is, however, an alternative line of thought which deserves some attention. This is that if designers do in fact depend on mental images of solutions, such images may be consolidated into patterns which relate consistently to functional analyses. In this way designers would enjoy the best of all possible worlds. They would be able to respond freshly to each new situation, be aware of what exactly is happening in it, draw upon their past experience, expressed rationally in terms of patterns, and assemble from these patterns new and acceptable wholes. If there is any strength in this argument, then the analysis presented in this paper is one possible framework for such an assembly of patterns.

First published as "A method of analysing and charting relationships in the office", *Architects' Journal* Information Library, 12 March 1969, pp. 693–699.

3 Office Design and Organizations (1974)

"We make our buildings, and afterwards our buildings make us" (Churchill, 1924). The relationship between people and buildings is reciprocal. This does not make research any easier since there is always likely to be an overlap between explanations of the factors that lead to certain design choices and explorations of how people respond to, perceive, or are affected by design.

One outstanding characteristic of the relationship between buildings and people is what Amos Rapoport (1969) calls the "low criticality" of building design. There is, in other words, usually a wide range of choice available in any design situation. Generally several solutions are possible, all of which satisfy such basic physical requirements as controlling temperature and excluding rain, and which all meet basic user requirements for convenience, space, and essential adjacencies. Once a fit has been provided between design and these simple "critical" requirements and once economic and technological problems have been solved, an area of "slack" is available within which design decisions are a matter of the expression of values: conveying meanings, indulging design whims, expressing individual creativity or simply being arbitrary. It is obvious that design consists of manipulating several environmental properties in a hierarchy of decreasing criticality. From a research point of view, low criticality means that the relationship between buildings and people is a wide, ill-defined field which can be studied in as many ways as there are branches of social science – from cultural anthropology to the boundaries of clinical psychology – but with little chance of clear-cut or guaranteed success.

Gutman has listed eight properties of the physical environment which may have some significance for behaviour. These are the location of facilities and structures (spatial organization), circulation and communication systems (circulation and communication), whatever environmental features maintain the physiological and psychological functions of the human organism (ambient properties), the environment as it is perceived (visual properties), facilities which are built into the environment (amenities), the social values, attitudes, statuses, and cultural norms which are represented or expressed by the environment (symbolic properties), and finally the peculiar sensory and aesthetic properties of the environment (architectonic properties). In their different ways all of these properties have the capacity to affect or change human life to some extent.

Criticality is a scale on which the importance of effects of these properties can be measured. Practical men will think that spatial organization, ambient properties, and amenities are the most critical. These features of buildings are valued even by estate agents, the least ethereal of beings, who call them location, area, and services. Users will argue that a building's capacity to provide circulation and communications systems is critical under certain circumstances and is capable of providing operational advantages. Architectonic properties are less likely to be thought critical by clients than by architects. Symbolic properties are, sadly, rarely thought critical either by architects or clients.

In general even the criticality of the most obvious properties of the physical environment seems to be not very high compared to other factors in people's working lives such as good pay and prospects. Langdon (1966a) has shown this in his investigations of user satisfaction with such ambient properties of office buildings as heating, lighting, and freedom from noise.

Research on buildings and people is difficult because the relationship is ambiguous, because there are few instances where the relationship is critical, and because many other factors intervene which diminish the importance of buildings in users' eyes.

HISTORY OF ATTEMPTS TO RELATE ORGANIZATION AND DESIGN

It is striking, given these difficulties, that researchers in this field at the beginning of the century should have been so convinced of the possibility of quick returns. The early experimenters, such as the British Industrial Fatigue Research Board, began with the simple assumption that manipulation of such variables as hours of work, atmospheric conditions and heat and lighting would directly affect the productivity of industrial workers. This argument is analogous to the innovations in public health which led so successfully to the elimination of cholera in the nineteenth century by manipulating physical variables.

The assumptions that lay behind these experiments were those of industrial psychology founded by Taylor, Frank Gilbreth, and their numerous successors. That is to say, it was supposed that the worker must be studied as an isolated unit; that in certain important respects the worker resembled a machine whose efficiency could be scientifically estimated; and that the main factors influencing efficiency were (a) wasteful or ineffectual movements in doing the job, (b) fatigue which was believed to be a "physicochemical state" of the body due to the accumulation of waste products, and (c) defects in the physical environment, such as poor lighting, inadequate heating, excessive humidity, and so on.

(Brown, 1964, p.69)

Mayo (1933) explains that this early work, which was not without success and which contributed to legislation such as the various Factory Acts and even eventually to the British Office, Shops and Railway Premises Act, was the background to the investigations begun at the Hawthorne Works of the Western Electric Company in the 1920s.

The enquiry involved at one phase the segregation of two groups of workers, engaged upon the same task, in two rooms equally illuminated. The experimental diminution of the lighting in ordered quantities, in one room only, gave no sufficient difference, expressed in terms of measured output as compared with the other still fully-illuminated room. Somehow or other that complex of mutually dependent factors, the human organism, shifted its equilibrium and unintentionally defeated the purpose of the experiment.

(See Mayo, 1960, p. 54)

This was the moment at which environmental variables fell out of favour as a major research interest. Instead, relations between workers, and between management and workers (in other words "human relations") became far more important. In parallel, the methods used by the Hawthorne experimenters became more and more relaxed until the final phase of almost participant-observer studies in the bank wiring room (Roethlisberger and Dickson, 1939; Homans, 1950). In the last phase of the Hawthorne study a massive interview programme obtained data about the topics which employees voluntarily chose to discuss. These were divided into favourable and unfavourable. It is interesting that the majority of comments about the physical environment were unfavourable (Roethlisberger and Dickson, 1939).

This hint was taken up later by Herzberg (1959) with his famous division of the "work environment" (not just the physical environment) into two kinds of element – motivators and dissatisfiers.

Dissatisfiers are made up, essentially, of such matters as pay, supplemental benefits, company policy and administration, behaviour of supervision, working conditions and several other factors somewhat peripheral to the task. Though traditionally perceived by management as motivators of people, these factors were found to be more potent as dissatisfiers. High motivation does not result from their improvement, but dissatisfaction does result from their deterioration.

Motivators, for the most part, are the factors of achievement, recognition, responsibility, growth, advancement, and other matters associated with the self-actualization of the individual on the job. Job satisfaction and high production were associated with motivators, while disappointments and ineffectiveness were usually associated with dissatisfiers.

(Scott Myers, 1964)

In other words, the physical environment has an asymmetrical relation to organizational success – having the capacity to make things worse but not to improve worker satisfaction. Broady (1968) has made a very interesting comparison of the stages through which the study of the social organization of industry has gone. He compares these stages with similar, but far later, phases in the understanding of the relationship between people and buildings.

In the first phase, one can clearly discern the industrial equivalent of architectural determinism. In the classical theory of industrial organization, embodied in F. W. Taylor's concept of '"scientific management", the worker was regarded as a mere appendage to the machine and his efforts were thought to be determined by purely economic incentives. The analogy with an architectural theory which conceives social well-being as a direct product of good physical design is, I think, apparent. The second phase, which began in the 1930s with the work of Elton Mayo, concentrates upon relationships within working groups or the shop floor. The interest in fostering good human relations in industry to which this led in the 1930 and 1940s antedated by 30 years the planning profession's current concern with citizen participation. Since then, however, our theory has extended still further to take account of the wider structure of social organization – the pattern of conflict between worker and management, for instance, whose strains have frequently negated management's efforts to improve human relations on the shop floor. Industrial sociology has thus progressed from a narrow and very pragmatic to a broader and more theoretically cogent view of industrial organization.

(Broady, 1968)

Broady expects to find in current studies of the relationship between man and buildings a reflection of the view of the organization as a structure. Herzberg's work is one step towards this. What follows is intended to be a further step.

SOME RECENT STUDIES

So much for the general current of ideas in industrial sociology and industrial psychology. Generally speaking, in these disciplines the study of physical variables fell out of favour in the 1930s and has only recently been resurrected, and then only in a very minor way. That is the general view of social scientists looking at design. Looking in the other direction, researchers based in the design fields or in some way in contact with designers have conducted a number of investigations in several different ways. A survey of these will help to make clear by contrast the position of this study. Wherever possible the studies which are cited deal with office design in particular.

The search for effects

Some effort has been made to measure direct effects of the form of offices on behaviour. Canter (1968) has attempted without great success to demonstrate the effect of room size on clerical performance by administering clerical aptitude tests in different physical conditions. Fucigna (1967) was similarly unsuccessful in a study of the performance of some analysts before and after a new furniture system was provided. Here the measures were time spent on various kinds of activity such as telephone work and report writing.

More interesting is a series of sociometric studies. In the field of housing there have been several attempts, notably by Festinger *et al.* (1950), Merton (1948), Kuper (1951), and Case (1967) to show the effect of layout on patterns of contact and friendship. Similar studies, comparing small and large office spaces, have been conducted in offices notably by Gullahorn (1960) and Homans (1954) on a small scale and by Wells (1965b) on a larger scale. Wells found that the social organization of the sections working in small areas was internally more cohesive, though the proportion of isolates was higher, and the number of wider links with other members of the same department much smaller.

> The higher average number of preference choices made by members of the open areas, coupled with the lower proportions of reciprocation, show that the socio-occupational network existing in the two types of area are fundamentally different. In the small areas there exists a fairly tight social group, whereas the social links connecting people in the open areas are much less tightly knit.
>
> (Wells, 1965b)

Wells argues that these results must be related to area, since: "The sections working in both the open and the small areas are essentially similar in respect of the nature of the work and the composition of the sub-samples" (Wells, 1965b). However, since Wells does not describe in any detail what the nature of the work was, he leaves us in some doubt about what is meant by "similarity".

User-satisfaction studies attempt to relate specific statements of satisfaction to specific physical stimuli such as noise. The most thorough study of user satisfaction in offices has been by Langdon (1966a) in work characterized by a large sample, very thorough measurement, and an exclusive concentration on the thermal environment, noise, and lighting – the building variables usually associated with building services. The aim of the survey was to direct architects' attention to the performance of buildings. Little is said about organizations themselves or about the type of work, since

> attempts to measure office efficiency in the course of user research have tended to show that organizational and human relations factors bulk so large in the overall picture that differences which might be attributed to office design cannot be easily discerned. Moreover, it is barely, if ever, possible to eliminate these factors in order to concentrate upon differences caused by environment.
>
> (Langdon 1966a)

In other words, there are too many intervening variables between buildings and behaviour to encourage any attempt to measure effects in organizational terms. "Largely for these reasons, user studies have centred mainly on user satisfaction, either inferred or directly expressed, as a criterion of environmental quality" (Langdon 1966a: see also Langdon 1966b).

Langdon argues that since buildings are designed to satisfy users, assessment of comfort is justified. This is so. But Langdon, among others, takes pains to point out that the built environment does not loom large in the total picture of work satisfaction. Even between the simple environmental variables and user satisfaction lie large questions. Wells (1965a) has demonstrated that people working in offices cannot gauge the proportion of daylight to natural light at their workplaces. Is user satisfaction inevitably related to inaccurate estimates or to reality? Langdon (1965), dealing with the question of disturbance by noise, points out that different classes of worker report different degrees of disturbance. In order to deal with this he invents the concept of "job expectation". Clearly, user satisfaction is a more relative and slippery idea than it first seemed.

A more complex approach to the effect of buildings on people has been made possible by using the psychological technique of "semantic differential". What is measured here is not satisfaction but more fundamental responses to architectural stimuli. These have been shown to vary consistently in relation to similar architectural stimuli. Canter (1966–1967) has done work of this kind in offices by developing dimensions, by inventing ingenious methods of simulating design which allow systematic variation of such variables as window size and roof pitch, and by arguing for "appropriateness", that is, congruence between user expectations of a certain kind of place and the stimuli actually provided in such a place.

In these studies, however, the architectural variables are necessarily small scale and the responses are individual, telling little about the way social groups use space.

Criticism of studies of effects

The chief difficulty inherent in all studies of the effects of buildings on behaviour is that buildings are rarely, if ever, sufficiently critical to determine behaviour. Many variables intervene, some of which undoubtedly have more effect on behaviour than any property of the physical environment.

Another difficulty is that buildings are large and complex entities, inhabited not just by individuals but by social groups. Since people themselves are such useful and precise instruments, effects are usually measured in terms of individual responses.

This tells us little about what these individuals do together, what technology they use, or, in the case of sociometric studies, why people choose to cluster together in certain ways. Since buildings are so complex there has been little systematic work on developing an overall framework for descriptive analysis. At present, isolated aspects of building form – area of rooms, noise transmission of partitions, adjacencies – are studied individually without any attempt to relate one building variable to another.

Of the studies listed above, seven – Festinger *et al.* (1950), Merton (1948), Kuper (1951), Case (1967), Gullahorn (1960), Homans (1954), Wells (1965a) – are operational in that they are concerned with the properties of office buildings in order to affect communications; three – Langdon (1966b; 1965) and Wells (1965b) – deal with noise. heat, lighting and other ambient properties; two – Canter (1968) and Fucigna (1967) – deal with spatial organization. One – Canter (1966–1967) – deals with visual properties, but none with amenities, none with symbolic properties and none with architectonic properties. Effects of the more basic properties of buildings on social interaction and well-being have been more fully studied probably because such properties are easier to measure. We know little of the visual, symbolic, or architectonic properties of office buildings, and even less of the effect of these properties on behaviour.

Some simpler approaches

The study of effects is very difficult. A more compelling, prior task is the invention of suitable categories and descriptions of buildings and behaviour in a way which would allow correspondences to be made between them. An example is Barker's idea of behaviour settings (Barker and Wright, 1955). People have learned to act in specific ways in specific settings. To understand behaviour, argues Barker, it helps to relate units of place or "behaviour settings" to units of behaviour. This simple idea is capable of development because it suggests not only relationships but a method of tracing them. Goffman's (1961; 1963; 1964) "role settings" are similarly promising. Joiner (1971) has actually made operational a similar idea in his study of different kinds of office room. He found, for example, distinct differences between room furniture layouts preferred by academics and those preferred by people in business. Joiner measured in physical terms what the differences were. Hall's (1966) studies of personal space and Sommer's (1962; 1965; 1969) studies of seating preferences in such spaces as libraries and waiting rooms, also fit into this descriptive research category. Both are particularly interesting because they attempt cross-cultural comparisons – Hall between different societies and Sommer between such "cultures" as schizophrenics and others, and between male and female. A more analytical study is Black's (1972) analysis of group size in a number of organizations. The aim of the exercise was to question the need for large, open offices. How often did groups of certain sizes actually occur? The results suggest a very high incidence of small groups and thus, by inference, of the need for smaller rather than larger spaces. In some respects, these studies are looser than those in the "effects" category. They often lack rigour; not all of them have carried the physical description far enough; nowhere, except in Joiner's work, is the relationship between the physical and the social really thoroughly investigated. Yet in all of them is a sense of comparison which indicates an open-ended attitude to culture and to the expression of values in design. In all of them there is potential for the systematic examination of variations in building form in parallel with variations in society.

"Intersystems congruence"

Michelson (1970) in his valuable book *Man and his Urban Environment,* outlines an approach to the study of the relationship between people and buildings which he calls "intersystems congruence". Both society and buildings are considered as systems – that is, holistically, with a sense of the relationship between parts. The goal of the study is the investigation of congruence, that is, the broad limits within which the built environment affects the ease or difficulty of carrying out human activities, maintaining group boundaries and characteristics, achieving goals, and expressing values. Some settings make it easier to do certain things. Others limit possibilities. Congruence is experiential if it deals with the "actual" relation between people and the environment; it is mental if it deals with what people think about the environment. This is a sufficiently broad, if unrealized, programme for research. It is sufficiently cautious to set the search for effects into second place and to emphasize the importance of establishing correspondences or evidence of congruence between people and buildings. It is sufficiently broad not to exclude the contribution of any branch of social science. Above all, it emphasizes by the use of the vague but useful word "systems" the sense of both society and buildings as complex entities with many internal relationships. When this study was begun, a primary aim was to survey the correspondence between office organizations and office layouts. No attempt was made to look for effects.

Broady's (1968) hint about the value of organization theory as a model for research on people and building has been grasped. With this view of the structure of organizations as a whole, the same descriptive approach as used by Joiner (1971) or Black (1972) can be used, but in a way which relates to a much broader and richer set of ideas. In this way a correspondence, once established, immediately borrows a theoretical power which it would otherwise have lacked.

THE STUDY OF OFFICE WORK

One of the chief difficulties in achieving a perspective on office work is the difficulty of defining the office function. Communication and control are the essence (Haire, 1959). But when an organization is simple, like a small workshop, the office function is fully integrated with production. When an office organization is large, minor production processes such as printing and the making of artwork are often secreted within the office itself. The point has often been made that the office as an institution is relatively new even in the oldest industrial societies (Morgan, 1960). "The percentage of office workers in the total working population rose from 0.8 in 1851 to only 4.0 in 1901 and 7.2 in 1921" (Rhee, 1968). However, in more recent years in advanced industrial societies the growth of clerical labour as a component of the total labour force has been more obvious. In the UK between 1931 and 1961, according to Rhee, the total labour force increased by 25 per cent but the number of office employees increased by 130 per cent.

Among the issues raised by the growth of clerical labour which have attracted attention in recent years are:

• the increasing size of administrative units (Lockwood, 1969)
• the increasing proportion of women employed in offices (Rhee, 1968)
• the diminishing status of the office worker (Klingender, 1935; Seers, 1950; Mills, 1951)
• the increasing use of machines (Rhee, 1968)
• the increasing importance of rationalization forced by automatic data processing (Rhee, 1968)

- the alleged stresses created by automation (Hoos, 1961).

Important as these issues are, they have not been accompanied by any serious study of the varieties of office work. The initial difficulty of defining the office function except in the most general terms of "communication and control" seems to have had the effect of discouraging detailed examination of what office workers actually do all day or of how they are in fact organized.

The contribution of organization theory

That is not to say that the study of organizations in general has been neglected. A concept like "organizational structure" – that is, the interrelation of social positions and roles (Parsons, 1951) – seems abstract and apparently remote from the office, but is, nonetheless, very helpful in thinking about how a firm hangs together. Structure has become an increasingly important concern in organization theory. In contrast to the "classical management principles" of Urwick (1951) and others which are, in effect, rules for good organization, and to the body of work which emphasized "human relations" (Mayo, 1945) – the feelings which hold organizations together – much recent work in organization theory has tried to discover the "real" dimensions of structural variation between organizations. On the one hand these dimensions emphasize role relationships rather than the bonds of feeling, and on the other hand, in contrast to the rules of classical management, the dimensions are both empirically based and tested.

A good example of such an approach is Joan Woodward's (1965) work which relates structural variables, such as the number of levels of management, ratio of managers and supervisors to total personnel, and the ratio of direct to indirect labour, to a scale of technical complexity of the manufacturing process. Woodward succeeded in calling into question many of the assumptions which lie behind classical principles of management. Another example is the study of Burns and Stalker (1961) who drew attention to the greater appropriateness of an "organic" or decentralized structure for firms which are engaged in technical innovation. Conversely a "mechanistic" or more centralized form of administration is appropriate where change is less rapid.

Mason Haire (1959) found consistent patterns in a structural variable (ratio of clerical to administrative staff) in the growth of a number of firms. Broady (1968) has drawn particular attention to the value of organization theory in the study of the relationship between design and people. He argues that the analysis of the social environment has been particularly well developed in the field of organization theory, which has benefited chiefly from the detailed study of industrial plants.

> An organization is defined as a social unit 'deliberately constructed and reconstructed to seek specific goals' and organization theory seems to give an account of how such units work and, more specifically, of the social conditions that are appropriate for achieving different kinds of goals.
>
> (Broady, 1968)

Using some examples of architects' offices drawn from the RIBA study of practice, Broady demonstrates some recurrent structural features which distinguish one kind of office from another.

> In the design of architects' offices or industrial firms or hospitals, accordingly, the organizational structure needs to be considered as a factor affecting the achievement of the organization's goals. And since these kinds of structural differences have implications for architectural design, it is clear that social organization and physical design need to be considered as complementary aspects of the total environment.
>
> (Broady 1968)

Apart from the habit of thinking simultaneously about the whole organization in all its aspects – technological, social, and environmental – one of the most attractive aspects of this view of organizations is the tendency to categorize types of organization by variation along a few simple dimensions. Woodward (1965) for example, in her search for a link between technology and behaviour, decided "what was needed...was a natural history of industry, something in the nature of a botanist's 'Flora' that could be used to identify in technological terms the firms they had studied". For offices, as for other kinds of technology, no such taxonomy existed. The idea of categories based upon empirical observation and related to a total view of the organization is highly appealing.

Types of office work

Without the benefit of a survey or of any adequate taxonomy of types of office work, it is possible to get a sense of the variety of office work by imagining the differences between, for example, a typical advertising agency and a general accounting department, or between an executive group and a design office (Duffy and Cave, 1973; Cave and Duffy, 1973). These differences are complex and small scale. They do not immediately relate to the large ideas which have been the guidelines of much sociological research. They may not even constitute an organizational problem since it could be assumed that most organizations must find an appropriate structure in order to survive.

However, at the level of office layout which is the subject of this paper, differences between kinds of office work and styles of management could well be very important. If office layout is related to office organization, then the diagnosis by the designer of the wrong form of organization or choice of an inappropriate layout could be an error costed, perhaps, in loss of productivity or high staff turnover. For architects this argument, which is close to their *raison d'etre,* is of very great interest.

Shell and scenery

A word of warning to architects is necessary at this point. A point of view held particularly by followers of Christopher Alexander has been criticized correctly by March and Steadman (1971). This

> seemed to be claiming that the objective structural analysis of the functional requirements of a social organization would, *ipso facto,* generate the design of the building or environment to accommodate it. That is to say, if we knew enough about the elaborate relations existing between pupils, pupils and staff, members of staff, and so on, we could design a school.
> (March and Steadman, 1971, p.9)

March and Steadman point out that geometrical interest in design ideas and the reality of constructional techniques impose inevitable constraints on the human situation. Duffy and Freedman (1970) argue that the concept of "fit" between building form and functional requirements is less interesting than the absence of fit, that is "slack" – the area in building design devoted to style, the expression of values and so on. One could add that buildings are designed to last for many years. Even if it were possible to fit a building precisely to a set of requirements on opening day, those requirements would certainly have changed after several years. A gap will inevitably occur between developing requirements and the residual long-lasting building shell (Duffy, 1973a; 1973b).

Office design, as practised today, is a particularly interesting example of how this gap is filled. Office building shells – structure, skin, and core – are often designed and built as speculative ventures with a life expectation of several decade. Tenants take leases in office buildings for relatively short periods of five or seven years. For occupants of short tenancies, design can be an entirely separate activity which is often carried out by different designers. At this level of prediction, the "scenery" or short life interior design can realistically be fitted to short-term and particular requirements if the constraints of long-life building shells are respected.

Office scenery is likely to be closely related to organizational structure. Office shells are not. This distinction clearly defines, by span of expected life, the scope of the architectural variables to be studied here. These are the elements of short-life scenery.

One consequence of this definition is that nothing is said about the design of office building shells.

The origins of office planning

Office interiors have been consciously designed with systematic reference to patterns of office work since the days of Taylor and Gilbreth. The analogy between the use of motion studies in factories and in certain clerical departments was obvious from the first. The editor of *Industrial Engineering* had this moment of insight in 1911.

> The writer, in handling the successive installments of *Motion Study* (by Frank Gilbreth), became more and more impressed with the possibilities...He resolved to apply some of these principles in his own office. Naturally the first point of attack is...where the greatest saving can be accomplished. In our case, it happened to be the outgoing mail.
>
> (Kent, 1911)

By the 1920s several handbooks (Thompson, 1906: Alford, 1924; Leffingwell, 1925; Galloway, 1918; Schulze, 1914, 1919) were available which gave detailed instructions on how to plan the office, how to relate adjacent departments, how to calculate areas, how to take paper flow into account. One of these even suggests that

> it is occasionally necessary to trace the path of a piece of work, visualizing not only the steps but the parts of the office through which it passes. This can be accomplished by constructing an

isometric...in the example shown, a very radical rearrangement of the office was found necessary and the chart was therefore prepared to convince all concerned of the waste involved in the faulty arrangement.

(Leffingwell, 1925, p. 148)

The private office was considered a problem. "It is not easy to decide what positions or persons in an organization are entitled to such distinction" (Leffingwell, 1925, p. 292). Privacy was considered to be frequently overstressed. "The modern metropolitan bank has already almost abandoned private offices and major executives are located in the open on an officer's platform" (Leffingwell, 1925, p. 293). While Schulze thought that the office

should be an expression in physical form of the organization of the business – that is, it should show the lines of authority, the separation of functions, and the direction of work through the different departments.

(Schulze, 1919, p. 95)

Some consideration was given to different styles of work-planning and scheduling, corresponding and interviewing, accounting and record keeping, as well as "advertising agents, law offices, and other professional institutions which include many original mental workers, a class which, as a rule, detests clerical duties and performs them very badly" (Leffingwell, 1925, p. 15). The special position of the executive is realized:

an executive is usually provided with a desk and a table with his chair between them. He talks to visitors and dictates letters over his table, using it for whatever routine work he may do, but turns to his desk when he has to concentrate on any problem. The desk is placed against the wall and the table nearer the centre of the room, with chairs for visitors so located that their faces will be toward the light so it will be easy for the executive to study them.

(Alford, 1924, p. 394)

These rules, which were written only 20 or 30 years after the beginning of the first great period of American office building, are a completely adequate codification of the avowed aims of much current practice in office design in New York today. They are the basis on which later handbooks were written and rewritten (for example, Saphier, 1968).

Office landscaping

The origins of modern American office layout design clearly lie in Taylorism. Office landscaping, or bürolandschaft, the spectacular German contribution to office planning of the 1960s, added to a basically Tayloristic concern with measuring work flow a number of ideas drawn from later schools of managerial thought. For the first time in office planning, attention was drawn to the distinction between the informal and the formal organization. "Anyone using an organization chart which illustrates the divisive more than the unifying character of the organization, as a basis for office layout is on the wrong track" (Lorenzen and Jaeger, 1968). This argument reflects the concern of the human relations school with affective bonds, rather than "classical management principles", as the means by which organizations are held together. Also new is an emphasis on "communications" rather than on work flow – a broader, more positive, concept which is clearly derived from the general cybernetic environment of the 1960s.

> The lines of frequent communications seldom follow the lines of command in an organization chart. Although the planned structure provides for a flow of information between superior and subordinates, the daily activities...require frequent and instant communication between positions of equal and/or unequal rank within the work group...as well as across group or departmental boundaries.
>
> (Lorenzen and Jaeger, 1968)

Above all, office landscaping expresses, in a particularly didactic form, arguments for a participative management style. McGregor and Likert are often quoted by protagonists of office landscaping (Lorenzen and Jaeger, 1968). The old hierarchical structure, or so the argument goes, stands in the way of the interests of both management and workers. If physical barriers come down, and desks are arranged loosely according to need, not status, in the manner of office landscaping, true co-operation towards a common goal is likely to be encouraged if not engendered.

What is interesting about these arguments is not so much whether they are true or not but that they were made at all. They represent a conscious process of translating fashionable managerial ideas into what is considered appropriate physical form. This is exactly the same step as was taken when motion study ideas were introduced into office design at the beginning of the century. The reprehensible part of many arguments for office landscaping is the strong but tacit assumption that not only should all organizations be equally participative but also that all layouts should be equally landscaped.

It is unlikely that this is could be or ought to be the case. Given the comparative, structural approach outlined earlier it seems far more probable that some organizations are more participative than others; some value communications greatly; and some rely upon a severe formality. A wide variety of organizational structure and management style seems possible. If layout reflects the organization, we should expect as many design possibilities as there are variations in organizational structure.

Ideas from organization theory suggest that office organizations vary in certain fundamental "structural" ways. Why these variations occur is open to question. Nevertheless, it seems reasonable to categorize organizations according to these variations and to make comparisons between organizations using such categories.

Recent arguments for office landscaping would lead one to believe that only one form of organization should exist and that correspondingly only one form of office layout is appropriate. This cannot be so. In the same way that organizations vary, so office layouts are likely to vary, assuming, of course, some correspondence between organizations and design.

A hypothetical model was devised to test whether or not such correspondences exist. The results form the central part of the dissertation to which this paper is the introduction (Duffy 1974). Before turning to the results, however, it is useful to summarize some of the most important methodological rules which guided this investigation of the misty borderline where architecture and the social sciences meet.

• The research had to be relevant to topical issues which were of practical importance to architects and designers. The results were to be in a form which would either contradict or confirm assumptions which are the current basis of design action.
• The research had to be closely related to "ready-made" measures and concepts in social science. These measures and concepts did not necessarily have to be central but they had to be of "respectable" origins and to have been fully developed. There seemed to be more point in relating fully worked-out sociological ideas to design than in attempting to contribute to innovation in a non-architectural discipline.

- Equal weight had to be given to both social science and architectural variables. This is the most important rule of all. Without it the research would have lapsed into the common fault of losing sight of the relationship between people and buildings because of a bias towards investigation on one side or the other.
- Explanation of cause and effect was to be avoided. Simply establishing a relationship between people and buildings was the chief objective.
- The chief units of analysis had to be the organizational group and the corresponding office layout, not the individual nor the single workplace. However, the data had to be collected in such a way that statements about group and layout were based upon individual and workplace measures so that the data could be aggregated and disaggregated in several ways.
- Actual organizations and layouts had to be studied. A comparative format for both social science and architectural data was essential.
- Both social science and architectural data had to be quantifiable.

This paper is a version of a section of the author's dissertation presented to Princeton University for the Ph.D. degree in January 1974. Published in this form as "Office Design and Organizations: 1. Theoretical basis", in *Environment and Planning B*, 1974, vol 1, pp 105–118.

4 Buildings Never Lie (1976)

Frozen music, perhaps. Frozen culture, certainly. Architecture seems to have the capacity to absorb and reflect the values of the society that commissioned and made it. I wonder how often architects consider by what mysterious process they are able to design buildings that mirror so eloquently the society in which they live. This ability seems to be shared equally by established and revolutionary architects, by Edwin Lutyens and Le Corbusier – although one accepted society more or less as it was and the other did his best to remodel it. Only in developing countries does there seem, even after the passage of time, a wider discrepancy between what buildings say and what those societies actually are. Even there the schism accurately reflects tensions that really exist.

Nowhere does architecture reflect society more clearly than in the design of office interiors. Take two Dutch examples that I know well – the recently completed Plant Administration Centre for IBM in Amsterdam (interiors planned and designed by JFN Associates, and subsequently by DEGW), and the Centraal Beheer offices in Apeldoorn (designed by Herman Hertzberger). Both are excellent offices, but excellent in different ways. The IBM spaces are cool, orderly and correct: individual expression is tolerated, but what seems stronger is the crisp, efficient corporate image of IBM. In Centraal Beheer, individual expression is so important that it almost cancels out the robust architecture of the shell. The expression of the identity of the company itself is hard to find.

In both of these examples, a corporate style has been accurately caught by the interior architecture – in the former case because of an extremely thorough and disciplined process of briefing; in the latter, because the architect had the imagination to divine what the company wanted to achieve and succeeded in reconciling this with his own objectives and pushing it a little way further – perhaps – than his client expected. In neither case, however, was a conscious corporate identity imposed from a book of rules. Unfortunately, we have no means to describe precisely these differences in style. Nor can we precisely relate them to style of management. We know the differences exist, and we sense the rightness of each solution in each circumstance. But we cannot pin them down, and we would find it very difficult to replicate consciously either style in a new situation. This is particularly irritating in the case of Centraal Beheer, because Hertzberger deliberately used his building to express his own personal preoccupation (which was taken up and magnified by his client) with the relationship between the individual and the corporate whole. In the IBM layout, on the other hand, individual autonomy is less marked than corporate loyalty.

It is this relationship between the individual and the institution – so well reflected in the interior design of offices— which I should like to examine further here. Very little has been made of this correspondence. Instead, since the Hawthorne experiments before the War (Roethlisberger and Dickson 1939), the physical environment and all the clues it offers have been neglected by social scientists. A typical recent example is in Peter Clark's book *Organizational Design* (1972), which begins with the naive attempt of the client to use design in his service (will red or blue walls make the worker happier?) and ends in the social scientists turning architectural intervention on its head by insisting that the real design problem was not the building but the invention of the right shape and form for the organization – in other words, organizational design.

The plea I should like to make is for a greater understanding by architects of what organizational design implies. It is not an activity which is entirely independent of the design of buildings. In fact, it is particularly important to architects since, just as the organization is at least the sum of all the individuals within it, so the office interior is at least the sum of all the workplaces which make it up. Organizations are designed; sometimes, perhaps, they design themselves. Many organizational decisions – numbers of staff, relations between groups, group size, method of transmitting messages – have an obvious physical correlate which is well known to brief writers: for example, in the area required, configuration of the building shell, size of spaces, centrality of the core. Another kind of correlation between design and organization seems more esoteric but is equally real. This concerns the relations between the various members of the organization – who is important, who has power, who is marginal, who is directly concerned with production, who provides a service, who is independent, who is controlled. These relations are vividly expressed in the physical environment of the interior of offices. The correlation is clear because each person is attached to a piece of space through which he is able to express his position in the organization. Similarly, the whole organization occupies a large amount of space through which it is collectively able to express its values. The correspondence between organization and physical things is very close – the language of space and furniture is very well understood by the people who use them. That is why when we enter a government department and observe the slovenly entrances and the cosy workplaces we know that organizational design follows values which are quite different from those that govern the advertising agency with its splendid reception and public areas but mean and crowded back rooms for the staff.

It seems to me that there is an important area for enquiry for architects here. How much does the architect design, and how much, like automatic writing, is designed by pressures from within the organization which force decisions upon him or her? In the case of Hertzberger's Centraal Beheer, a clear distinction was made between the bold design decisions made by the architect and the areas of design control he delegated to the individual workers. In this example, most of the superficial interior design decisions (which, of course, is practically everything you see) were made by the occupants. In IBM, most design decisions were made by the architect, the agent of the corporate client. In other words, the strength with which the architect intervenes, and even the degree of freedom with which the architect can operate, are themselves reflections of the social structure and the values of the client organization.

To what extent can the architect be an innovator? How much are environmental designers the prisoners of their own environment? The more architects understand the nature of organizations, and the more sensitive they are to the stresses within them, the more likely they are to respond intelligently by providing them with the means by which values can be expressed internally and externally. They will be able to distinguish an IBM situation from a Centraal Beheer situation. They will never make the mistake of pouring the right organization into the wrong building and will never have to suffer the miserable process of watching an organization collectively and individually gradually destroy their work in order to make itself comfortable, to express itself in the way it wants to be. One has seen many interiors in which a clever design concept has in a short time been systematically eroded and overlaid by what is really valued by its users.

Organizations change; decisions are constantly being made and remade. But what is the right organizational form? The more architects understand organizations and the complex decision-making processes within them, the more likely they are to begin to participate to some extent in the process – not just as passive observers but as combatants fighting on one side or the other. Like Hertzberger they may act as defenders of individual liberty, persuading management to adapt their total view of the organization to accommodate individual quirks and predilections. Conversely they may be willing to be tools in the hands of management, forcing or insidiously persuading individual members of staff to conform to the values of the organization as a whole.

The architect's position is not neutral in this war between individual and institutional values. If buildings, and especially interiors, can convey messages, is it also possible that they may be used to tell lies? There is a saying in anthropology that the natives never lie. Under questioning by anthropologists, whatever untruths the natives may tell about the life and customs of their people – to flatter or make fun of the interrogator – these lies will in the end be as revealing about the way those people think as plain, unvarnished truth. It is probably the same with architecture. Buildings can lie, but the lie will only be tolerated as long as it is believed. Once disbelieved, the lie will sooner or later be destroyed. As long as it is believed, the lie in a sense is true. Distorted or not, buildings and especially interiors reflect some kind of organizational reality.

Architects have much to learn about organizations. They may eventually learn from them something of the limits of their own powers. They may learn the kind of message their work is used to convey. They may learn to increase the range of what may be said. But there may be as much to be learned by social scientists from architecture in use. The office interior, for example, seems to be an incredibly rich indicator of the interplay of the actors within an organization. This would be especially so if the interior is observed as it is changed through time, and not, as customarily, merely frozen at one point in time. The form in which an office is laid out and designed can be interpreted as a medium in which the interplay and conflict between the institution and the individual can be traced through time.

From a symbolic-interactionist perspective which tries to understand how we define the situation in which we find ourselves – how we impose our own values upon "reality", and how we select the ends we seek – the office environment should be particularly useful. The degree of control of individuals over the workplace, their attempts to use it to defend and define their own positions, the meaning they attach to it, and the way it is changed and developed over time as they themselves change and the organization around them changes, should illuminate the place of the individual within the institution, helping to answer the Hobbesian question of how it is that rational but distrustful and sometimes deceitful men can live peacefully together in society. If the right methodology can be developed, the study of the relationship between individual and institution, between management style and architectural style, between architecture and organizations ought to prove unexpectedly and late in the day fruitful for both architectural and organizational theory.

First published as "Buildings never lie", *Architectural Design*, February 1976.

5 Systems Thinking (1991)

If one word can encapsulate a whole quarter of a century, "systems" sums up the years between 1950 and 1975, when disciplines ran riot, renounced conventional boundaries, sought interconnections between phenomena, thought big, started again from scratch. They began, in short, to connect the kneebone to the thighbone. Architects – never backward in such pursuits – sought through this whole period for a fresh vision. Many expected this to emerge from a radical analysis of their clients' needs. For most, the vision never quite materialized. For some, as the skylines of innumerable cities testify, an all-too-concrete imagery emerged in the all-too-unforgettable form of a thousand tower blocks. Norman Foster, in contrast, not only embraced wholeheartedly the idea of systems architecture but came away in 1975 with a clutch of buildings that were not only different but obviously superior, with his reputation enhanced and his hands entirely spotless.

Why was the idea of systems so attractive to architects in this period? Perhaps more important, what is it about Norman Foster that has enabled him to turn the systems idea, which turned out to be so empty an inspiration for so many architects, into utterly convincing architecture? Did Foster need the idea, or was he so good that anything he did would be turned to gold?

These questions need to be answered if the foundations of Norman Foster's particular architectural contribution are to be properly surveyed and understood. With the right answers, Foster's early career can also be used to illuminate what is likely to become an increasingly hard-to-understand episode in cultural history.

SYSTEMS IDEAS

Systems were in the air. Related to the interdisciplinary thinking which in the early 1940s was the basis of the invention of operational research, systems thinking carried an aura of big programmes implicit within it (Tennessee Valley Authority, Combined Ops, the Manhattan Project). The very word was worth a lot: it had the effect of a simultaneous claim to intellectual respectability and practicality.

Consider a parallel from another field – Eric Trist of the Tavistock Institute (interdisciplinary by definition) is a typical systems intellectual of the period. In the late 1940s, when British social science still meant something, he demonstrated that systems thinking could be profitably applied to designing the interface between men and machines in the newly nationalized collieries. He showed that it was not enough just to import the latest American coal-cutting technology: it had to be introduced in such a way that it did not destroy the mutual support in risk taking between colliers that had grown up over centuries in the Durham coalfields. Men and machines were an "open socio-technical system". Social systems, reward systems, technological systems – this all had to be carefully interwoven to make it possible for the newly-founded National Coal Board to achieve its organizational objectives.

Architectural antecedents

Five key examples are enough to show how similar systems ideas were introduced into architecture.

The three best examples are American. Charles Eames created a brilliant metaphor of systems thinking in his own house – all standard components from builders' catalogues and *objets trouvés* – as well as highly innovative product design and exhibitions. Buckminster Fuller's whole career was in itself a core study of the abolition of intellectual boundaries and the search for innovative solutions. A little later, Robert Propst, the furniture designer, invented the revolutionary Action Office furniture for Herman Miller – based on his direct and systematic observations of how people worked.

In Britain the obvious contemporary parallel is the work of the development groups in the old Ministry of Education, so well described by Andrew Saint in *Towards a Social Architecture*. Resources are scarce, demand for school places is heavy: how can a miracle in the procurement of school buildings be achieved? By systems thinking, of course: bringing together architects and educationists, physicists and builders, boffins and quantity surveyors, to rethink not just how to build the old kind of school faster, but new schools, with new curricula, new plan forms, new ways of teaching, new methods of building. The logic is simple: relax the old constraints, bring pure intellect to bear, rethink the problem, and out it all comes, clickety-click: new teaching, new architecture, a bright, oh so bright, new world.

Not only in Britain and not only in education did such miracles of the modern movement happen. The fifth example is drawn from Germany in the mid-1950s, when the Schnelle brothers began to think about office buildings from first principles. The same conditions applied: great economic stringency, a heavy demand for office spaces because of the rapid rebuilding of the German economy, a crossing and intermingling of disciplines, the urgent need for cheap physical solutions to pressing organizational problems. The result was the dazzling new concept of bürolandschaft, the famous open plan office layouts designed to maximize organizational communications and which, from the inside out, determined the shape of what became a totally new generation of office buildings. Once seen, never forgotten. Bürolandschaft instantly encapsulated generations of management thinking from Taylorism to human relations to cybernetics – an image of systems thinking.

All five examples owe their success to a balance of memorable imagery and a fully-articulated intellectual programme. Foster's work is best understood in the context of this dualism. He can be compared, for example, to contemporaries who seemed, in earlier phases of their career, to be equally promising and for the same reasons. With his eloquence, radicalism and rage for a more soundly-based, more rational architecture, Cedric Price is the best British example. Ezra Ehrenkrantz, who had absorbed the radical British tradition in his years at the Building Research Station, appeared as a star in the Californian skies in the early 1960s with his innovative "performance specification" approach to procuring school buildings (SCSD). In fact, just as Foster was quick to specify Propst's Action Office furniture, so certain images from the SCSD programme – which had a certain Californian, Craig Elwood-like authenticity – were present as icons in Foster's earliest office in Covent Garden.

Neither Cedric Price's nor Ezra Ehrenkrantz's built work, however, ever succeeded in capturing the systems idea strongly enough in architectural terms – ideology always seemed stronger than imagery (and in Ehrenkrantz's case the ideology, too, seems to have faded with time).

Late starter

Foster had all the advantages of single-mindedness and a late start. The position from which he began in the late 1960s allowed him to establish – quickly – his own version of what buildings ought to be like. The models were available, an architectural language existed and an appropriate ideology was also in place. As is clear from several waves of school building, however, while this language was modernist, always austere and practical in construction, it was usually relaxed and even romantic in plan form. Only occasionally were the results memorable or elegant.

Neither ideology nor architecture lacked anything in high seriousness. But they did lack passion – two decades of earnest architectural endeavour in Britain had not produced a poet.

The extent of Foster's acceptance of this inheritance is abundantly clear in the Newport schools competition of 1967. Billed as a "sophisticated package within DES cost limits", the proposal managed to combine the lively and imaginative interest in users so characteristic of the best DES work of the time with an enthusiastic acceptance of the deep open plan that owed a lot to North American influence and an energetic and practical sense of the way buildings should be put together. There is, however, a toughness and rigour about Foster's work that is new. Care is taken to demonstrate that the rigid rectangular building envelope can accommodate both "traditional classroom layout" and "plan arrangement based on new educational techniques". While the sketches hint that the latter style is preferred, the "basic systems network" has foreseen and foresuffered all. Something of what Newport promised for school building was achieved in the School for Handicapped Children, Liverpool (1973–6). This is the school building conceived as shed – five linked portal frames, with four service cores "to define the various zones of activity". The project combines all the key canonical features of this period – a glum, unpromising site, the severe, deep plan, the taut, nervous, almost aerodynamic building skin, the construction kit grid, the visible integration of services and structure, the relatively loose, rhapsodic interior planning. Somehow, the children and their paraphernalia are independent of and yet counterpoint the architecture.

Similar features can be found in the schools of the 1940s, 1950s and 1960s illustrated by Andrew Saint in *Towards a Social Architecture*. None of these buildings, however, has the obsessive, holistic quality that already defines Foster's genius.

BEYOND A SOCIAL ARCHITECTURE

The first commercial building Foster ever built (with Richard Rogers and the rest of Team 4) carried this holistic passion into a different world – one that had previously tolerated very low standards of building and design. This is the steel-framed electronics factory for Reliance Controls at Swindon (1967) – for which Sir Peter Parker was the enlightened, and fortunate, client.

Foster and his colleagues in Team 4 rose to the challenge of a dynamic client in an emerging, dynamic industry – fast track design, speedy erection, low cost, flexibility to accommodate growth and change, progressive image. In plan, the distinction between office and factory was swept away. In section, the priority was for the provision for adaptability and for services.

Three factors in this building are indicative of the future direction of Foster's work. First, stretching the use of components far beyond conventional views of their capacity – for example, the use of corrugated deck units with no intermediate supporting rails. Second, the integration of all components into a comprehensive system – for example, the reflective nature of the underside of the roof decking. And third, the extreme, practical, minimalist elegance of the construction. Nothing superfluous, everything deft, all components working together. This is why Foster's perspective section is so important: it is as much a heuristic device to eliminate redundancy as a means of explaining what was done.

The projects for Fred Olsen at Millwall Docks follow directly in this line. Now the architect has hit his form, diagramming, reducing, explaining all at once. The new challenge (in what is now Docklands) was operational – how to move large numbers of people from taxis and coaches, through ticketing and customs on to their boat, and how to provide amenities for Fred Olsen's staff. The shell design is simplified to the search for the least number of the simplest possible components. The planning, equally, becomes a process of remorseless simplification. Nothing is left unresolved: everything is made into an intellectual challenge and solved with the least effort in the most elegant way.

Nothing will come of nothing

"Less is more" is a familiar – perhaps overfamiliar – mantra. But nothing in Mies's work prepares one for the nervy, obsessive, impatient quality that by this time was already characteristic of Foster's work. Mies, translated to Chicago, was attractive to developers because his view of architecture did not particularly contradict theirs. Foster, in a much more positive way, had become by this stage highly attractive to certain sophisticated industrial user clients because it had become obvious that he was capable of thinking about exploiting scarce resources to achieve organizational objectives in very much the same way as they did. Fred Olsen showed how Foster was able not just to build economically but also to plan intelligently with management to achieve operational goals – in which working collaboratively with the dockers was as important as anticipating passenger requirements.

IBM is the epitome of the enlightened client. For an architect to work with IBM is to experience excellent project management – just as capable in procuring buildings as in developing new computer systems, of using the corporation's immense experience as well as seeking innovative ways of solving new problems. So given his recent experiences in the electronics industry, it is not surprising that in 1970 they picked Foster to design "temporary" offices at Cosham. Those temporary offices are still there today as crisp and sharp as ever.

The plan form is almost exactly that of the Newport School (if you are Norman Foster you never waste a good idea): a huge, single-storey rectangle, 146m by 73m, with absolutely clear access and circulation, served by asymmetrically placed cores and highly-serviced areas.

Here is the ghost of the Hertfordshire schools but with their soft romanticism purged and their clumsy detailing transmuted into the most exquisite delicacy and lightness of construction. Birkin Haward's drawing of the section is itself a masterpiece and one of the great architectural images of all time. (Even the brochure produced by Foster to describe the scheme is a didactic masterpiece.) The slowly accumulated experience of two decades of public sector work has been captured and raised to another power in the service of the most sophisticated computer company in the world. This was achieved not by elaboration but by reduction, by the simplest and most intensely focused means.

Clarity is everything. Data and electrical services are integrated into the column grid which in turn neatly complements the layout of desks and of internal rooms. The distribution of air conditioning in units on the roof follows a precise and confident plan – so unlike the clutter that still disfigures buildings 20 years later in business parks. Site planning, services, structure, construction, layout – all have been comprehended and ordered. So simple, so direct. Why isn't all building like this?

Progressive refinement

Two other deep, commercial projects of this period should be mentioned: the building for Modern Art Glass at Thamesmead (1973) and the earlier building (or, rather, degree zero of building) for Computer Technology Ltd (1973). Modern Art Glass – a warehouse and office storeroom – demonstrates Foster's habit of seizing whenever he can the opportunity to develop component design as far as he can take it. The client had been a subcontractor on earlier Foster projects and wanted to use his own building as a showcase for glazing technology. Foster rose to the challenge: "12mm bronze-tinted toughened glass supported on lugs welded to tubular steel supports, with vertical mullions of bolted neoprene and horizontal joints filled with silicone – all pretty impressive". Modern Art Glass may be a showcase but it is still unabashedly an industrial shed. In the end, what impresses is the extraordinary way with which ordinary components have been put together. Unlike, for example, Rogers at the Corporation of Lloyd's, innovating grandly on a hundred fronts simultaneously, Foster is content to improve the humdrum by focusing on the least number of most feasible means.

His most radical exercise in minimalist design in this period was the temporary air structure for Computer Technology Ltd at Hemel Hempstead – 8000 sq ft commenced, achieved and occupied within eight weeks – to provide basic office accommodation while the more permanent (and, one has to admit, rather less memorable) structures were erected.

This extraordinary period from 1968 to 1974 – during which Foster turned shed design into an art form – is summed up in a diagram from *The Architectural Review* which tacitly claims, project by project, an almost Darwinian line of refinement very much in the Buckminster Fuller tradition, from Reliance to Computer Technology. D'Arcy Thompson would have been tempted to display this as an example of progressive adaptation and improvement of one of the most basic components of architectural enclosure – steel. The diagram reveals the extent of understatement in the Foster style – by a sleight of hand, technological progress is made to look impersonal and inevitable. In fact, such continuing refinement can only be the consequence of an individual vision, of one man's overriding drive.

ALL HEAVEN IN A GRAIN OF SAND

By 1975, Foster had demonstrated in the unglamorous and highly competitive arena of the design of deep plan industrial sheds that:

• he had not only learned everything there was to know from two decades of patient development work in the public sector but was capable of transferring it to another sphere
• his particular architectural skills were relevant to achieving clients' operational goals in the fastest growing sector of the economy at that time
• he could transcend each individual project to achieve the equivalent

of a continuing programme of development
• building components could be as easily and effectively developed as building types.

That all this was possible on low cost industrial projects on dismal industrial estates in unfashionable locations simply adds to the magnitude of the achievement. The groundwork had been done and the objectives established for subsequent, far more conspicuous and complex projects such as IBM's Distribution Centre at Greenford and Willis Faber Dumas in Ipswich. If one analyses Foster's major achievements of the late-1980s, such as Stansted, the genesis of the approach can be traced back to the same integrating and reductionist obsessions that led to the success of Reliance Controls.

Very early in his career, Foster had found a systems-based ideology that combined satisfying client requirements with innovatory thinking about how to put buildings together. It is a severe, puritanical, purging kind of ideology with little scope for sentimentality or second thoughts. Under its scorching, excoriating glare, there could be little room for the wilfulness of bürolandschaft layouts – a tougher, service-based discipline had to be found. Nor could there be any sympathy for the romantic elaboration of the thick, messy concrete buffer that lies at the heart of Hertzberger's contemporary attempt to reconcile long-term corporate culture with short-term individual worker discretions. The objective is always to do the most with the least. There is, in fact, scant evidence of tolerance of whimsy or choice on the part of the end users – corporate clarity always tends to dominate. There is no attempt to emulate the growing German interest in complex building forms intended to articulate and reinforce group spaces. It always seems more important to stress the rationalist, corporate orthogonal than to explore the potential of outlandish grids. Given its lightness and precision, steel is the ideal material. In this way, Foster avoids in a stroke the overcomplexity and rigidity of Arup Associates' attempt to integrate services with concrete structures (for example, Gateway 1, designed for Wiggins Teape at Basingstoke). Meeting short term objectives is always more challenging than vague notions of long-term capacity. There is no attempt, except in the most abstract terms, to follow Louis Kahn's love of the articulation of building form to express served and service spaces. Understatement is more attractive to Foster than an architecture that needs mass to expound its meaning. There is no playfulness, no waste, no redundancy, no attempt to speak in any Babylonish dialect. Simplicity is the thing.

All the buildings discussed in this essay have deep open plans. The significance of the deep plan is not just that such plan configurations are sensible for the purposes these particular buildings serve (as they certainly are) but for three underlying and much more important reasons. The first is that the deep open plan represented at this time an ideology, a particular, no-nonsense approach to building design. Breaking down barriers – between offices and workshops, between front and back, between high and low status – was very much an open "systems" attitude of the time: "long life, low energy, loose fit". Secondly, and more important, the radical simplification that open planning entailed allowed Foster to concentrate on the development and refinement of certain recurrent constructional details – in a sense, he removed planning from the problem: all the plans referred to in this chapter are the same. Thirdly, and most importantly, deepness and openness allowed Foster to make visible his intention to integrate systems. There is a strong, partly unconscious, didactic programme that runs through all of these buildings – "systems integration is good; therefore they should be seen". For this mission, smaller, more fragmented building types would not have suited Foster's purposes at all. The accident (or the single-mindedness) of being commissioned to design a series of similar buildings made Foster the architect he is. These buildings both chose and made him.

Did Foster really need the intellectual baggage of systems thinking? The answer is undoubtedly "yes". Without this open-ended, conceptual framework, Foster's energies would have been both dissipated and too narrowly channelled.

Would systems thinking in itself have been enough to create what Foster has achieved? The answer is certainly "no". The legacy of the British school building programme is sufficient testament to the weakness of good intentions without great talent.

Foster's reductionist genius required a starting point. In the end, this series of projects leaves one breathless at the intensity of imagination, at the alchemy that could distil such ordinary material, such temporary and mundane projects, into purest gold.

First published in *Norman Foster, Team 4 and Foster Associates, Building Projects Vol. I: 1964–73*, 1991.

6 Bürolandschaft 1958–1978 (1979)

Many architects will remember very well the shock of seeing office landscaping for the first time. In the early 1960s the essence of office design was to stack homogenized net lettable area into Miesian towers. Nothing had prepared us for those curious German drawings which actually showed desks, hundreds of desks, randomly arranged in great open spaces. In schools or housing everyone agonized about the brief but never in office design. All at once, these new and unforgettable layouts seemed to prove not only that offices were for people but that a superior understanding of how those people worked could lead to revolutionary changes in the shape of the buildings. Office landscaping layouts were diagrams of organizational form first and buildings only second. A victory of reason and method over preconceived design solutions: so it seemed at the time.

Seeing the German offices themselves a little later was no disappointment. The Schnelle brothers who invented bürolandschaft in the late 1950s had done their work well. Carpets and continuous ceilings, new furniture, plants and a sense of space and order were a revelation in office design in the context of that time. Few Europeans then had a clear idea of the higher standards which were expected in American office buildings. The relatively poor conditions customary in the UK can still be easily recaptured by leafing through old issues of architectural and interior design magazines in which even the best office examples seem to our present vision hard, glaring, poky and uncomfortable. The German offices – the BP prototype in Hamburg, Ninoflax in Nordhorn, Buch und Ton, Krupps, Boehringer, Osram – seemed incomparably more sophisticated. Their look burned itself into the retina. This was the office of the future.

If the image was not enough to convince, there was always the rationale – beautifully presented arguments which gradually unfolded into a codebook of procedures. "This is how it is done. Follow these rules and all will be well." So much had been anticipated and yet there was no limit to debate as issue after issue of *Kommunikation*, the Schnelle's own journal, dealt with cybernetics, decision making, information theory, and above all the theory of organization. No detail was too small to be ignored; no branch of science too esoteric to be relevant to the problem of designing better offices for better organizations. This was not a small achievement. Perhaps it is irreverent to make the comparison but Le Corbusier on a larger scale is an exact parallel to the originators of office landscaping in his skill in combining vivid design initiatives with plausible justifications. When the skills of the pamphleteer and the slogan writer join the vision of the designer, the combination is deadly. Unforgettable image, convincing storyline, clear rules for putting it into effect. It is hardly surprising that office landscaping has been such a success. It was an offer you could not refuse without branding yourself as unprogressive or a bureaucrat or a paper hoarder or undemocratic or mean. Every objection was anticipated, every argument tested and tried. From Germany to Scandinavia to the United Kingdom, then to the US by 1967, to Italy by 1970, and to Spain slightly later; the ripples are still spreading onwards and outwards today.

In the centre, in Germany where bürolandschaft started and in Scandinavia where it was so widely adopted so quickly, there is hardly the same general and unqualified approval for the concept as there was ten years ago. "Reversible" space which can be either open plan or cellular is now much talked about in Germany; in Sweden there have recently been some spectacular instances of projects which originally had been intended to be open plan and which have ended up highly cellular. In Holland the best known office building of the decade, Centraal Beheer, is open plan but is nevertheless, in bürolandschaft terms, entirely heretical, breaking all the rules about lighting, circulation and depth of space which once were so fundamental. In the US there are plenty of open plan offices and much discussion of office landscaping but it would take a very subtle mind to distinguish between the native tradition of open office planning and what has been imported from Europe. What are the reasons for these reactions and what light do they throw on the original concept?

IS OFFICE LANDSCAPING A CONCEPT?

"Pure" office landscaping has been distinguished from impure varieties which are sullied by orthogonal desk layout grids or enclosed individual offices. This is a dangerous argument which can be reduced to insisting that pure office landscaping is good and that anything which is not good is impure – a very convenient way of making sure that critics don't take your unsuccessful projects too seriously.

In fact it is impossible to use any rock bottom criterion to establish what office landscaping is. A better quality environment? Perhaps: but relative to what standard? Random layout reflecting patterns of work flow? But it is possible to devise many forms of layout which respect work flow and whose randomness varies widely. Of course, randomness of layout is directly related to layout density. You can't have desks in irregular formation if you are putting a lot of people in a floor. Is it really true that only layouts below a certain density are landscaped? Degree of enclosure also varies widely from project to project especially since the coming of screen-based furniture systems and more and more enclosures for meetings and equipment. At what degree of enclosure does landscaping cease to be viable? Building shells which have been landscaped vary enormously from depths of over 100m to less than 12m. Is the magic office depth of 20m within which landscaping is said to be possible really valid?

Inspect a few score office landscapes and the rules evaporate; the degree of variation is greater than the common factors. What remains? A ragbag of physical features such as rubber plants and break areas and a low murmur of slogans about better communications, more equality, more team spirit. The easily identifiable image turns out to be a shimmering mirage held together by organizational ideas which, once questioned, begin to lose their coherent power.

What we have observed is the success of a brilliant piece of management consultancy which brought together a number of disparate managerial ideas and wrapped them up in an attractive physical package. None of the ideas in the package – except perhaps some aspects of physical design – is new. The emphasis on work flow can be traced back to the first flowering of scientific Taylorist work study in the US just before the First World War. American manuals for the office administrators of this period are full of rudimentary versions of the flow charts which office landscaping made so familiar 50 years later. The ideas about equality and team spirit are derived from the great upsurge in American interest in human relations at the work place following the failure of the Hawthorne experiments to relate productivity to the physical environment except through the mediation of human contact, manager to worker. On top of these two historical strata of American managerial ideas lies a third – the cybernetic and systems notions of the 1950s which saw the office as a control mechanism. Three distinct strata of managerial ideas were put together within the context of an American technical innovation possible now for the first time in Europe, the use of deep air-conditioned space for offices. Imagine the impact of these American ideas on post-war Germany when a new and burgeoning economy required a vast building programme. Add to this the relative rarity of speculative development in Germany and the strong tradition of purpose-built office buildings. The only missing factor and the one which is the hardest to explain is the genius of the Schnelle brothers in realizing that all these diverse and alien elements could be packaged in a way which would appeal to powerful managerial clients.

CONSEQUENCES OF OFFICE LANDSCAPING

The bad consequences of office landscaping are very obvious. A package design solution sooner or later must be wrong. It cannot be sensitive to variation in organizational form. Implicit in bürolandschaft is the idea that all organizations are or ought to be the same with an equal emphasis on communications, lack of hierarchy, flexibility, team spirit. This is obviously false. Different kinds of business are structured in many different ways, have different technologies and values and above all different traditions of accommodating themselves in offices. There is a world of difference between insurance and the law, between a sales office and a research establishment. No one type of office layout or even office building shell can accommodate them all.

Worse still, the enthusiasm for the bürolandschaft package has led to a vast number of expensive and highly inflexible building shells which are far too deep to be useful. That they are full of super-flexible furniture must be a small consolation to their owners since the labour of maintaining these layouts is now very apparent. With skill and dedication, bürolandschaft can be controlled; without these resources densities rise, circulation clogs and the quality of the environment declines. Nothing is more fragile than an open plan office layout.

The good consequences are less clear but more far reaching. Office landscaping has taught Europeans the American lesson that office planning should be taken seriously, that planning and talking to the user are vital, that the user is prior to the design of the building shell, that buildings can be made to reflect organizational requirements. American office planners had learned to cope with deep air-conditioned office space and large organizations well before the advent of bürolandschaft. This relative sophistication explains why office landscaping was less of a shock in the States than in Germany and why it has been welcomed as one more alternative rather than the one uniquely important solution.

Bürolandschaft has stimulated furniture design. New open plan offices provide excellent arguments for refurnishing and many ranges of office furniture have been designed specially to meet the demands of new offices. Office furniture was given design attention it never had before and from being providers of desks and chairs, office furniture manufacturers see themselves as selling "systems" of interconnected components to accommodate all office tasks. It is clear that office furniture is absorbing many functions such as partitioning, lighting and servicing distribution which formerly were performed by architecture itself. Many offices are now better furnished than office workers' homes. Expectations of design and comfort in the office have risen. While this is partly a consequence and partly a cause of office landscaping, the trend is irreversible.

CHANGING CONDITIONS

Architecture is an image of society; office layout of organizational form. That bürolandschaft was invented and widely accepted in the 1960s can be explained by the conjunction of an unusual set of circumstances. Office technology was still relatively simple despite the Schnelles' talk of cybernetics. The typical early landscaped office was a clerical factory in which work groups were large and simply structured. Office organizations were not changing very fast so that while participation, teamwork and equality were bywords, the underlying reality was still that power was held very tightly by a small number of forward-looking but very senior managers. Their unilateral decision to introduce a democratic layout without status distinctions would be unthinkingly obeyed. Office staff were passive in those days. Office buildings were architecturally weak and were becoming even more recessive, trying very hard with widely-spaced, rounded columns and off-centre cores to disappear altogether. Office planning and maintenance could be expected to be carried out by staff of a high order particularly if they were supported by skilled consultants. It was in this context that bürolandschaft was possible. These conditions cannot remain. Bürolandschaft is under threat. Everyone knows that office work is changing very rapidly. Computer terminals are now very common in the office but the full impact of automation in changing the balance of office skills and in removing the need for large concentrations of low-level clerical staff has yet to be felt. It is quite possible that the small, untidy professional office is more a model of the typical future organization than the vast hygienic clerical formations of the 1960s. If this is so, what relevance will office landscaping have?

The balance of power in office organizations is shifting. This is clearly shown by the growing demand for personal space, pictures, mementoes, pets which Centraal Beheer exemplifies. These demands are not trivial. You can only keep your office as tidy as a battleship if you have as much power as an admiral. Once management has shown itself willing to negotiate with the ratings' individual decor, the next step is to negotiate about the shape of the building itself – about windows, partitions, lighting, heating: physical, palpable objects which are highly quantifiable and highly attractive to argue about. Of course, such negotiation is only superficially about the office environment. Underneath is a struggle to invent new organizational forms which take into account a new vision of industrial society in which power is shared more widely and a new reality of an office labour force composed of awkward, skilled, self-reliant, self-opinionated professionals.

Centraal Beheer is a watershed. Hertzberger's building is one of the last of the great corporate open office plans and one of the first of a new era of personal, individualized, domestic office environments. But the freedom given to staff is still only possible within a strong organizational (and building) structure. Had staff been involved – as they frequently are nowadays in Sweden – with decisions about the shape of the building shell and not just the decor and colour of the walls, a far more cellular, conservative building form would have been the likely result.

Meanwhile the shape of office buildings is changing for other, more architectural reasons. Deep, highly-serviced office buildings are only one theme in the history of office design. There is another thread which could be traced back through many nineteenth-century projects to Soane's Halls in the Bank of England, and certainly to Frank Lloyd Wright's three seminal office buildings – Larkin, Johnson Wax, and Marin County. This is the theme of the strong, three-dimensional, highly-structured, highly-particular interior space.

Centraal Beheer is directly in this tradition and so are many new American office projects, sometimes new buildings and sometimes adaptations of big existing buildings. Bürolandschaft was not designed to sit within such bold spaces.

Finally, many problems of facilities management have obviously not been solved by office landscaping. Flexibility is not just a matter of moving light portable furniture; it needs to be controlled and managed at a more fundamental level. Large, open-plan layouts take many hours of skill and care to keep in order – a secret cost. Surely buildings could be designed which allow change and yet control layout almost automatically? Here again Centraal Beheer, with its interwoven structure and fixed circulation, provides a possible clue.

Office tasks, organization, building, space management are all changing. No one formula, even one so brilliantly conceived as bürolandschaft, can possibly cope with the wide diversity of present conditions, let alone those of the future. Invention is badly needed both in the design and the development of interior furniture and fittings and in the design of office building shells. This is what makes the late 1970s such an extremely interesting period in office design. Two major lessons for architects can be derived from two decades of bürolandschaft.

• Architects have, on the whole, lost the initiative. They have allowed new forms of design and briefing services provided sometimes by consultants and sometimes by furniture manufacturers to interpose themselves between the client and the layout. Unless architects are close to clients they cannot understand their problems.
• Architects have failed to distinguish between clients' short and long-term requirements. Too many buildings have been cast in eternal concrete on the basis of transient managerial or architectural whims with far too little thought about inevitable changes in management style and structure. The myth of flexible, universal open-plan space has led us all astray.

Bürolandschaft has come to a dead end. This is a challenge, not a set-back. We can build on this experience. To go back to dumb partitioned offices, to the low level of thinking about office design which was tolerated in the UK in the early 1960s and which led to the miserable stock of speculative and custom-built offices which we see all around us, would be a disaster. We must be able to do better than that.

First published as "Bürolandschaft", *Architectural Review,* January 1979.

Part 2   1979 – 1991

THE

PRACTICE

OF

ARCHITECTURE

Brian Griffin / Davenport Associates

The generation growing up in Britain after World War II saw planning as humanizing and the market as free-booting – close to piracy – with privatizing treading the same fine, killing and casuistical line as that between pirate and privateer. For many it was somehow counterintuitive to see Thatcher's deregulatory revolution as liberalizing rather than licence – the extension of privilege – and inevitable that the very things that were wrong with Britain (a financial system based on a greedy, short-termist stock market and faint-hearted clearing banks reluctant to support investment in production) would be untouched or even aggravated by the New Right reforms. As architects were released from the paradoxes and accommodations of planning, the paradoxes of non-planning were about to take hold.

The Profession in the Marketplace

The year 1979 was, of course, a watershed in Britain – but not a waterfall: intellectually discredited and politically moribund, the welfare state/mixed economy/world role consensus that had sustained post-war Britain had been leaking authority for years. Perhaps the dam-burst of dreams began with the 1975 Healey cuts designed to resolve the sterling crisis, perhaps it first spurted in some Tory grandee's king-making ambitions for his brutal protegée – but by 1979 the consensus had run dry. The market would provide. Instead of control and centralization – fragmentation. Instead of accountability to a network of values, subservience to one – the market.

"It is important to be quite clear about this: the modern movement for planning is a movement against competition as such, a new flag under which all the old enemies of competition have rallied" (Hayek, *The Road to Serfdom*). Hayek is of course talking about economic planning – by which he means, in essence, "only that planning which is against competition" – but the juxtaposition with the words "modern movement" is no accident: adventitious, perhaps, but revealing. Planning, competition, *laissez-faire* – professionals as a whole were in for a bumpy ride but clearly architects in particular were to be disabused of their special status. They were not master builders; they were the enemy of the people.

As the Thatcher administration set about self-consciously testing the ethical and practical limits of its fundamentalist agenda, there may have been doubts about the purity of deregulatory motivation and the even-handedness of the way in which it was wielded – but, particularly post-Falklands, there was no doubt about the effect, which was unremittingly selective and polarizing, producing a series of have and have-not schisms across the country. There were, then, inevitably to be casualties in this reductivist evolutionary test of the fittest. Would one of them be the essential architectural element of design in use? A crucial test would be whether architecture allowed itself to be borne downstream through the uninflecting conduit of the market. Or would it dam up a few sticks of integrity? In the built environment, nowhere was the torrent stronger than in the City of London in the mid-1980s, in its pre-spawning rush to put on weight before the Big Bang marked the race to the headwaters of globalized trade.

A key plank of belief for the New Right was the pulling back of the boundaries of the state and a key part of that belief was the need to deregulate the money markets in the City of London. From October 1986 banks would be permitted to trade and traders could still trade – but in competition with banks. Underlying this move was the acknowledgement of the internationalization of finance and the desire for access to the global marketplace. That globalization depended on electronics and electronics had to be housed. Ironically, this ubiquity of information made the old location, location, location chant more critical than it had ever been.

On the world stage, the implications were that – if the reasoning was sound – London would take its place at the apex of the trading golden triangle, both spatially and in terms of significance, between New York and Tokyo. On the local stage, it meant that those deregulated banks and stockbrokers had to be allowed to let rip with the space they needed if they were to occupy that profitable and strategic tip and see off their competitors, Paris or Frankfurt. Gigantism and mergers were inevitable – were, it is fair to say, planned: and so Big Bang, as this liberalizing measure was called, was from the start intricately tied up with the English planning system.

Michael Cassidy, chairman of the City of London planning committee, explained the process to a Japanese audience in 1987:

> The local planning authority has the power to withhold consent for development – refurbishment as well as new building. It also considers applications for demolition of protected buildings. The City of London planning committee has 35 members, meeting fortnightly, with the power to confer or refuse consent. During the course of 1986 the securities market was deregulated, meaning that market making could be undertaken directly with the company concerned rather than through an intermediary. Market makers merged with banks and international securities houses creating huge new financial services conglomerates and the demand for a new type of space – space with large, open area floors, good floor to ceiling heights, minimum of columns, low squat designs (groundscrapers rather than skyscrapers for more efficient use of space) and sophisticated servicing provision both to improve the working environment and to ensure 24-hour operation.
>
> (Cassidy, 1987)

City developers got the consent to meet that demand. After all, "In no system that could be rationally defended would the state just do nothing" (Hayek, *op. cit.*). Hosting huge acreages of infrastructurally-demanding offices in some of the smallest, most cramped and most primitively-serviced space in the capital was simply too important to be left to the market mechanism.

The market could have provided: getting things wrong, allowing the fittest to survive – buildings as well as individuals – and consigning the unfittest to the garbage dump. It would have been expensive, inhumane, cruel and wasteful, but it would have worked in architecture as it did in other areas, leaving the landscape littered with the husks of redundant practices alongside the corpses of unsuitable projects. Some areas of the built environment would have been and indeed were irredeemably blighted as they lost out to market forces (and not surprisingly they included social housing and school building, chief beneficiaries of the planned economy). Others, however, were essential to the smooth manipulation of the new religion of non-manipulation and were therefore too important to be left to chance. This was one of those areas.

Big Bang had to be planned for from a very low base in quantity, quality and suitability of space. Organizations, buildings and information technology – the poor relations of the decades after the war – had to work together perfectly, first time. To make sure that they did, a revolution in the thinking of the construction industry – not just architects: agents, developers, tenants – had to take place. But if evolution is the dance, revolution is the step, and the step had to come first. It came with the acknowledgement that information technology – IT – had simultaneously changed the game and upped the stakes. By October 1986 that space had to work, and not iteratively but in one stride – and it was architects who had to make it work. They were back in control of design, use and procurement.

During the period of centralized state control, architects could drift, riding the public bandwagon without questioning the loss of soul, or self-determination, involved. When the New Right took their turn in the wallow, most architects plunged into the concept of the market – in ways satirized by Nathanael West in the 1930s (the self-immolating Lemuel Pitkin in *A Cool Million*) and Terry Southern in the 1960s (the dollar bills in the shit-and sulphuric acid tank in *The Magic Christian*) – without counting the cost of such a unitary solution to such complex questions. Between the end of the war and the rise of Thatcherism what sustained the profession was a quite unfashionable concern with elements of craft that introduced the figure of the user to the magic circle of client-as-investor, builder-as-tradesman and architect-as-Fountainhead. In this second period, the dead man's handle was set by the punctiliousness with which those new lessons, that new wisdom, were applied in practice, when the temptation was to go along with the pioneering, Gold Rush morality – to hell with poverty, give the cat another Canary Wharf.

Did professionalism act as a corrective to this rush? Were architects – as a profession – prepared for information technology? The change in status of women in the workplace? The importance of the environment and energy conservation? The shift from public to private ownership?

The rough answer has to be that although strong and principled positions were taken by individual architects and isolated practices – intellectually, commercially, politically – most members of the profession smugly behaved like predators for years after they had been marked out as prey by an unsympathetic or antagonistic government and the beginnings of what would be the longest and deepest recession for half a century.

The length of time between the self-defining, self-protecting initiatives made by the profession in the 1960s and the next cycle of self-analysis begun at the end of the 1980s betrays a complacency that compares unfavourably with the vigorousness and combativeness of the earlier years of the profession: that, indeed, created the profession in a clash of violent private enterprise and rigorous public accountability – when the industrial, political and social developments of the nineteenth century were shadowed by professional development; when the new institutions of democracy created new building types such as museums, zoos, arcades, hospitals, cemeteries; when innovations in trade and transport gave rise to canals, railway stations, hotels, banks, offices, restaurants, parks; and when public works like Bazalgette's Metropolitan Board of Works emerged to counter unsheathed Victorian *laissez-faire.*

For most of the 1980s the energy that had driven through that formative period seemed to be no longer available even to resist threats to the continued existence of the profession created in such easily traceable, hard-to-achieve steps: 1863, RIBA voluntary exams; 1882, compulsory exams for associateship;1895, first school – Liverpool; 1902, system of recognition of schools/exemption of their students – AA and Liverpool; 1904, RIBA Board of Architectural Education; 1923, RIBA visiting boards; 1931 and 1938, the Architects' Registration Acts.

For a few years around the turn of the decade architecture as a vocation, as a discipline, as a profession fusing time and space, was on the brink of extinction. To fit in with government orthodoxy it would be neater all round if it renounced those high callings and became a service provider. What, after all, was so special about architects?

Les Hutton

7 Office Buildings and Society (1981)

Buildings betray what we value. Offices in particular reveal the values of those who build them and work in them. No one who passed down the main street of Thomas Hardy's Casterbridge had any doubts about which corn merchants or bankers or solicitors considered themselves of weight and prominence. In any plan of an office interior layout that shows furniture as well as room size it is equally easy to detect those managers who have been powerful enough to appropriate spatial as well as organizational influence. What image best captures the capacity of buildings to reflect society? Buildings are like mirrors – grotesque distorting mirrors, that exaggerate some features of life and diminish others. Some aspects of social relationships, such as rank, are expressed in spatial terms in an almost unambiguous fashion. Yet this is certainly not always the case. What appears to be a predictable correspondence between space and society can be contradicted, inverted or transformed into another medium. Nothing can be taken for granted. Less like mirrors than the changing surface of a lake, buildings reflect only fleetingly and even then distort as much as they depict. There are at least two causes of confusion. The first is that buildings can be used to say things about society which, if not lies, are statements of aspirations or propaganda rather than facts. Hitler and Speer, as they drew plans for a new Berlin, knew this.

The second cause of confusion is that buildings themselves are not a neutral medium: they have the capacity, because of the images they project and through the powerful associations which cling about them, to acquire a significance which transcends and transforms what they contain. Gibbon's description of the moment "at Rome, on the 15th of October, 1764, as I sat musing amidst the ruins of Capitol, while the barefooted friars were singing vespers in the Temple of Jupiter, that the idea of writing the decline and fall of the city first started to my mind", captures the significance invested even in ruins.

Office buildings have changed our cities; office work has revolutionized our society. Manhattan or Frankfurt or the City of London are evidence of the enormous impact the office has had upon our lives. How can we explain these spectacular aggregations of expensive building materials?

Despite distinguished contributions to parts of the story, the history of the development of the office as a social system has still to be written. We have a handful of company histories that give a glimpse of how companies were accommodated. There is pioneer work on the development of office technology and some interesting work on the history of white-collar unions. An inherent difficulty in writing the history of the office building is that for historians there is perhaps too fine a distinction between the office as a building or collection of buildings and the office as the arena for the activities of an enterprise.

For architects, the history of the office building has been partially studied, but largely as a by-product of an interest in certain architects' careers, or technical developments such as the invention of the elevator and the steel frame which made the skyscraper possible. The history of the office building as a reflection of changing office organizations and the basis on which they came to exist has hardly been attempted.

The difficulties are formidable. We have no full theoretical understanding of the way in which buildings relate to office organizations. We do not know which aspects of building form – height, width, degree of enclosure, richness, texture – relate to which aspects of organizational life. Why do rich stockbrokers work three or four together in a shared office while partners in accountants' firms work in single rooms? Is it technology, or social structure, or simply tradition that explains such habits? Without explanation it is very hard to avoid either exaggerating or minimizing the significance of a particular building for office organizations. Moreover, data are scarce and not fully worked over. It is hard, for example, to find plans which show how buildings were used since few architects have ever interested themselves in this aspect of their own buildings let alone of buildings in general. It is hard enough, as Banham has shown (in *The Architecture of the Well-Tempered Environment*), to explain the development of such non-constructional aspects of office design as air conditioning. Finally, the office as a focus for social and economic history has not yet proved attractive to historians.The groundwork for a coherent explanation of the relations between developing office organizations and changing office buildings has yet to be prepared. All this is required: knowledge of building design as well as of organizational structure; a comparative understanding of economic, social and business development in the major industrial societies; a grasp of economics, organization theory and sociology; a trained historical imagination. The introduction of the study of office buildings into the social and economic history of office organization could make important contributions to our understanding of aspects of modern society. In office buildings, unlike factories, schools and shops, there is a close correspondence – at least on a functional level – between workers and those small areas of space that are theirs and theirs alone: individually owned desks, chairs and workplaces. Like traces of some primitive form of life, the remains of workplaces and the enterprises which were the aggregates of many workplaces are still evident in the form of the buildings in which people used to labour. Workplaces were clustered together to become whole leases or buildings, while the workers combined into many shapes and structures of organization. The clerks are gone now. Lupin as well as Mr Pooter is dead. But the office buildings which were designed to meet their needs and foster their fantasies still exist and still contain their ghosts. Despite the considerable difficulty of relating building form to social life, because of the importance of the workplace it should be possible to trace such a relationship in a particularly pure and simple form in office buildings.

Office space is found in units of every size, from the tiny solicitor's office to great monuments of industry like the Shell Centre on London's South Bank, which contains over 42 acres of space. It is therefore possible to make comparisons between all manner of social and organizational units and their use of space.

The study of office space focuses attention in a particularly acute way on a vast section of the economy and working population which is otherwise hazily and inadequately defined. That a special form of accommodation was set aside for these workers gives them a more effective and all-embracing definition than the technical label "clerical" or the social tag of "white-collar". Because of this spatial perspective, questions about modern society can be raised in a sharpened way. To explain why certain buildings came to be, we need to know a lot about the people who worked in them.

The final advantage is that the physical office, although inadequately recorded and photographed, adds a vast amount of data to the study of changes in organization. Buildings and their interiors are rich in evidence and could be to social historians what a dig is to an archaeologist, or a tribe's artefacts are to an anthropologist. As a practising architect rather than historian, I must leave to others the preparation of a comprehensive history of how office building has reflected organizational form. However, on the basis of some reading and a little experience, three fragments of the kind of history I should like to see might be attempted. Underlying these attempts are such general questions as "Why isn't all office space always the same?" and "If office design does change, why does it?"

Obviously, office buildings have changed in many ways in the last

100 years. Each generation of new enterprises seems to have had its own organizational and technological problems to solve. In more precise terms, my questions become:

• What were the prevailing social ideas about relationships in office organizations and, indeed, in society at large?
• To what extent does the form of office buildings and office interiors reveal changes in office technology and office organization?
• To what degree is the form of office buildings and of their interior arrangements dependent upon available building construction and real estate practice?
• What is the more powerful agent of change in office design: internal factors related to building use or external factors to do with building technology or real estate practice?

Some definitions are necessary. First, a sharp distinction is customarily made in office design between the building – that is, the main structural and core elements designed to last for many years – and the interior, including internal spatial divisions, the furniture, fittings and furnishings which make an office inhabitable and which are frequently renewed. This is a relatively modern distinction and should be used with care in connection with early buildings.

Office technology covers the tasks performed in the office, the machines and equipment needed to carry them out, the flow of work and the pattern of communications between the parts. This is the system engineer's way of looking at the office. In contrast, office organization is the manager's or union's view of the office as a complex of relationships between people, some powerful and others weak. What is it that holds the office organization together when so many forces tend to pull it apart? In what ways can managers design organizations to improve their effectiveness? What impact does industrial democracy have upon organizational structure? These are the kind of questions which have been debated throughout the century by men like Fayol, McGregor, Jacques and Mayo. Some social scientists would argue that it is necessary to consider technology and organization together as aspects of a socio-technical system: without such a holistic approach, nothing makes sense. Building construction covers the materials and methods available to the building industry, to build, for example, steel frames up to 40 storeys high or to air condition spaces 100m deep. Real estate factors are the conditions under which office properties are bought, leased and valued.

These four major factors seem to have been the most important influences on the design of offices. Office technology and organization relate directly to building users and are therefore internal factors. Building technology and real estate relate to users through the medium of agents who are not directly under their control and who intervene only intermittently in their organizational lives. They are therefore external factors. The relationship between external and internal factors is critical.

THREE CONTRASTED CASES

To examine the play of these factors upon the office building, three contrasted pairs of buildings have been selected. Each pair is roughly contemporary. Each example reveals something of the way technology or organization or building construction or real estate practice has had an impact upon the form of the office.

The Sun Life Insurance Company Office (1849)/Oriel Chambers (1864)

The exchange is one of the great prototypes of the office – a kind of marketplace where, instead of buying and selling goods, complex financial arrangements are set up. Lloyd's coffee shop was where insurance risks were calculated and cover negotiated. Lloyd's Exchange is now a vast hall where, in benches which are not too different from those in the original coffee house, hundreds of brokers and syndicates transact their business. Round the edges of Lloyd's have grown up other parts of the insurance industry which have had to find a way of accommodating themselves.

A relatively well-documented example of an insurance company's office building history is that of the Sun Life Insurance Company, founded in the early eighteenth century and the world's oldest insurance office. The "technology" of a fire insurance office at this time involved a variety of people: besides the clerks, busily engaged in filling in policies, receiving premiums, and paying claims, a small staff of collectors or, as they were called after 1791, messengers, was needed to deliver and take directions for London policies, to collect the premiums on them from those who did not pay in person at the office, to deliver and bring in letters, and to affix the firemark to insured premises.

Above these members of staff were the treasurer, secretary and the managers, who exercised control over the capital structure of the company, the clerks' business activities, and other aspects of business through a series of general meetings and sub-committees. Until the early nineteenth century, the company had always leased buildings in close proximity to the Royal Exchange. In 1849, however, it moved into new architect-designed premises. These were designed by C. R. Cockerell, whose elder brother John was one of the Sun's managers and had designed two other insurance offices in London.

It is worth noting that this new building, which cost, in the money of that time, the enormous sum of over £1000 per workplace (and a total of £55 842, including the cost of the freeholds) was built for an organization which, by modern standards, was extremely small and, again by today's standards, growing only slowly.

What kind of a building was thought appropriate by the Sun Insurance Company? It was still relatively unusual and, therefore, a sign of some prosperity for a company to build its own offices. Location and presence seem to have mattered a great deal and perhaps more than any other factor. But this was the Sun's building; its robust classical detailing hardly removed it from its palazzo prototypes, although it was thought necessary to slip in two unclassical extra floors.There seems little contradiction between the serene mercantile hierarchy of the Sun Insurance Company in which the secretary (who originally had chambers in the building), the managers, the clerks and the messengers all took their places, and a building form which took the *piano nobile* for granted. Nor is there any difficulty in fitting such an organization of small stable groups of six to ten clerks into a plan not far removed from that of a fine house, with its sequence of great rooms, in the most fashionable parts of London such as Berkeley Square. The organization of the Sun Insurance Company might be seen as a small household. Because of their skills, which were scarce and hard to replace, clerks had a high status in the early nineteenth century. Charles Lamb, for example, was such a clerk in East India House, retiring in 1825 on a pension of £450 a year. Dickens catches the atmosphere of different businesses as well as the subtle relationship between space and status:

> Between Mr Dombey and the common world, as it was accessible through the medium of the other office – to which Mr Dombey's presence in his own room may be said to have struck like damp, or cold air – there were two degrees of descent. Mr Carker in his own office was the first step; Mr Morfin, in his own office, was the second. Each of these gentlemen occupied a little chamber like a bathroom, opening from a passage outside Mr Dombey's door. Mr Carker, as Grand Vizier, inhabited the room that was nearest to the Sultan. Mr Morfin, as an officer of inferior state,

inhabited the room that was nearest to the clerks.

(Charles Dickens, *Dombey and Son,* p. 207)

In the early nineteenth century, according to Pevsner, office buildings were first built to be let. In the view of the architect, Edward l'Anson, such buildings were a relative novelty in the 1850s. This I find hard to believe in the face of evidence such as the building history of the Sun Insurance Company, the commercial development in Newcastle-upon-Tyne by Dobson in the 1840s or the longstanding example of lawyers' accommodation in the Inns of Court. Most of these speculative lettable offices are hard to distinguish in external form from the purpose-built Sun Insurance Company.

The Oriel Chambers building in Liverpool (1864), both in plan and elevation, is sharply different. Oriel Chambers *are* chambers; that is, the building was designed to provide small suites of accommodation for very small firms. The two or three-man office must have been a far more typical form of accommodation than the purpose-built Sun office providing for 40 or 50 people. These small offices were absolutely right for the Dickensian world of the Cheeryble Brothers or Ralph Nickleby, small entrepreneurs, financiers or professional men, each supported by one or two indispensable clerks. Such small units could easily be accommodated in domestic structures, as Gray's Inn shows very clearly. What is remarkable about Oriel Chambers is that the architect, Peter Ellis, seems to have wanted neither the Georgian, domestic-cum-college solution of the Inns of Court nor the normal sub-palazzo façade with all its implications of the one proud organization standing alone. Oriel Chambers, both in plan and elevation, is almost programmatically modular – a neat aggregation of small undifferentiated units, which is exactly what it is. This is the novelty of Oriel Chambers: not only is the plan a succession of small office suites which are highly adapted to the needs of small businesses, but the façade also carries the same message.

Neither palace nor college, Oriel Chambers created a stylistic precedent for countless office buildings.

The Larkin building (1904) and the Guaranty building (1894–5)

The most important fact about the Larkin building (Frank Lloyd Wright, Buffalo, 1904) is that it was built for a mail order house. The mail order company is typical of the new kinds of enterprise which sprang up towards the end of the nineteenth century and depended upon three essential preconditions: the economies of scale which vast co-ordinating purchasing could achieve, excellent communications for ordering and distribution, and, finally, a large, malleable, well-organized and above all cheap workforce capable of handling hundreds and thousands of minute transactions quickly. The Larkin building is an office built by a corporation to accommodate hundreds of clerks. The scale of the operation was entirely different from what had been usual earlier in the nineteenth century: the technology was far more routinized and factory-like; the employees were low in status, and the corporate owner was even more dominant.

It is no accident that the Larkin building was used to illustrate an exemplary, if anonymous, "modern office building" in one of the many handbooks for office managers published in the United States at the beginning of the century. Both the building and these handbooks are products of the same movement, the application to the growing clerical workforce of "scientific management" principles developed in industry. Employees were seen as so many units of production who responded only to financial reward. The task of the manager was to break down any operation into its simplest constituent parts and achieve great productivity by the application of scientific methods. (See Chapter 3, pp. 46–47.) This is how machines are designed; so also could offices be run. Such an approach is a far cry from Charles Lamb hidden among his ledgers in East India House. The scale of the operation is much larger, the proportion of young women employees is very high, the level of clerical skill required much less, the techniques of handling information far more developed, the use of office machinery far greater. We do not know enough about these changes except that they were very rapid and were first employed in the United States.

The typewriter was developed in the US in the early 1870s. In 1879 Remingtons sold 146 machines; in 1881, 3300 and in 1890, 65 000. In the same year, the YWCA in New York introduced the first course in typewriting. Similar rapid growth characterized the use of the telephone. Two years after the granting of a patent to Alexander Graham Bell in 1876, the first telephone line was in operation between Boston and Cambridge, Massachusetts. By the end of the century there were one million telephones in use in the US.

The Larkin building is an original building not only because of its design but as evidence of the same rapid commercial growth. In comparison to all earlier office buildings, it is vast, accommodating several hundred people. Early office prototypes were based, like the Sun office, either on the palace-like model of grand, sequential spaces or on simple repetitive spaces like Oriel Chambers. The Larkin building is different. Just as it is one building externally, so internally it is one space proclaiming the unity of organization. Slogans on the walls affirmed corporate values. Within this organization everyone takes his place. This is apparent not only from the tight and rigid planning of the desks but by the seats themselves, which are pivoted from the desk allowing only a minimum of movement: an eloquent statement of the abdication of freedom on the part of the clerks in the early years of Taylorism. A similar example of this application of scientific ideas to the rationalization of space and activity can be seen in the way in which filing cabinets are built into the balustrades and outer walls and become an architectural feature in their own right. The absence of small enclosed spaces possibly resulted from the mechanical ventilation which, at this time, could cope with high spaces in department stores and theatres but not small rooms. However, it might also suggest the new importance of supervision.

Far less is known about what happened inside another type of office building which is, at least in its external form, as spectacular as Larkin. This is the skyscraper. By the late 1880s there were many buildings in Chicago and New York which were colossal versions of the tiny speculative office building such as the Oriel Chambers of the 1860s. Instead of a built area three or four times the area of the site, the Chicago skyscrapers had achieved a ratio of 1:20 by the end of the century. This was possible because of the development of steel frame construction (from the 1860s) and the elevator. At a more fundamental level, these buildings were the result of a real estate market in which the key factor was that building costs were less significant than the cost of the land. The economic forces that governed the size of the Sun Life Assurance building in the 1860s were certainly not the same as those that drove Chicago developers onwards and upwards.

In other ways the speculative Chicago office buildings of the 1880s and 1890s, unlike the Larkin building, were not innovative in office use. They were designed on exactly the same principle as Oriel Chambers, aggregations of small rooms for small firms. The critical problem for the architect was to invent forms which mastered both great bulk and the endless repetition of similar windows.

The skyscraper was a product of real estate practice and technology. If not the result of a change in the size of organizations, it was perhaps a reflection of the growth in number of different enterprises. This was apparently recognized by one of the most prominent skyscraper architects, whose career was founded on these developments, Louis Sullivan: "an indefinite number of storeys of offices piled tier upon tier, one tier just like another tier, one office just like all the other offices – an office being similar to a cell in a honey-comb, merely a compartment, nothing more" (Sullivan, 1896).

These early skyscrapers were probably let to small firms, each not much larger than those at which Oriel Chambers were aimed. The difference was that the basic unit of accommodation could be multiplied endlessly. This is evident from the plans of original buildings such as the Reliance (1895), the Monadock building (1891) and the Garrick building (1892). Even buildings of deeper plan such as the Fischer building (1896) could easily be subdivided into small units of office accommodation.

The Guaranty building, built in bustling Buffalo in 1895 and designed by Frank Lloyd Wright's *lieber meister* Louis Sullivan, can be allowed to sum up this great development in real estate practice. Despite its mass and apparent unity, its twelve U-shaped storeys provide a very large number of small offices on a very restricted site. The contrast with Larkin, built nine years later in the same city, could hardly be greater.

The Seagram building, New York (1954) and Ninoflax, Nordhorn (1963)

The office building is a building of work, of organization, of transparency, of economy. Bright spacious working areas, open, unpartitioned, zoned only according to the organism of the company.

(Mies van der Rohe)

Despite these fine words of the 1920s, the evidence seems to point to Mies van der Rohe, the architect of the Seagram building, being more interested in the formal possibilities of reflective glass than any real organizational requirements or actual developmental possibilities. When this architect was able eventually to build such an office skyscraper in New York in 1954 the result is extremely refined but nevertheless entirely local, as much a product of New York or Chicago real estate practices as Sullivan's Guaranty building of 1895. Like the Guaranty building, each floor apart from the podium is quite small; but by 1954 total air conditioning was possible and even small rooms could be controlled quite separately from all other spaces. Because of this, internal rooms and therefore a relatively deep space are possible within a compact plan form. In this respect alone, the Seagram building is different from Guaranty. However, in all other ways, and particularly in the vision of the office as one building with one entrance which is eminently capable of being subdivided and let off in many small units, it is the same. To an architect, the relatively unimportant details of the façade allow Seagram to be distinguished from Guaranty. Inside things are not quite the same.

The experience of moving from floor to floor in the Seagram building is surreal. Within the immaculately-detailed bronze frame, the very blinds of which are controlled to reduce accidental variety in external appearance, there exist as many as twenty different firms, each occupying at least one floor. Each of these tenants acting within the normal conventions of New York real estate practice has fitted out or rather decorated its own floor in its own way. One firm is a glass company and celebrates its product with elaborate display. The law practice of an eminent senator radiates wealth and solidity. Only one architectural practice reveals the building, as the architect conceived it. Moving by elevator from one floor to another is to move from one wildly different corporate culture to another.

While the Seagram building was being built in the early 1950s in the US, a far more spectacular development in office design was taking place in Germany. This was the invention of bürolandschaft or office landscaping, an attempt to achieve an organic freedom both in organizational and building form – without precedents or constraints.

The origins of office landscaping lie outside architecture. The basic ideas stem from management consultancy. These have three diverse origins. First, the basic Taylorist ideas of scientific work study with their immense impact on the Larkin building in the early years of the century; second, attempts to translate into a relaxed and status-free form of layout the "human relations" thinking which superseded Taylorism and which emphasized the importance of non-instrumental aspects of work, such as smiling and addressing staff by their first names; third, the cybernetic idea of the office as a kind of communication device or control system. These ideas were developed as part of the management consultancy movement of the 1950s. They were applied in particular by the Schnelles who invented the unforgettable imagery of random desk arrangement, plants, relaxation areas and light, portable furniture. Less known is that this form of layout was made possible only by an advance in building technology: the potential, for the first time in Europe, of using air conditioning to make deep space habitable. Even more obscure is that such radical advances in building form were possible in the German real estate tradition with its emphasis on custom-built buildings.

The Ninoflax office is a typical early example of a bürolandschaft building. It is the administration building for a textile company in Nordhorn, a small town on the Dutch border. Most activities are clerical. The offices are entirely open-plan: the building form and constructional grids are non-orthogonal, unlike the highly modular discipline which marks the Seagram building. Standards are uniform and high. Unlike Seagram, with its different tenancies, the building is a product of organizational ideas in a particularly obvious way, and is almost a diagram of a large clerical organization run with a certain management style. No deviation from the corporate style is tolerated. It is also the product of a real estate tradition that values the importance of custom-built offices almost to the exclusion of speculative development. This basic condition ensured that architect's ideas would be subordinate to the ideas behind bürolandschaft. Building forms were moulded to express the intentions of the client. The final conditioning factor was the industrial climate of the time, in which staff discipline and obedience could be relied upon and senior management were able to adopt "advanced" policies without question. Open layout as well as open management were imposed from above. These conditions no longer prevail in northern Europe. With increasing scepticism about office landscaping, tougher attitudes to real estate practice and, above all, a new attitude among employees who are far more anxious to negotiate about the physical working environment, Ninoflax and hundreds of other similar buildings have become obsolescent within ten years.

CONCLUSION

To compare three pairs of buildings is not enough. Other examples could have been used to make different points and to mark different stages in the history of office buildings. Offices are not the same. Measured by practically any scale, Oriel Chambers and Ninoflax, Guaranty and Seagram, Sun Life and Larkin vary enormously in size, in site coverage, in relative emphasis on exterior and interior, in subdivision, in lettability, in relation to the outside world. Why do they vary? Office organization and office technology – the internal factors – have clearly played their part. Without the spectacular growth and change in office size and organization since the beginning of the nineteenth century, the huge office complexes of today would be inexplicable. Even today, the increasing impact of participation, or, more fundamentally, the shift of power from management to staff, is making office landscaping an untenable concept in northern Europe. A form of planning of which the openness and completeness reflect powerful centralized management thinking cannot be reconciled with the new ability of staff to negotiate about the physical conditions they would like to appropriate for themselves such as partitions, access to windows, and privacy. Centraal Beheer, an open plan office for an insurance company in Holland, and famous for the intervention of staff in design – painting their own walls, bringing in posters and even pets – marked the end of the period when total management control was possible. Current anti-office landscaping and highly cellular projects in Scandinavia are the direct consequence of new labour laws.

The most interesting crux in this history is the conflict between these internal organizational factors and external real estate forces. Unlike North American projects, European buildings have generally tended to reflect architectural or stylistic trends and, in more recent times, managerial fashions rather quickly and accurately. This is because of the relative weakness of the external forces. From Mies van der Rohe's glass skyscraper to the Pirelli building and Centre Point we can observe European buildings which are an imitation of American practice without the tough grip of real estate rules which pervades American offices. In Ninoflax and other open-plan buildings we see the direct impact of managerial fashion on building forms. In the US, despite the enormous fertility in organizational ideas, external real estate factors have tended to be dominant. Buildings have been seen as negotiable commodities first and objects of use secondarily. This is obvious in the impact of land values on building bulk in Chicago and New York and later in the strong emphasis on modular construction which is designed to make subdivision and subletting easy. These disciplines, which are practically universal in the United States, are even now relatively little understood in Europe.

Why external constraints were weak in one context and at one time, and strong in another can be explained only in terms of fundamental economic forces. Explanations of why, within these constraints, certain building forms were possible and preferred must be undertaken through an understanding of the structure and organization of business society. When both levels of explanation, external and internal, are exhausted, we can then begin to ask questions about the particular design contribution of Ellis, Sullivan, Wright, Mies van der Rohe. How much freedom these architects enjoyed within the economic and social circumstances of their time is open to question. In many ways they had little freedom and their design energy was expended on relatively trivial details. The buildings discussed here tell us far more about the societies which built them than about their architects.

First published as "Office buildings and organizational change", in *Buildings and Society*, King, A. D. ed., Routledge. 1981.

8 Organizations, Buildings and Information Technology (1983)

Computer people probably do not worry very much about architecture except perhaps as a convenient metaphor to describe the structure of systems. Certainly architects have not troubled themselves a great deal, until recently, about the needs of computers.

The popular conception that most information technology equipment can operate in the conventional office environment is optimistic and misleading. The computer has escaped from the computer rooms in which architects had become accustomed to believe it had been tamed.

Far from it. Information technology is wild and likely to occur randomly in more or less problematical concentrations anywhere within a building. This is all the more so because the concentration of decision making about computers in the data processing department is breaking down very fast.

The current problems that firms are experiencing are not short term ones. Developments in technology such as more powerful, thinner cables and smaller, less environmentally demanding equipment will not – at least before the end of this decade – cure these problems. New equipment such as flat screens will only partially replace models in current use. Rather than become much smaller, machines will tend to become more powerful relative to their size.

While cabling will become more powerful and elegant, there will be more interconnected equipment and more networks and it is interconnection that will create most cable problems. Needs for power and other connections will also increase as the density of information technology equipment in the office increases many times over.

Perhaps it is useful to remind readers who are more familiar with computers than with buildings, why these new demands are so difficult to satisfy. The most obvious and important fact is that most of our office building stock already exists: we only replace something like 3 per cent a year. In other words, buildings are built to last many, many years, which is fine unless there is a sudden and major change in user requirements. Unfortunately, this is exactly what information technology has induced. Not only are many of our buildings old, but even recent buildings have been designed without thought for the rapidly increasing level of servicing, cabling and cooling which information technology demands.

What air conditioning or lighting exists is almost certain to have been designed on the assumption that only highly predictable external conditions – summer and winter, night and day, solar gain on the eastern face moving during the day to the west – will change while insider user demands will be relatively constant.

With the new, rapidly changing office with entirely unpredictable use of highly demanding equipment, the old certainties no longer hold. Thus many buildings quite suddenly are becoming obsolete.

How many buildings are in danger we do not know. Nor do we know exactly what the overall pattern of demand from information technology will be in various sectors of the office population. But we do know, from a report called Orbit (Office research into buildings and information technology), carried out by DEGW and Eosys, that it is extremely expensive to renovate some office buildings to accommodate information technology (IT). Refurbishment involving major changes to electrical and air conditioning systems could easily cost £200 to £300/sq m, and in certain cases could very well approach the cost of building a new building.

Perhaps the most useful tool to emerge from Orbit is a predictive device – the technique of building appraisal. The various studies carried out by the team led to a set of requirement which can be used to determine whether or not any given building has the capacity to accommodate various densities of IT use. These requirements have been turned into a series of rating scales which have been applied experimentally to a wide range of typical British office buildings of various ages and configurations.

Some, like the new Lloyd's building by Richard Rogers in the City of London, perform very well. Others turn out to be as dismal as they look.

Features to look out for include:

• finely zoned and highly adaptable air conditioning, which can cool local concentrations of heat producing equipment
• the ability to deal with more and more compartmentation for people and equipment (it is surprising how difficult this is to achieve in many buildings)
• above all, generous ducting, both vertical and horizontal, to accommodate great amounts of interconnected cabling.

Features to avoid include:

- low floor-to-ceiling heights (very common in 1960s offices)
- air conditioning which is centrally controlled and cannot be made to respond to local demands
- services embedded into the building shell so that modification is difficult.

Building appraisal allows building owners to determine the potential of existing and proposed buildings to accommodate electronic equipment. It provides what Orbit set out to find – a systematic basis for planning the physical accommodation of information technology.

But the lessons of Orbit go further. The structure, physical fabric and servicing systems of the office building – the hardware – are all in the process of massive rethinking and redesign. The office as we know it was invented in Chicago almost exactly 100 years ago in response to an explosion in organizational and technical invention. What is happening now in office technology and organizations is the most fundamental change since that time, and we confidently expect a corresponding surge of architectural invention in this country, in the US and in Europe.

In terms of software, it is probably hard for computer people to realize that while office buildings seem such large and impressive objects, the level of expertise devoted to managing offices and planning their use through time, the software of office design, is still extremely primitive. The crisis that Orbit highlights – of extremely costly obsolescence and the risk to organizational success of inadequate buildings hindering the introduction of information technology – will force a closer link between the management of office technology and the management of space. A new level of professionalism in space management is certain.

The origins of Orbit lie in an attempt to bring together the views of architects and computer people. By late 1981 David Firnberg, who had been managing director of the National Computing Centre and now heads Eosys, the information technology consultancy, had become very concerned that many office buildings were a severe impediment to the introduction of information technology. Architects and space planners had quite independently seen the computer, and especially the proliferation of terminals, as a growing impediment to the design of successful and effective office environments. Consequently Eosys and DEGW decided at the end of 1981 to join forces to study how the physical office environment was being affected by information technology and to recommend whatever could be done to ease the introduction of electronic equipment and networks into the office.

The focus of our attention was the office building itself, rather than office locations, which had already attracted much research attention. Nobody, anywhere, however, had taken a hard look at the working environment of the electronic office.

Before Orbit very few people had developed a consistent view about the pattern and rate of development of information technology in the office over the next 10 years in the UK. No one had systematically tested such a point of view against the reality of what was actually happening in the ordinary British office building.

Myths abounded – some fed by the "hope it will go away" attitudes of consumers, others by the "softly softly catchee monkey" tactics of some equipment vendors.

Among architects the debate, to the extent that it existed, polarized between impossibly glamorous visions of high-tech environments – in which glittering new equipment (wireless, of course) floated without visible means of support – and another contradictory attitude, equally destructive to detailed enquiry, the assumption that the office function would soon be entirely decentralized into every home.

For end users, and particularly unions, the myth that mattered was fear of loss of jobs as the office became automated.

The "seven grim volumes" of Orbit, as the *Financial Times* called them, are made up of six appendices, each of which represents a separate investigation by part of the multidisciplinary research team, and a main report which weaves all the data together, assesses their significance and recommends what ought to be done.

Appendix 1, for example, prepared by David Firnberg, Diana Duggan and Richard Oades of Eosys, is in part a taxonomy of IT equipment with particular emphasis on describing physical characteristics such as weight, dimensions and heat output. Signal media are discussed, from twisted pair cables to fibre-optics.

Most importantly, this appendix sums up Eosys' own surveys of management opinion on how quickly various kinds of IT equipment will come into widespread use in British offices. It is projected that by the end of the decade about four million of the roughly 10 million British office workplaces will accommodate some kind of electronic device – that is, about half the take-up rate being experienced in the US and yet quite enough to put enormous strain on our stock of office space.

The case studies in Appendix 2 – of the experiences of leading edge organizations in introducing information technology into their offices

– represent another cut into the problem. The situation described in the majority of cases is of barely-controlled chaos, with management struggling to get the new equipment to work, and giving scant regard to the messy, incremental and inevitably expensive process of fitting it into the physical environment.

The ironies are multiple: no evidence here of the paperless, wireless, high-tech office but instead burgeoning demands for space, storage, special environmental conditions, (such as cooling, freedom from dust, noise control) outlets for power and data, and above all for ways of accommodating mile after mile of cable.

In Orbit the direct and indirect effects of IT were distinguished – the former being the simple physical demands of equipment for space, ducting and environmental control; the latter being the potentially far more significant effects of the changes IT is bringing to office workers through changing their status and expectations.

The study of, for example, the ergonomics of the use of visual display units (VDUs), particularly in relation to lighting and chair design, is now of critical importance. However, the case studies show very clearly that ergonomics in practice is light years away from the theory. IT is already creating very large problems among the organizations most well-equipped to plan ahead and cope with its introduction to the office. How well will smaller, less experienced firms manage?

First published as "Taming the beast from the wild", in *Computer Weekly*, 19 January 1983.

9 The Changing Role of the Architect (1984)

I wander thro' each charter'd street
Near where the charter'd Thames does flow,
And mark in every face I meet
Marks of weakness, marks of woe.

William Blake

Perhaps it's true that eventually we become what we eat. We charter'd architects certainly behave as we are paid. I don't mean to say that architects are particularly venal or corrupt. Nor that we will do *anything* that we are paid to do. Collectively we are far too wilful for even our worst enemies to accuse us of that. The point I want to make is more subtle, more fundamental: that we architects have become imprisoned by the professional structure we erected for ourselves 150 years ago in order to preserve our freedom.

That supposed liberty was based on two constraints – separation from the builder and independence of the client. To keep ourselves from commercial contamination, horrified as only early Victorians could be by the scandals hovering round such shady fellows as Nash, we elected to sever our connection with the complex of trades that now we call the building industry. Simultaneously we cut ourselves off from the client by adopting a position of spurious neutrality to allow us to arbitrate between him and the contractor. In nobody's pocket, our status as gentlemen was such that eventually it became no longer necessary even to mention money – the more or less automatic fee based on a percentage of the contract sum dissolved any embarrassment. Why should it ever have to end?

Well, quite apart from external pressure from the Monopolies Commission, the system we devised so long ago has become totally inappropriate because architects' relations with both builder and client are under a new kind of pressure. Time, or rather a new understanding of the implications of how buildings are used through time, is the generator of this pressure.

Take the client's point of view first. For clients a new building, however exciting, or even unforgettable, is only an isolated event. Their real design problem is to accommodate changing activities, for some organizations in several buildings old and new, over long periods of time. This is likely to be the case whether clients are commercial organizations leasing office space, or financial institutions investing in property, or housing managers in local authorities, or administrators in the health service meditating on a lack of cash or an excess of obsolescent property.

To old-fashioned architects brought up during the big-spending splendours of the Welfare State, this information is of no value. Such people don't want to become jobbing architects. They were trained to design new buildings on new sites that solve new problems. Unfortunately such attitudes make them less than useful – even obsolescent. The real design problem – and I might say the really interesting design problem – is to help such clients make best use of their continuing stock of space by understanding how to balance building new against rehabilitation, by making clear the economics of costs in use, by gauging buildings' capacities for different kinds of use, by constantly adjusting the stock to meet new needs. In other words the architect is threatened by having to learn to design with and through time. The old fee scale doesn't help at all in such matters. Nor does it equip the architect to cope with the political realities of participative design either in public projects such as housing or community projects or in the commercial world which is less monolithic and far more political than many architects believe.

Design is the allocation of scarce resources. More and more people want a say in how those resources are used and the architect will have to learn how to respond. One thing is certain: neither the old *Conditions of Engagement* nor, even worse, the new *Architect's Appointment,* give any guidance beyond reiterating the fatuous and increasingly irrelevant certainties of the old *Plan of Work.* No builder will ever forget who is taking the financial risk, who is responsible for timetable and budget; who signs the contract with the client.

Now take the builder's point of view. Architects have always been more frightened of the builder than of the client. Like the British in Singapore, we have built our defences on the seaward front, pointing out towards the Dreadnoughts of the building industry, and have taken for granted that all is well in the quiet backwaters that face the client. Such confrontationalist tactics haven't taught us very much. They have cut us off from a proper understanding of the management of the building process (perhaps the most important lesson of the systems disasters of the 1960s). They have also prevented us from exploiting what should have been our strongest point – our sensitivity to user demands. Had we really understood how the client uses buildings we should have been able to exploit this knowledge to ensure that buildings are constructed so that they are efficient to run, easy to use and simple to adapt. We have not succeeded in pleasing the client nor in mastering our 150-year-old enemy. In fact it could be said that we have demonstrated very effectively that client and builder together could get on very well without us. Perhaps it is cold comfort that the builders seem even less well equipped to cope with changeable clients than we are. Package deals, fast track, design and build make this regrettable argument even less likely to be true.

The crux both builders and architects face is coming to terms with time. In technical terms this means shifting from a profession and industry based on the assumption that the relationship with the client is synchronic (that is, each transaction is separate and each comes at a unique moment in time) whereas we should be trying to devise professional and technical services which are diachronic (that is, continuing and developing through time).

It is as if we are moving from the primitive form of agriculture found in the wilder parts of South America where Indians burn and hack out a new clearing in the forest for each year's new crop of maize and then next year move on. The next stage in our development should be to discover, through the rotation of crops, stable and more intensive forms of culture.

Seen in this light what are thought to be fringe or even eccentric activities such as community architecture, space planning, consultancy on energy and costs in use, participative design, and facilities are now of central importance. Normal architecture, as defined by our outmoded professional codes, suddenly seems vulnerable, in a dead end, on a hiding to nothing. To achieve a new kind of relationship with the client will not be at all easy. Models are few and far between. It may very well be that some clients are as unready as we are, hostile to a new level of intimacy and competence. We architects will have to prove ourselves by devising new forms of service; we will have to invent new techniques for information gathering and design; we will be forced to prove our ability by laboriously gathering far better data on building use than is available today; above all we will have to devise a totally new aesthetic based not on the bright, sterile and peopleless moment of move in but on the gradual adaptation of space through time, an aesthetic of process and maturity.

When I think how far our schools of architecture are from being able to service or even comprehend this opportunity I am tempted to despair. The argument I have made is expansionist: there is no limit to the use to which architectural talent could be put if we break out of our bad old ways. I don't know what the students think but their professors, wringing their hands in fear of closures, certainly seem to love their chains.

First published as "The changing role of the architect," *RIBA London Region Yearbook 1984.*

10 Responding to Change (1985)

Nothing is more vulnerable to change than the workplace. Interior designers have known for a long time that users handle their interior environment so roughly that it is often hard to distinguish the results from vandalism. Few interior design concepts survive the enormous pressures of change any better than a railway carriage survives a Saturday football crowd: and few designers have the courage or the imagination to cope with such pressures. Lamentably, the problem is becoming more serious every day. Not only do most of the working population now work in offices, but office technology is changing more rapidly than ever before.

Orbit-2 is an attempt to come to terms with change in the office. Like its predecessor, the British Orbit study, completed in 1982, the North American Orbit-2 is an attempt to gauge the most likely impact of information technology on the office environment before it hits us. It is particularly relevant to British architects today; not only are American architectural ideas being imported – the City of London is an obvious example – but the take-up of information technology in the US has been so much more rapid and widespread than in the UK that American experience provides useful precedents.

Orbit-1 made a broad survey of what was happening: taking an inventory of information technology devices and media; establishing a timetable for the take-up of informational technology in different organizations; scanning the organizational literature for clues about the direction and pace of change; and surveying the offices of leading organizations to detect the environmental consequences of high technology equipment. Now, in North America, such caution is not necessary. No one cares or dares to make the argument that was still confidently advanced in Britain three years ago – that technology will solve its own problems, cleaning up its own environmental mess, before it even happens.

Orbit-2 is more directly concerned with turning building assessment into a practical tool. It has been devised not just to measure the capacity of buildings to respond to changes in information technology and organizational structure, but also to help any office building user or developer in deciding exactly what sort of office design contributes most effectively to organizational success.

Measurement is critical because office buildings are substantial investments. Far less accurate, consistent and comparative information is available about the expenditure of £10 million or £100 million on a major office building than about the £10 000 needed for a new car or the £1000 that still buys a whole array of domestic appliances. *Motor* provides better analyses of key variables to indicate the performance of cars. *Which?* conveys accurate, statistically-refined information about dishwashers. Nowhere can one find similar user-based information about office buildings – that is, until Orbit-2 set about developing a method of building assessment, pioneered in the original study.

TWO KEY IDEAS

Two ideas lie behind this method. The first is that of organizational typology. Not all organizations are the same and it is highly improbable that one form of office building can satisfy all organizations equally well. It is equally improbable that the requirements of all organizations will remain constant. Change is inevitable and the office environment must respond.

The Orbit-2 team developed an organizational typology based on two elements – the nature of work (routine or non-routine) and the nature of change (slow or rapid). Low-change/routine work is undertaken by, for example, the back office of a bank. High-change/routine work could be carried out by a project-driven engineering business in the oil industry. Low-change/non-routine would be work carried out by a research institute such as the Rand Corporation. High-change/non-routine work is exemplified by a high-tech electronics firm in its growth phase. In the middle of the models is the mid-change/mid-routine organization, like many corporate headquarters offices, which suffers from every sort of design problem.

This typology allows the direction of change to be charted. Most speculative office buildings have been designed for the simplest case – the clerical organization with an unchanging routine that until recently was the staple of the office building market. Orbit-2's prediction is that most organizations are shifting at different paces towards less routine and more change and are likely to make greater demands on environmental resources.

The second key element is design strategy. With the aim of balancing the supply of office accommodation with the demands of users, the Orbit-2 team soon realized the futility of categorizing office buildings by the usual real estate terms, which describe space as a commodity, or in architectural language, which deals with the elements from which they are built. Something else was needed to define the combinations of building elements (for example, ceilings and lighting and systems furniture) that are actually deployed to solve user problems. This was the origin of the concept of the design strategy – combinations of physical resources, assembled to solve particular organizational and technological problems.

PRACTICAL TEST-BEDS

At this stage in the study the 18 sponsors (The World Bank, Honeywell, Interface Flooring Systems, TRW, Steelcase, Mobil, Tate Architectural Products, Xerox, Mead, Arthur Young, Public Works Canada, Houston Design Centre, Exxon, Donn Corporation, Building Owners and Managers Institute, Birtcher, Alberta Public Works and Sunar Hauserman) made a most useful contribution. Each sponsor put forward one or two buildings for assessment, in all shapes and sizes, representing current office design in North America. In addition, the survey methods were thoroughly tested on the sponsors themselves, providing an equally wide range of organizational types.

To measure the demand for change in these different kinds of organization, a series of questionnaires was devised. These were based on 16 key issues identified by the Orbit-2 team. Nine deal with the environmental consequences of change in organizational structure, and seven with the direct demands made by information technology.

Organizational issues

- Population size: is it changing?
- Churn: how often are people moved from one workplace to another within the organization?
- Human factors/environment: how important to operations is the quality of the office environment – lighting, air conditioning and so on?
- Attracting and keeping staff: is it important to the organization's success?
- Interaction: how important are interaction and face-to-face communication among staff?
- Communication of hierarchy: how important is it for people to

recognize differences in rank, status and power within the organization?
• Image to visitors: how important is it?
• Security to outside: is there a need to protect information and other valuable objects from outsiders?
• Security to inside: is there a need to protect information from insiders?

Information technology issues

• Environmentally-demanding equipment: do special environmental conditions have to be provided for information technology equipment?
• Heat-producing equipment: does it need to be moved within the offices?
• Demand for power: what is the need for primary and secondary electrical power capacity and feed, including vertical and horizontal distribution?
• Protecting hardware operations: how important is it for operations not to be interrupted, even for a few seconds, or for data never to be lost, delayed, changed or misrecorded, due to hardware problems?
• Connecting equipment: how important is it that all or most electronic workstations are connected to networks, mainframes or other electronic equipment not at the workstations?
• Moving cables: how easy it is to move the end-points of cables that connect electronic equipment?
• Human factors/workstations: workstations should be provided with ergonomically-appropriate furniture, equipment and task lighting, and enough horizontal and vertical space for all necessary information technology equipment.

EXAMPLES OF CHANGE

The responses of different organizations to these issues, that is, how important each issue is to them now and in the future, can be portrayed graphically as demand profiles, making them easy to compare. These show, for example, that the routine/low-change organization faces greater technical than organizational demands, whereas in the low-routine/high-change firm, technical and organizational demands are about equal. What is common to all the different types of organization, however, is that all demands are predicted to increase. Such profiles indicate the level of demand, but what about supply: what implications does increased demand have for office design?

To illustrate the thinking behind Orbit-2, three examples of change have been prepared. The back office of a bank (routine/low-change); the corporate headquarters (mid-routine/mid-change); and the high-tech firm in its growth phase (low routine/high change). What kind of organizations are they, and what sort of environmental resources will they need as they develop and change?

Typical back office

This office is large and the number of staff is expected to remain stable. The workforce is clerical but gradually the proportion of professionals is increasing. Departments are large and rarely change: hardly one in ten staff changes their workstation each year. Attracting the right kind of skilled clerical staff in this suburban area has never been a problem, but there is growing dissatisfaction with working conditions. These will be improved, since management believes that attention to ergonomics will improve productivity. Meetings are not important. Visitors are infrequent but the bank believes that care should be taken to give them a good impression. Management style, although formal, is not inhuman. Security to the outside is an increasing problem.

Few organizational issues are critical: information technology is another matter. The very heavy investment in equipment that the bank has made in the last five years (terminals linked to a mainframe by a local area network) must be kept going at all costs, so the greatest concern of the back office is to protect hardware operations. Operational adjustments to equipment are frequent and easy access to the cabling network for maintenance and repair is extremely important. The equipment's need for cooling and power is very great. The working day is gradually lengthening and shiftwork will be established eventually. Workstation design will be given increasing attention for humane as well as productivity reasons. No major replacement of equipment is planned in the next decade.

Typical corporate headquarters

Accommodated in a new building in the corporate heartland, this very large headquarters (2000 staff) is going through major structural changes. Much thought is being given to who should be in the corporate headquarters departments, and sections come and go. Churn is not so high. Most people expect to change their workplace only once every other year, usually as a result of promotion rather than any reorganization of their duties. Concern with human factors is high – as much because of corporate policy as any demand from the staff – and is expected to increase. The company is extremely anxious to improve internal communications, both between departments and between various key classes of senior and professional staff. Image to visitors is all-important, followed, only a little way behind, by security to the outside world and between various internal and increasingly competitive groups.

The headquarters is going through an ambitious programme of computerization. The new network is complete, and many managers and professionals are already habitual users of terminals. As these new patterns of work are extended and reinforced over the next five years or so, every aspect of information technology will become more critical: the need to connect, reconnect and adapt cabling and equipment; to protect hardware operations from power failures and static; to supply ever more power; and to cope with random but severe heat loads. Great care will be taken to ensure that the working environment for using high-technology equipment will satisfy the latest ergonomic criteria.

Typical high-tech firm

Established in the late 1970s, this highly-specialized and extremely successful firm in Silicon Valley is now 500-strong and expects to double the number of employees in the next three years. Reorganization to the verges of chaos has always been the habit of the firm: no structure, no relationships, no projects survive for long. Everyone moves workstation several times a year; some have no settled workplace at all. Although people often work in extremely crowded and uncomfortable conditions (explained by rapid growth and change) the firm cares deeply about the welfare of the highly paid workforce, not just out of paternalism but also because it must attract and retain the very best scientific and marketing talent. An enormous premium is put on achieving interaction between everyone in the firm. Informal meetings, weekend sessions, constant arguing and discussion are essential to successful projects, and every means is used to encourage them. Much thought is being given to how to maintain this pattern, despite a worrying tendency to introduce more formality in day-to-day business. This trend towards settling down is expected to continue in at least some parts of the firm, because some financial scares have made it necessary to introduce older, wiser heads into the financial section. Security is already a nightmare; industrial espionage will make it much more so.

No thought has been given to human factors. However, it is likely that they will be taken much more seriously in the next few years since staff morale (the staff is ageing – the average age is now as high as 30) may depend upon it. In every other respect the firm is a laboratory for environmental problems created by information technology, with massive concentrations of equipment, several networks, innumerable wires and constant change and adaptation. No one expects anything but an increase in each type of problem as current development plans are put into effect.

IMPLICATIONS FOR OFFICE DESIGN

Design strategies most likely to be affected can be simplified and grouped under four headings – shell, services, scenery and sets. These roughly correspond to the four most important areas of design activity in office buildings: elements such as the structure and skin which endure for the full 50-year life of the building; major services, which last for 15–20 years; the scenery or fitting-out elements such as finishes and partitions, which last for no longer than a lease; and finally the sets, the arrangements of equipment and furniture, which change increasingly rapidly. For the shell, the key decisions are about the location and shape of the building. Servicing strategies are designed to ensure that cooling and cabling capacities are adequate for the building as a whole. Scenery addresses issues of privacy and local environmental control. Sets are concerned with the immediate area of the workplace – wire management in furniture, ergonomics. Evidently, the high-tech organization is changing rapidly. In contrast, the back office is relatively static, shifting slightly towards a more technical but more humane environment as time goes on. The corporate headquarters has to cope with moving from the city to the suburbs as well as with technological and organizational challenges.

DANGERS OF OBSOLESCENCE

In 1983, the Orbit study pointed out the dangers of premature obsolescence in British office buildings as a result of accelerating change in information technology and in the social organization of offices. The evidence from Orbit-2 is that the same pressures exist in North America but are stronger. The timescale of change is similar; no improvements in the design of electronic devices or in the standardization of media are likely to outpace the environmental consequences of the rapid diffusion of information technology throughout all US offices over the next decade.

Despite very great differences between North American and European offices in the size of servicing and method of construction, it is clear that in many ways (lighting, cable distribution and even air conditioning) the general standard of specification is no more suitable for accommodating information technology. In some respects (aspect, power outlets, workstation design, anything to do with human factors) the general standard is below that in Scandinavia and West Germany, for example.

OFFICES FOR CHANGE

Different types of organization, in different circumstances, at different stages in the take-up of information technology, require different environmental resources. It is extremely unlikely that any one building, or any one set of prescriptions for design, can accommodate the full range of organizational and technological changes being experienced in the world of office work. However, there is no doubt that companies are becoming increasingly dissatisfied with the standard office building designed for low-change, routine organizations. They want offices that can satisfy the far stiffer demands created by more rapid change and less routine.

Offices designed for change will be:

• diverse, responding to the needs of a much wider variety of organizations than is acknowledged today, with quite different timetables and patterns of use
• simple, so that many generations of change can take place within them, and interiors can be rearranged quickly
• highly serviced, with mechanical, electrical and telecommunications services providing not only the infrastructure for use but also the rationale for the overall design
• responsive to change, able to mature and improve as users adapt environmental resources to their changing needs
• decentralized, so that users can make of the office what they want, and not be programmed by some superior intelligence – whether it is the designer or the corporate hierarchy.

Such buildings will depend on good facilities management, and on finding better ways of procuring and fitting them out. In doing so, not only users but also architects and suppliers will have ample opportunity to reconsider their contributions and their roles. There are plenty of opportunities here for invention. Perhaps office design will be able to escape from the double strait-jacket of rigid corporate values and pinchpenny developers which has made it impossible, at least until very recently, to imagine how to make architecture out of change.

Published as "Growing concerns", Francis Duffy and Paul Stansall, *Designers' Journal*, October 1985. Orbit-2 was carried out in 1985, principally by Gerald, Davis, Franklin Becker, William Sims and Francis Duffy.

11 A Case For More Collaboration (1986)

It is hard for one discipline to recognize the full breadth and scope of the work of another, especially in times of change when professions such as architecture and surveying are so busy redefining and renegotiating their own hard-won positions. Some negative turf protecting consequences of this uncertainty are evident in the recent squabble between Norman Foster and the RICS about the use of a photograph of the recently-completed Hongkong and Shanghai Bank in a brochure on project management. More positive consequences in the form of possible new forms of collaboration between architects and surveyors seem to me in everyone's interest – not least that of the client. It is the intention of this article to outline some of these, particularly in the context of the vital and challenging field of office design.

A little bit of history is necessary to explain to surveyors why architects behave and think as they do, and why some architects feel so threatened. When you sell your soul the cost is usually painful, as Dr Faustus discovered after his unfortunate deal with Mephistopheles. So it has been with architecture. When architectural training was formalized at the turn of this century, depth was abandoned for the sake of breadth: architects claimed equal competence in all building types and organized their training and professional qualifications to achieve this claim. Wide and comprehensive training was won at the cost of depth, as became clear when architects subsequently abandoned their claims to comprehend surveying, building costs, structural and other forms of engineering, project management, interior design, space planning and facilities management and so on. Given this long, self-inflicted retreat from mastery it is small wonder that architects feel their position to be so insecure.

A theoretical alternative form of our profession – one that has never really existed – would have been vertically rather than horizontally structured: it would have integrated many skills (design, engineering, user studies, economics, project management) to solve problems on a series of narrow fronts such as housing or the design of hospitals.

The two glories of architecture are that the profession has never abandoned commitment to design, nor responsibility for the user. If only it were possible to combine these ancient responsibilities with a deeper, more integrated array of skills more precisely related to solving user problems. It is this vertical organization of competence that I want to recommend to architects – and, of course, with equal enthusiasm, to chartered surveyors.

THE PROBLEM OF OBSOLESCENCE

The particular focus of my concern is the office building. Office design seems to be recovering from the bad old days when architects (as well as developers and surveyors) assumed that the funds knew best. Farseeing (if totally anonymous and invisible) gnomes were able to foresee all and put everything in place. Turbulent changes in office demand over the past two or three years have shown that, even if such gnomes existed, they would be wrong today. Instead we have a free hand to rewrite the rules of office design – and, in consequence, rebuild the commercial fabric of our cities.

The bad old days of British office design are encapsulated by the brochure from the major pension fund that found its way to my desk as we were completing the original Orbit study in 1983. We had expressed our fear that many British offices were functionally obsolete, unable to accommodate the cables, cooling and partitioning that information technology would inevitably bring. Emboldened by the calculation that the cost of refitting many of these dreadful buildings of the 1960s to bring them back to useful life could easily outweigh the cost of rebuilding them, we then made the modest proposal that funding institutions should, in all honesty, subtract the cost of retrofitting from the value of such buildings in their books. The brochure from the pension fund featured, of course, Technicolour photographs of six of the most typically vulnerable offices, together with an invitation to invest my partners' hard-earned cash. We declined. This problem of obsolescence has not gone away in the past three years. The same dilemma that faced my partnership in microcosm in 1983 now looks every funding institution firmly in the eye.

USE VALUE OR EXCHANGE VALUE

It has been generally assumed in Britain that office buildings will increase in value. Normal depreciation does not apply – unlike cars, machine tools, or factories which are systematically down-graded in value throughout their lifetime. The exchange value of offices (and of course the land on which they sit) has always tended to increase. What has been learned since Orbit is that, because of the new and unexpected demands on the office fabric and location of information technology, the use value of office buildings is much more important than had been generally thought.

This plays, of course, right into architects' hands. If use value is as important as or even more important than exchange value, then the skill of the designer becomes much more critical. No longer is office design simply a matter of assembling the site and fixing the planners: the real need is to understand what offices are for and how they are used. Poorly designed, ill-conceived, unusable offices will stick: well-thought-out, skilfully designed and highly usable ones will be let.

Good design does not simply come at one point in time. The utility of an office building can only be properly measured throughout its whole lifetime and in relation to the duration of its various components – the long-term shell, the 20 years of the life of major servicing elements, the five or seven-year-term "scenery" (fixtures and fitting out) and the constantly changing rearrangements of furniture and equipment by users.

The economic results of thinking about use through time are very significant for architects. In the mid-1960s a typical good-quality British office building (if I can make such a broad generalization for the purpose of isolating a trend) would cost something like £425/sq m (in mid-1980s prices). Twenty years later a new office of a fairly basic standard costs £650/sq m – a big increase that reflects a generally better-quality working environment. Far more significant, however, is how these costs are apportioned, In 1965, 70 per cent of the building cost would be spent on the shell, 20 per cent on services and, say, 10 per cent on scenery. Today the proportions are quite different: 40 per cent on shell, 40 per cent on services and 20 per cent on scenery. In other words, good old-fashioned architecture is diminishing in importance and services and scenery are absorbing more and more of an already large and increasing budget. Moreover, if expenditure on all these items is seen in the context of the life of the office building, the relative insignificance of the shell becomes more apparent: cumulatively, far more money is spent on services that are replaced every 15 to 20 years, and on scenery that is totally replaced six or seven times in the life of a building. The lesson for architects is obvious: we have overrated the traditional skill of building new buildings on greenfield sites and have totally underestimated the potential for design in office services and office scenery. In economic terms the great bulk of the profession is still, quite simply, facing in the wrong direction.

A Case For More Collaboration (1986) 113

SUPPLY AND DEMAND

Consumers of office space have not made the same mistake. One major consequence of the revolution in information technology which is changing the fabric of the office building so dramatically is that facilities managers, who are responsible for procuring and maintaining the physical environment of the office, are no longer treated as of small consequence. The success of most enterprises now hangs on the electronic transfer of data. Maintaining the infrastructure of services means that facilities management is now critical for organizational survival. The prestige and power of this new profession have grown enormously.

As consumers, facilities managers are beginning to understand all about use value. In larger organizations – and particularly in American firms – they are capable of exerting great pressure on vendors of office services and products (among whom architects and surveyors are numbered) to provide what is required. The day of the amateur purchaser of office buildings is almost over.

CENTRALIZED ACTIVITY

Much of this sophisticated development activity seems to be currently concentrated in the City of London, as the consequences of the Big Bang and the creation of the British branch of the international financial services industry work their way through the office building stock. No doubt a crop of novel and interesting buildings will be the result and the geography of the City of London will be radically changed as a consequence.

The picture in Leeds, Hull or Brighton is much less exhilarating. Traditional low rental levels effectively block any hope of retrofitting or redevelopment on certain sites. Local developers argue that no change is possible. And yet information technology has one obvious characteristic. It is universal, as likely to be applied sooner or later in a solicitor's office in Leeds as in a City bank. The clear implication is that the same technologically-driven and facilities-managed processes that are changing the City of London will eventually change offices in the centre of Newcastle, Swindon or Cardiff – or destroy them if it becomes possible to work from newer, better and cheaper buildings on dispersed suburban sites.

The linking of supply and demand should result in better office buildings. They are likely to be very different from those we are accustomed to, not only in the City but on the M25, in business parks and in suburban locations – new types of buildings designed for newly-understood sectors of the office market.

Systematically linking supply and demand amid all the complexities of building design and real estate means research – an unfashionable concept in the market-led 1980s and never a favourite pastime of either architects or surveyors. Disregard all this. Not only is research essential but it offers scope for new kinds of collaboration between architects and surveyors.

The kind of research I have in mind has these characteristics:

- It relates to user concerns.
- It stresses building capacity – the ability of any given building to accommodate certain uses.
- It is inherently multidisciplinary and interactive.
- It is not at all passive, but designed to lead to action.

Examples that are close to hand are the two Orbit studies and a recent series of user-based research projects for developers, particularly Rosehaugh Stanhope and Stockley. This research includes extensive interviews with potential tenants in both financial services and high-tech industries as well as surveys of existing physical conditions to provide not only a picture of future needs but also a datum against which environmental improvements can be measured. Implicit in the approach is the idea of the tenant profile – the classic demands for environmental resources of different sectors of the office market. Not only can buildings be categorized in terms of their utility, but users can be classified according to their needs.

Orbit-1 and the North American Orbit-2 are not concerned with particular developments. What started in 1981 as a study of the impact of information technology on office buildings has developed into a kind of tool kit of building appraisal. Orbit-2 provides a set of rough and ready instruments with which any potential tenant or user can determine the likely pattern or change in requirements for their organization and simultaneously measure how well any given building – built or still on the drawing board – can satisfy those requirements. While such a comparative tool kit is valuable to corporate owners of multiple properties, it must be said that it is not entirely without relevance to developers, as they set about exploring the needs of each particular sector of the office market.

To me, such consumerist investigations are essential to develop architects' understanding of users of a particular building type – the office building. It could easily be misconstrued by surveyors as an invasion of their patch, an attempt to muscle in on the delicate handling of the relationship between buyers and sellers of property. In fact the opposite is surely the case: these techniques of building appraisal should complement and support the letting agent and should throw a brilliant light upon aspects of valuation.

Moreover, in order to make full use of these techniques, the skill and knowledge of the surveyor is essential.

A NEW SCIENCE OF BUILDING USE

It is hard not to feel when describing this kind of approach a little like Charles Darwin, who felt after his visit to the Galapagos Islands that the geologists and botanists of his day were like chickens scratching away in the corner of an enormous farmyard of underused data. Both surveyors and architects have so far failed to take advantage of the data about building capacity and building use which is piled high in every one of their offices. Architects and surveyors can help each other by:

• building up a shared data base, perhaps on the lines of Orbit-2, about the requirements of different user sectors and the performance of generic types of office building
• sharing information on what users actually do in their offices, how rapidly they change and the pressures to which they subject the building fabric
• systematically studying and comparing profiles of user needs in sectors such as insurance, foreign banks and electronics
• establishing more rigorous criteria and specifications for office building design
• working together, on the drawing board and earlier, and making sure that building designs meet user needs.

To traditional architects who sometimes hate letting agents, this may sound like selling the pass once again. To me the magic of design is real, important and undoubtedly the province of architecture, but none the less capable of being enhanced by scientific understanding of user requirements. Only in this way can the vertical, the in-depth, the collaborative, the multi-disciplinary professional service which I should like to see be used to provide increasingly sophisticated users with sufficiently responsive and adaptable accommodation.

The alternative is disintegration, a rerun of the failure of the 1960s, the loss of the chance which we will never have again in our lifetimes to create a new, better and more useful kind of city.

First published as "A case for more collaboration," *Estates Gazette,* 18 October 1986.

12 Architectural Practice (1989)

Robert Gutman's new book on architectural practice in the United States is an important and distressing work which, if its argument were to be listened to and its implications understood, would lead to the closure of hundreds of schools of architecture and the public disgrace of thousands who call themselves teachers of architecture. What the book implies, in short, is that there is now no connection between what happens in architectural practice and what is taught in the schools, except the bitter tears of those tens of thousands of disappointed people who have suffered from a misdirected system.

Gutman is far too wise to express his argument in such emotive terms. He hardly need do so, for the story is plain enough. Gutman is a distinguished sociologist who understands architects, having been the leader in the USA of the field of the sociology of architecture. He also likes architects, counts many of the most distinguished members of the profession in America among his friends, and has taught for more than twenty years at Princeton University, in what is considered to be one of the very best architectural schools in North America.

His tale is about a profession which is changing spectacularly in response to remorseless economic and social pressures, but which cannot, for profound psychological as well as historical reasons, acknowledge that change. The study has been funded by the National Endowment for the Arts, and is the result partly of Gutman's own wide knowledge of the architectural profession, partly of extensive use of national and professional surveys and statistics, and partly of discussions with some professional degree students in the school of architecture at Princeton, "who were interested in a more accurate assessment of contemporary design and building practice than studio education provides"

Not everything about the story is black – an expanding demand for architectural services, the increased size and complexity of buildings, the consolidation and professionalization of the construction industry, the greater rationality and sophistication of client organizations, and the changing expectations, by no means all bad, of architecture among the public. Most British architects would recognize these trends, and many would agree that the last years of this century are potentially a wonderful decade for architects. What they will also recognize is the effect these trends are having upon the shape of the profession, for example the increasing polarization between the sharks and the minnows. Half of the 25 000 architectural offices in the US employ no more than one person. Of the 12 000 firms that employ more than one person, only 250 employ more than 50 people. These firms, "which constitute only two per cent of all the architectural firms in the country, collect 30 per cent of the fees for architectural service". The remaining 11 750 offices divide the remaining 70 per cent of the receipts. And even within the glorious 250, only a handful – SOM, John Portman, HOK, for example – are truly enormous, adequately capitalized and, inevitably, increasingly dominant.

Why should these dry economic statistics matter in the studio? The answer jumps out in a plangent sentence on the penultimate page: "The combination of diversity and fragmentation is a major factor that helps to explain why architecture is populated by a higher proportion of alienated and disappointed men and women than any other major profession, why so many firms are badly managed, and why, when offices are managed efficiently, they achieve work of dubious architectural quality." Alienation and disappointment: the consequences of an unreformed, but not unreformable, situation. The schools of architecture still have the opportunity to think through the challenges that Gutman describes. So far they have almost universally failed to do so, preferring instead to exaggerate further and further the star system, that is, the tendency to undervalue great areas of architectural skill in favour of a single criterion, that of originality of design, which sometimes results in freshness, but more often in nothing more than lightness of touch. This, by definition, is the root cause of so many unrealistic expectations and such widespread disappointment.

The star system is basically defensive, a retreat into magic. Reality is too threatening, and rethinking the teaching of architecture too much like hard work, to be attractive to the weird mixture of the weary and the inexperienced who staff our academies. To be fair, their problem is a difficult one: the widening gap between the schools and contemporary architectural practice, the diversity and complexity of which goes far beyond the experience of the majority of practising architects, makes it seem practically impossible to prepare students adequately. Which should change, practice or the schools? Practice certainly needs major reforms, but the schools are worse. By behaving as if nothing has changed in the practice of architecture during the last twenty years, by refusing to acknowledge the contradictions which stare them in the face, they perpetuate a system which is not only irrelevant but false and cruel.

Robert Gutman does not draw his conclusion so vehemently. He is more optimistic, deep down, about the future of architecture. To close all the schools and to devise an improved form of pupillage (such as that proposed by Richard Weston of Leicester) would seem to him an unappealing and too Thatcherite way of addressing the challenges which he so eloquently describes. Nevertheless he has done an excellent job of reminding us that both the teaching and the practice of architecture are firmly embedded in society and, when society changes, both must follow. Which, ironically, is precisely why Robert Kerr and his radical friends, disenchanted with both the Pecksniffs and the academies of their day, founded the Architectural Association in 1847.

Review in *AA Files 17*, Spring 1989, of *Architectural Practice: A Critical View*, by Robert Gutman, Princeton Architectural Press,. 1988.

13 The Professional in the Built Environment (1991)

Acceptance of the second-rate in Britain has been a dominant factor in poor economic performance – in inefficiency, which has resulted in all manner of waste, and above all in widespread failure to create tolerable urban standards, leading to consequential social problems and divisiveness. In commerce and manufacture, failure to build upon the early successes of the industrial revolution has been much remarked since the mid-nineteenth century. Apart from products of war, advanced science, artistic and intellectual pursuits, the absence of concern for quality has been a common factor in British society. It is significant that these three exceptions are all in areas where the free market mechanism, dominated by minimum cost without regard to other attributes, does not operate.

There is a difference between the judgement of quality by individuals and by society. For personal transactions, comparative experience is helped by exchange of views, aided by *Which?*-type advertising based on quality. Once higher quality is recognized and appreciated, the consumer expects it as a matter of course. For social transactions, however, it has proved far more difficult in Britain for government and corporate consumers to develop the appropriate level of sophisticated judgement. Transactions are large, complex, and relatively rare for each purchasing body.

Hence there is little direct comparative experience. Projects are interdependent, with complex and often multiple customer-contractor relationships. Benefits are long term and, to be appreciated, require predictive capability. The tangible element of cost is unrelated to the more important, but more complex, calculations of value-for-money so that continuity is lost in great projects and aims are readily diverted by political expediency. Social objectives, which are essentially inter-related, are too frequently fragmented, sub-optimized, and inadequately co-ordinated. Expertise, foresight, analysis, synthesis are undervalued. In fact the media encourage widespread suspicion of such skills to conceal their own ignorance – the "simple man knows best" approach.

It is essential to reverse these trends and to renew in the built environment a reaffirmation of the roles of the professional, architect, planner and engineer. These professionals ought to act as interpreters of requirements, guides towards means, seers for future change and co-ordinators of other elements for success, and organizers of consequential projects. It can hardly be claimed that they are currently fulfilling these roles successfully.

Why is this? What is to be done? Who is to do it? To answer these questions these professionals need first to identify the elements of their own inadequacy.

FRAGMENTATION

In private practice, each species has traditionally retreated behind an actual or metaphorical brass plate, emerging only in response to specific demands. Such responses are often confined to a specialist function or are over-extended to shallow generalizations. No responsibility (other than directly physical) is assumed for consequential effects. They use yesterday's technology and yesterday's products, responding slowly to change rather than acting decisively to stimulate it.

In the public sector, the irresponsibility has been split between departments, with little co-ordination and no synthesis of individual and often contradictory objectives.

In the private sector, architects working for private developers in general have been insufficiently engaged in issues of policy. They have worked as single-project designers and detailers, obeying narrowly-conceived commercial criteria.

Fragmentation of functions and of relations between professions has been assisted by separate education and training (from the age of 15). Each profession has failed to recognize complementary competences. Divisions and the false notions of incompatibility (for example artistry versus numeracy) breed mutual contempt, a subset of the widely-accepted polarity between science and the humanities. Research and development have been largely looked upon as the responsibility of government, until almost too late. Unfamiliarity with new materials and processes has at last been perceived as a handicap affecting the professional's ability to deliver an optimal product.

It is significant that, left to themselves, architects will focus on drawings, planners will concentrate on proceduralism and engineers will occupy themseves with calculations, norms and safety factors. They all expect to tussle with the management of the constructional process but with diminishing expectations of achieving success, related no doubt to the increasingly tense and adversarial nature of interface with various kinds of contractor and subcontractor. Nowhere in the world have contractual procedures been so elaborated as they are in Britain – and we do not believe this to be evidence of great success in our construction industry. The principal defect is that success is justified by cost and not by volume.

Meanwhile, where are the clients? Building industry professionals, absorbed by their own professional concerns or by the excitement of confrontations with colleagues in the construction industry, have taken clients for granted. Muzzled clients are by no means rare – it is, for example, still considered good practice to freeze changes in client requirements for the convenience of the construction process without need for broader assessment.

Not unnaturally, some clients have reacted by developing their own skills in the procurement of the built environment – sometimes, such as through design/construct contracts, by side-stepping the traditional services. Most significant has been the rise of a new profession, facilities management, whose practitioners lay special claim to competence in the ongoing management for organizational ends of the vast stock of existing commercial buildings. This development is of enormous strategic importance to the traditional professional.

THE CASE FOR AN INTELLIGENT MARKET

Political extremes lead to the Manichaean view that society's needs have to be met either wholly by free-market mechanisms or by central planning: "a country where property, profit and advertising dominate the collective consciousness, where law is fiercely adversarial and unscrupulous" is seen as the only alternative to "the centralized planning of the socialist state" (Roger Scruton, *The Times* 31.12.85). Such attitudes are wholly destructive to the building environment, where planning at all scales and for varying time horizons represents an absolutely essential element, ultimately to be afforded by the surplus value of marketable products.

Recent concentration on marketing, accountancy, management – divorced from the particular functions to be managed – has not been matched by qualities of judgement, by synthesis which lead to optimization, nor by the recognition of multiple objectives. For far too many clients, decisions are made on the basis of the cheapest option, in fear of the critical accountant or auditor.

The environmental professional should have a vital place in the market economy, with the ability to help to transform market aspirations towards the notion of an intelligent market. How to achieve this objective is the main concern of this contribution.

THE ENVIRONMENTAL PROFESSIONAL IN THE MARKET ECONOMY

Essentially, the intelligent market concentrates on the overall set of transactions that contribute to achieving value-for-money in an integrated manner. The intelligent market recognizes that this objective is defeated by applying over-simple market evaluations to individual transactions that should themselves be co-ordinated towards the main objective.

Two simple truths should prevail. First, the quality of professional service defies contractual frameworks. Time is simply wasted by attempting to do so. While major incompetence may occasionally become apparent, there is vast scope – and in practice great differences in result – between marginal competence and true enlightenment. Second, the drafting of terms of reference for the work of professionals involves considerable skill based on understanding of the requisite activities and phases of work. It is a wise client who evolves terms of reference in co-operation with the professional.

A remarkable recent trend in both public and private sectors has been the irrational adoption, by accountant-dominated project promoters, of increasing fragmentation of the project and the appointment of different design professionals for different phases, each at least cost. These arbitrary divisions disregard not only the essential iteration and continuity between phases but also ignore the need for the overall operation to be directed with enlightenment, a quality blighted by the least-cost criterion.

If professionals are appointed on price competition, there is an immediate dilemma for the most talented and proficient. They will be competing against those whose commercial attitudes will incline them to undertaking the minimum (disengaged from any wider concerns with consequences) while still showing a profit. Yet this is the fundamental relationship between the parties in any development from which the success of all else should flow. A professional should advise on the appointment of all other parties, to ensure overall achievement of objectives, as the agent for continuity and synthesis.

There are two parallel dangers in the opening up of the design process to the consumer: the first is to delude ourselves that the veracities of outmoded professionalism will be enough to carry us through, constantly renegotiating needs within a changing society. The second is to succumb to overgeneralized and simplistic pressures of the market place represented by dependence upon the primitive level of "consumer" information in retailing which has found its expression in the *Sun*, the *Mirror* and the TV ratings. Professionalism has to be based on something much more substantial than the choice between believing that either we or the public must by definition be right.

The answer must be a rapid build up in the intellectual basis on which professional judgement relies.

REDEFINING PROFESSIONALISM

Environmental professionals are society's gateway to the construction industry. In order to act effectively in channelling the huge resources of constructional technology to meet the requirements of society, it is essential to build up a much more systematic body of knowledge than is currently available on:

• user needs at every level, and particularly the underlying forces, which are likely to change people's expectations, forms of social organization, ways of working, living and leisure, all of which are directly related to the substantial use of environmental resource
• ways of measuring the capacity of the built environment to meet these needs
• the performance in use of buildings (and cities) to allow feedback not only to improve the design of buildings and building components at every scale from the door knob to the city (the hardware of building design) but also to create more effective facilities management (software) to make possible better use of the built environment for individuals as well as for every scale of social organization.

Wherever there is a design decision, there is the need to link physical resources to human needs. Professionals will only achieve respect and eventually the power to achieve change if they can demonstrate that they know more about managing this interface than the users of buildings themselves and certainly more than the vendors of real estate or buildings or building components.

Only through maintaining an autonomous, constantly renewed, continuously validated body of knowledge about buildings, building users, and buildings in use will they be able to justify the free exercise of their professional judgement.

EDUCATION

Given such a starting point there is every opportunity to educate individual as well as corporate clients. There will be just as much need to educate the public client in the best use of the built environment. Clients should be helped to acquire the distinguishing features of HM Treasury's definition of the "enlightened purchaser", a role complementary to that of the professionals acting in the knowledge-based professional capacity, described above.

The essential issue remains the identification of the intelligent market against which changes to the built environment need to be tested, and an understanding of the essential symbiosis between commercial property and quality of life that the built environment can promote or obstruct.

These professionals need to acquire a wider appreciation of the factors that lie outside their particular disciplines, be able to synthesize knowledge across disciplines, and be prepared to apply techniques of appraisal of alternative solutions to problems. They also need to understand the nature of innovation, the contribution to be expected from research and development and how to contribute to such work. Their role should be transparent for both the public and private client, subordinating personal interests to maintain an objective view of the interests of other parties.

Above all, they must communicate clearly, using language appropriate to their audience. Professional predilections should not be cloaked in mystery to enhance respect.

PRACTICAL NEXT STEPS

Given such a reorganization, such a knowledge base, and such a commitment to both the short and the long-term interests of the user, these professionals could be in a position to :

• stimulate and educate the client
• initiate new ways of working that are less supply-side dominated and far more consumerist
• adopt research-based, and thus testable, positions on matters of local regional and national policy
• resist market-driven pressures towards short-term solutions
• integrate the several disciplines and resources concerned with the future of the built environment

- lead the planning process at every level.

If professionals for the twenty-first century are to achieve their full potential, the relationship between them and society must be intimate, complementary and complete.

Delivered as a speech co-written with Sir Alan Muir Wood at an Ove Arup Foundation Madingley seminar on education for the professional in the built environment, 11 June 1991.

Part 3   1992 – 1997

THE

PROFESSION

OF

ARCHITECTURE

Simon Head

The overt ideology of planning had given way to the occult ideology of non-planning and the majority of architects had soldiered, alone, through the changes of fortune. By the turn of the decade even the most complacent, and complaisant, foresaw the next battle as decisive: it was time for teamwork.

Partnership in an Intelligent Market

The fresh air of 1979 was now stale, its few ideas exhausted by the oxygen-hungry hypocaust that as early as 1987, in the interlude between the Big Bang and the Big Crash, showed signs of burning the coaches to keep the train running – on the *Herald* (or Valediction) *of Free Enterprise* in Zeebrugge harbour, and then in the reinsuring greed that pushed amateur profit-takers into the path of the British hurricane, Piper Alpha, the firestorms of the Bronx holocaust, the ticket hall of King's Cross. A new wind of change may have been blowing once again through Africa (and Eastern Europe) but it took its time getting to Britain.

One institution after another had bowed to the dictates of the market, given up the struggle as uneven. People wanted public institutions – like the BBC, like the health service – to be accountable: they didn't really resent their being responsible. The Government, however, didn't seem to care if no one was accountable, so long as responsibility lay in private rather than state hands. So that it was inevitable that architecture – which to the lay person (and no one was more aesthetically lay than Thatcher and her bottom-line administration) must have looked like a protected species – would have a fight on its hands to prove that it was unique and cherishable and not just more meat on the hoof.

The attack on the architectural profession by government was quite concerted and came on three fronts. The first attack was on the basis of architects' fees – it was proposed to extend compulsory competitive tendering (CPI) to architectural services in order to regulate procurement procedures by both government and local government. In principle reasonable enough, this measure had the unintended effect of forcing government officials always to choose the lowest tender, irrespective of quality – something that most architects rightly felt would inevitably produce an ever deteriorating public environment (and reminiscent of John Glenn's last thoughts before he blasted off: that he was sitting on a liquid nitrogen bomb produced to the cheapest tender). The second attack was on the funding of the five-year architectural course – something architectural students in the UK had learned to take for granted. Here the Government's motive was entirely financial – one year from five would save 20 per cent, self-evidently a good thing to cost cutting civil servants – and again architects rightly feared for the qualitative consequences of this proposal. Architects were also profoundly stirred by a sense of their own collective ownership of and responsibility for the education of future members of their profession. The third attack, and the most serious, was on the right of architects to the exclusive use of their title, the regulation of architects in the UK being not directly by function but by title. The major justification for this attack was the fundamentally Thatcherite glorification of unbridled market forces. The minor justification was consistency: If no other body in the construction industry enjoyed an equivalent privilege, why should architects, and thus by inference design, be singled out as worthy of special attention?

In the same way that the safety of the City of London's space demands were too important to be left to the market's slash and burn, the notion of architectural professionalism as just another self-interest group – to survive or fall – was too important to go down without a fight. In the deepest runnel of the trough of free enterprise, the RIBA stemmed the tide of slurry – instituted a research policy that paved the way for a strategic study of the profession, set up its own enquiry into architectural education, set its face against marginalization, looked forward to the intelligent market. Back to protection, certainly. But the Monopolies and Mergers Commission and the Government simplified things for architects by the bluntness of their attack – a violent intervention by a violently anti-interventionist government. The effect was galvanic.

In the 1960s there had been a flurry of self-analysis, driven by reforming zeal in the public interest. In the late 1980s the inducement was the series of external threats that mobilized architects into precisely targeted pre-emptive strikes. The *Burton Report,* commissioned by the RIBA Steering Group on Education in 1991, hoped to pre-empt the loss of a fifth of the government-funded education period for architects. The *RIBA Strategic Study,* covering the same period, hoped to pre-empt questions about architecture's role by getting its retaliation in first. The main conclusion of the study, when all the pessimistic details of current and recurrent failures are stripped away, is that design imagination is a commodity still highly valued by clients but not enough on its own to allow architects to recapture their former importance in the procurement process and certainly not throughout the mass of the construction industry. For architects, real power and influence depend upon their acting as the hinge between users and the construction industry. This position depends in turn upon architects systematically building up, on the basis of their design-based training and their privileged vantage point, as they never have before, an unparalleled body of knowledge, sector by sector, about how design really does help users to achieve their social and business objectives. In this sense the strategic study concludes that architectural knowledge is the key to power. When it reported in 1991, the charging she-bear was already dead and her cubs were living on borrowed time but – a grizzly covering ground at 44ft/sec – was about to land on the smoking gun of the protected species and crush the life out of it anyway, for posthumous spite. The *Warne Report* into the Architects' Registration Acts would ask, What's so special about architects? The *Latham Report* – not an answer but another mobilization – emphasized the scale and contribution of the whole construction industry to the nation's economy and stressed the importance of team work, the need to end an adversarial, litigious culture of blame. (Although blame is just the provisional wing of accountability.)

These fundamental questions were being asked at the height of a harsh recession, and it is to the credit of the profession that it accepted the long-term challenge when it could have kept a death-grip on what little remained: because although certain sectors had prospered in the marketplace – certain high-profile individuals and individual practices – the profession as a whole was on the brink of fragmentation. The world was changing for everyone – but slightly sooner for architects. Before harbingers were just a metaphor for hard times ahead, they were real advance guards of ill omen – army provisioners, quartermasters visiting food and accommodation fears on reluctantly-supportive villagers. Scavenging ahead, architects knew in February 1989 that the boom was over: like parachuting for the blind, architects were the guide dogs who hit the ground first and alerted developers to the hard reality that was rushing up to meet them. Many did continue to play the game of competition – succumbed to the temptation of fee-bidding. Rejecting the offer to gamble, Hermann in Pushkin's "The Queen of Spades" makes the killjoy but prescient comment, "I am not in the position of being able to risk the necessary in the hope of acquiring the superfluous." Architects who engaged in nil fee bids, giving up professional design fees in the hope of acquiring future clerical work, made fee-cutting look like throat-cutting: and it wasn't always the opposition's throat. The necessary they were risking was their design uniqueness; the superfluous the work that would allow them to continue as a service industry. For many it was too great a price to pay, and for all it was a bad bargain.

But architects, like everyone else in the 1980s, had been politicized –

or, rather, they had been economized: they may not have been ashamed of their finer, non-quantifiable impulses but, like everyone else, they knew better than to think they represented any kind of winnable argument. That naivety was gone from public life. Made up of well-educated, dedicated, committed and single-minded people, the profession mobilized to make a business case for a position that for most of them, for most of their lives, had simply come with the rations – the necessity of an extensive education period, the need for a protected title, a construction industry as a team with architects a vital and valued but not overweening presence within it, allied to project managers, facilities managers, construction managers.

Practice had had its run. It was time for self-conscious professionalism – deployed, ultimately successfully, by successive RIBA presidents Max Hutchinson, Richard MacCormac and Frank Duffy. These successes were gratifying – on quality and fees achieved through persistence, on education through the law courts, on registration through a brilliant campaign of lobbying, a model of what can be achieved against great odds by a relatively small but well-organized professional body. The real success, however, was the revivifying of the ideals of the architectural profession. It was through the beneficial result of these three campaigns that many architects began to see the importance of architectural knowledge which links design and users, which is inherently interdisciplinary, and which is best developed in the context of action. They also began to understand the connection between architectural knowledge and vitally necessary developments in the practice of architecture and in the architectural profession as a whole. Necessary, that is, if both practices and profession are to survive to serve clients and to help an increasingly knowledge-based and more demanding society to prosper.

Les Hutton

14 Knowledge – Defining the Professional (1992)

Mandatory fees, unlimited liability, prohibition of advertising by architects and of architects holding directorships or indeed having any commercial relations with property developers, estate agents, product manufacturers, or builders – these exclusive rules, which once were thought to be the enduring marks of professionalism, have all been swept away in the last decade or so. What remains? Is there anything that distinguishes architects from the other members of the construction team?

Do students, when they enter schools of architecture – and architecture is increasingly attracting the brightest and the best – have any idea that they are entering a profession? Do they know what that step implies? Clever as they are, I sometimes doubt it. And does it matter? The concept of a profession is easy to mock, hard to pin down. Like many other nineteenth-century inventions, it is taken for granted as long as it works.

In the abstract, sociological sense, a profession is an institution designed to regulate standards of competence in the more complex and challenging fields of human endeavour while simultaneously protecting the public from abuse by laying down standards of conduct for its members. Typically professions are vitally interested in education through which levels of entry are controlled. In order to consolidate their power they tend to elaborate codes of conduct and to manage the interface of their members with each other and with their clients.

In practice, professions inspire mixed feelings: that the adjective "professional" generally connotes excellence is evidence that the objective (and achievement) of the protection of standards of competence in difficult fields is popularly respected; that professions are recurrently accused of being closed shops, trades unions, cartels enjoying and exploiting the benefits of monopoly on certain kinds of knowledge, shows that a less attractive kind of protectionism is also widely recognized.

The strength and the vice of all professions used to be exclusivity. Maintaining tight professional boundaries was a source of power – excellent if used to maintain standards, not so good if used to achieve what used to be quaintly called "the feathering of nests", despicable if used to conspire against the public interest. In the case of architecture, as the profession formed itself in the early years of the nineteenth century, what mattered greatly to the founders of the RIBA was very much in the public interest – the protection of clients from corruption in building and property. The great objective of the apparatus of codes, ethics, and fee scales invented by architects was to make the architect "the client's friend" – the one person who could be relied upon not to deceive. It was Dr Johnson, towards the end of the eighteenth century, who said with feeling that "to build is to be robbed". Many members of the public still feel the same today.

AN ALTERNATIVE TO EXCLUSIVITY?

Nevertheless, things have changed a lot. The relations between architects, the client, and the construction industry – often caricatured, sometimes idealized, always complex – have gone through many permutations in the last 150 years. The rise and fall of the public sector as the dominant procurer of buildings in the UK changed and then changed again the architect's role and status in the middle years of this century. Other building professions have grown up and made their presence felt: architects have lost some of the monopoly of attention, the special relationship, once enjoyed with clients as well as some of the respect bestowed on them as a matter of right by builders who thought they knew their place.

Thatcherism made it impossible for architects to ignore the logic of the free market – which acted, incidentally, by no means entirely to their disfavour, commercially as well as artistically. The increasing urgency and complexity of the ways in which clients of various sorts, users as well as developers, now expect to procure buildings are making enormous demands on the whole construction industry. Building itself has become much more diverse – de-skilled in parts and yet sophisticated and well managed in others. Above all, there are few places left in the UK today where you can still safely entertain the fantasy that British architects are insulated from the world economy.

Within such complexity, to take the "independence" of the architect for granted is a big claim – and, some would argue, a foolhardy one. In a world comprehensible only through "systems" thinking, for one profession in the construction industry to claim complete autonomy flies in the face of reality, especially for architects who are, after all, trained to think about most other things holistically.

Two examples illustrate the shifting balance of power. When I read recently in a brochure from Shimizu (one of the largest of the great Japanese construction companies) that they employ over 1300 "first class registered architects" I knew at once that a redefinition of professional boundaries was needed if I were ever to comprehend the Japanese construction industry. Closer to home it was even more destabilizing to be told by the chairman of one of Britain's biggest construction groups that he would happily listen to what I had to say about design provided I was prepared to recognize that he himself employed 7500 designers.

It is impossible to avoid confronting the argument – coming from the direction of NEDO, the National Contractors' Group, and the Construction Management Department at Reading University – that professional exclusivism has had its day and that what is now needed to strengthen the British construction industry in an increasingly competitive world is a new logic of co-operative professionalism, based on particular skills and specific knowledge, but biased towards a more welcoming, inclusive approach to neighbouring and allied disciplines.

THE CORE OF THE DISCIPLINE

Nothing could be more timely and welcome for architects. We need this challenge and we are willing to co-operate. But to be able to collaborate successfully we have to know where we are coming from. Warm feelings and the desire to get on with colleagues are not enough when the objective for architects and for the entire construction industry is not just economic survival but much, much more – the responsibility for a large part of our national, and international, culture.

Design is the core. The design of buildings is an imaginative process. It is also highly practical, involving an inventive grasp of user requirements so that they can be given – by the clever allocation of always too scarce resources – popular and appropriate spatial expression. Architects have the seemingly impossible task of discovering the future – buildings are designed to endure for decades, far beyond the practicality of ordinary business prediction. Architectural education is very special for a very cogent reason – architectural design involves taking responsibility for the long-term shape of buildings and cities, but always on the basis of imperfect information about what is needed. Uncertainty is very great; action essential. Deep issues are conjured up. Many people are involved, not all of whom agree and, if they do, it is not usually for very long.

Building design is inherently collaborative but is always conducted in shifting and sometimes treacherous circumstances. Design, as General Wolfe said about war, is an option of difficulties.

Not surprisingly, given these difficulties, architects have invented over the centuries peculiar techniques for teaching design which are not just based on seminars, lectures, essays, laboratories but on all these things plus the studio-based design project, the simulation of as many aspects of real design as possible – including the public debate of alternatives and the vigorous analysis of competing objectives. The life of the studio has shaped the architectural psyche. Project-based teaching is our invention and our glory. Propositions for action are always the result. What many who have not experienced the project-based studio system may not realize is the sophisticated way in which such propositions are derived. Architectural propositions are always holistic. They bridge gaps that other disciplines are free to avoid – for example, between:

• past and future – architects are taught to remember that not only are they part of a great tradition, companions, as it were, of Alberti, Ledoux, and Lethaby, but that they are equally responsible for extending that tradition into the future
• art and science – architects see themselves as artists but to design they must grapple with the practical applications of immensely complex scientific knowledge
• demand and supply – architects are inherently part of the construction industry but design (which in the end is impossible to distinguish from briefing) is also inevitably and intimately bound up with helping clients to determine priorities about requirements. Design faces both ways. The architect's position is by definition ambivalent.
• decision making and reflection – it is necessary but not sufficient for architects to propose design action. Looking back and thinking ahead are also needed to complete and continue feedback loop between society and the construction industry.

One could go on. The first point is that architectural education is different and complex not out of inefficiency or muddle or perversity but because the grand but elusive nature of architecture cannot be captured in the neat conventional boxes which are so attractive to bureaucracy, to commerce, and sometimes even to the academic world. The second point is that learning to design is not at all easy. Discovering architecture is a public process, which continues throughout all architects' careers, of nerve-racking presentations followed by intense peer-group criticism. The third point is that the architectural tradition of project-based, action-orientated, design-impregnated education is a major pedagogical achievement in its own right. Which is not to say that architectural practice and architectural education cannot be improved but before you improve them reformers must be prepared to acknowledge the central, subtle and sometimes subversive nature of design. Design is the core.

TOWARDS A NEW CONCEPT OF PROFESSIONALISM

"He who gives most is King" (Marcel Mauss, *Le Don*). Generosity and openness come with confidence. What stands out is that the only lasting and sound justification for a profession is no longer exclusivism, essential as it was in the nineteenth century – but knowledge. Architectural knowledge has a very distinctive nature because it is based on design and because it unites – in the context of action – past and future, science and art, demand and supply, decision making and reflection. Consequently the husbanding of that body of knowledge, its continual improvement, and its passing on through education to future generations are the essential functions of the architectural profession – our *raison d'etre*, our responsibility, our collective destiny.

No other kind of institution besides a profession is equipped to undertake this task in each given field of complex endeavour and judgement. The State – and this includes the European Commission as well as Westminster – is not sufficiently wise or competent or omnipresent. Commerce – which in effect means our colleagues in the construction and property industries and the product manufacturers – tends, in our kind of economy, to be far too short term in its thinking and planning even to see the need except perhaps in fragments. The universities and polytechnics are vital allies in the task but they are limited in their ability to comprehend the world of action which is inevitably a large part of the architect's environment. Perhaps our best potential friends are the clients and users but they, too, are fragmented and cannot be expected to do our job for us.

This concept of a learning profession, with its clear sense of a co-operative and cultural purpose, transcends the mistaken definition of the architectural profession as the sum of its units of production – the practices large and small, the local government offices, and the residual government architects which are currently our visible presence in the UK. In fact, not only is architectural practice much more varied than loose talk about misleading stereotypes has led clients and colleagues to believe, but there are many architects and architecturally-formed individuals themselves working as developers, as project managers, as researchers, as specialists of various kinds, as interior designers, as social scientists, historians, writers and journalists, as facilities managers, as teachers, as community architects and builders, as client representatives, as product designers. All these architects and architecturally-trained people must be considered as essentially part of the learning profession: what binds them together with more traditional or visible aspects of architectural endeavour is their original design formation which makes it impossible, once the design habit has taken hold, for them to look at the physical world without wanting to change it imaginatively for the better for themselves, for their employers, or for society. The deontic habit is very special and runs very deep.

Nor can a learning profession operate alone. It needs a network of intense alliances with other disciplines and professions because it is always curious, pushing outwards, interrogating its environment. Buildings and cities are huge and complex entities and to construct them as well as to understand them there is no limit to the help that must be sought. But a learning profession, however outgoing, can never lose its essential identity because it has its own principle of action – in the case of architecture, the design imagination. Without the confidence that design, the essential spring for action, gives to architects they would either turn inwards into their own diminishing private concerns or become indistinguishable from people in other disciplines – in both cases equally useless. Above all, architecture as a learning profession depends upon the love of knowledge – the cumulative building up of systematic bodies of knowledge about those three aspects of the architect's task, so succinctly characterized by Sir Henry Wotton in 1624: "The end is to build well. Well building hath three Conditions. Commodity, Firmness, and Delight."

GREAT CONSEQUENCES

Great as the success of the British architectural profession has been in the last 100 years in building up and monitoring an international system of architectural education – which is proving almost embarrassingly popular not only with students but with foreign governments – it cannot yet be said to exhibit all the characteristics of the educational programme of a true learning profession. The system as it has evolved so far is strong but it is really no more than a robust base for further advance. As Richard Burton's Steering Group prepares the architectural profession's response to the Secretary of State for Education and Science, a great deal of evidence has emerged in the discussions of lively and open-minded innovation along the lines sketched above. There is, for example, already:

- wide diversity of emphasis and interest between the schools
- considerable experience in some schools of funding joint courses with other disciplines, especially engineering
- a lively research tradition in several schools and some practices
- a considerable interest and increasing success in continuing professional development (CPD)
- successful links with practice, sometimes through teaching practitioners, but also through the RIBA's programme of a minimum of two years practical training – much envied abroad.

No doubt there could be much, much more. The common knowledge base is still too weak, the collective memory still riddled with amnesia, the links with practice and with other disciplines, and particularly building economics, still too tentative, random and fragmentary. But the will and the precedents exist. Moreover, on the one essential underlying factor there is total unanimity: design is the core.

With that rock-hard common core, architecture as a learning profession with its own destiny, its own distinctive character, its own knowledge base, and its own government can flourish. Given the reformed, confident, generous and open foundation that a learning profession implies, the kind of co-operation that architects need – and that other equal professions and the construction industry seek – is readily forthcoming. Boundaries between traditional architectural practice and new ways of working will cease to matter. Architects will increasingly work in non-traditional ways throughout the construction industry and within client bodies. They will seek even more frequently than today, joint qualifications with other professions. They will not hesitate to focus their specialized attention on emerging problems and opportunities in diverse and un-traditional ways. Design-based and user-orientated research will be the basis of increasingly fertile relations with users and clients – demonstrating, if it still needs to be proved, that the architectural imagination really is the best gateway of clients to the construction industry, and vice versa.

A well-regulated architectural profession must deliver not security, nor meal tickets, nor an orthodoxy but instead open, well-informed, and liberal debate to resolve inevitable conflicts, internal as well as external, on issues to do with artistic responsibility, duty to society, and above all the construction of the future. The pursuit of knowledge allied to design purpose should not be exclusive but open to everyone. Nothing is permanent; nothing can be taken for granted; recognition and success have to be earned. The truthful answer to students who are sceptical about professionalism is that a learning profession does not give them the right to anything – except knowledge.

Published as "The Right to Know" in *Building Design,* 13 March, 1992.

15 Fighting Deregulation (1993)

Such a successful word, "architect", more and more frequently cropping up in the press, especially in the political and business pages, and always used to honour the initiators of great projects and enterprises. Real architects have got used in practice to more down-to-earth assessments of our capabilities – but, my goodness, don't we love our title, the three crisp syllables of which convey so much authority.

"The overwhelming majority of architects, either individually or through professional organizations, who offered observations in the review of the Architects Registration Acts 1931–1969, argued that statutory registration and the protection of the title 'architect' should be retained." So writes John Warne, the assessor for the Department of the Environment, whose lucid report, published and accepted by government on Wednesday 3 February 1993, nevertheless found no impediment to the theft – or liberation – of the title which we architects had come to believe was uniquely ours. Whether this loss will be so neatly achieved is still very much a matter for lobbying and debate. The RIBA will certainly fight stoutly for the maintenance of a register by the Institute itself, especially as Warne himself says, "There would seem to be no insuperable practical or constitutional obstacle to designating the RIBA as the registration body."

But what is registration and what does it mean? While I like much of John Warne's logic and warm to his obvious admiration for the work of the RIBA, there are two features of the architect's world view which he underestimates: first, the role of the architect as champion of the consumer and, second, the integrating, holistic, and all-permeating nature of design. Imperfect as our present system of registration certainly is, I believe it was invented both to defend the user and to recognize society's continuing need and respect for the inventive and Promethean nature of the architectural intellect. Both factors played, I believe, an important part in the 1931 Act. Registration was nothing more than a primitive form of consumerism – the best that could be done in that simpler age "to protect the good name of the profession and therefore the public by excluding 'charlatans'". How simple was the 1930s assumption that the interests of profession and public were coterminous. But has the fundamental nature of architecture changed at all in the last 60 years – whatever our competitors say about changing boundaries? In the more complex 1990s do architects in Bute or Inverness, in large or small practice, specialists or generalists, suffer any less from unfair competition? Are consumers any more immune to sharp practice? Has the charlatan quotient – the ratio of duds to hot shots – really been reduced? Is the environment, which architects exist to sustain, really a jot less vulnerable today than it was in 1931?

WARNE'S THREE VOICES

It is not, I believe, generally known that there are three John Warnes whose separate views have been ingeniously stitched together in this Review of the Architects (Registration) Acts 1931–1969.

Warne Mark 1 is undoubtedly consumerist in inclination and intention. He tends to assume that market forces will set things right, that unrestrained competition will lead to the best of all possible worlds. He does not hesitate to apply this simple 1980s belief to the complexities of professional judgement. He does not ask himself how the synchronic logic of the market can be applied to such long-term, intractable, and value-laden issues as the improvement of the quality of life, the regeneration of our cities and the transmitting of cultural values from one generation to the next. Who does know best for the future? Should everyone have an equal say? Is the market intelligent enough to create anything more substantial for society, more worthwhile than the sum of so many deals?

Warne Mark 2 is wiser and milder. He has a better basis for answering such questions. It is obvious throughout the report that this better Warne believes in the essential nature of professionalism – in the knowledge, the foresight, the courage and the judgement to say "no" even to the client's dearest wish if it is not right. Warne Mark 2 subscribes to a finer ideal than that of the marketplace – that of the self-regulating profession that is responsible for the maintenance of its own values, that conducts its own intellectual, and in our case social, artistic, and technological programme. Such independence – and Warne Mark 2 expresses it very well – is only possible by paying the price of constant self-examination through continuous dialogue with users, clients, society and governments.

If a profession such as architecture dares claim in the 1990s to have access to special skills and insights, its members should not be surprised when they are challenged to prove their claims. The cosy assumption of authority implicit in the 1930s professionals' claim to special status is hollow unless it is based upon superior and ever-expanding and improving knowledge. To develop and hand on such knowledge – action based, open to scrutiny, theoretically testable and, above all, ethical – is why professional bodies exist.

Warne Mark 3 is timidly egalitarian. He has been down the road to talk to architects' competitors and has been shaken by their not totally disinterested critique of architects' claims. It is also fair to say that this Warne has also been talking to our clients who are also not universally dazzled by the application of our ideals in practice. Warne Mark 3 asks whether architecture really does deserve special status as the only registered body within the construction industry. Surely, he says, this special status creates a disequilibrium which makes worse the divisions within a hopelessly-fragmented and unevenly-skilled industry. Registration perpetuates ancient quarrels and stands in the way of reform. Wrong, we have to say. The problem of division that Warne Mark 3 is beginning to tackle goes far deeper than registration: it is the fundamental problem of an introverted and supply-side dominated industry in coming to terms with the customer. Architects in this ancient mess have consistently stood out for user values. Architects have not only dared hold the pencil; they have spoken out for the client and for society, their past and their future. Architects, when they follow their professional ideals, have been, are and will continue to be the real consumerists within the construction industry. No wonder architects are disliked. No wonder this real and uncomfortable, design-based and user-oriented status is marked out in our particular society by registration. You cannot dismantle the responsibility and leadership that is inherent in the act of design. You don't solve this problem of inherent conflict between supplier and consumer in which architects are so inconveniently, uncomfortably and sometimes gloriously caught by abolishing the Act. Reality goes even deeper than the law. Abolish registration: the ancient and special nature of the architect's position will not change.

VALUES TO FIGHT FOR

What is strange, in an increasingly fragmented and complicated world, is the persistence and consistency of architectural values. Whatever forms of regulation and fee payment architects are subjected to, their values tend to be the same. Whatever educational regime or form of funding is in place, architectural education somehow survives. The universality of the architectural programme is most evident in the success of certain forms of architectural teaching – project-based, long in maturation, interdisciplinary in nature – which are found all over the world. This became very evident to me last year in the preparation of the Burton Report on the duration, the intensity and the content of the architectural course. These ideas about the special and universal nature of the architect's calling were also the foundation of the two very optimistic conclusions of the *RIBA Strategic Study, Phase 1.*

• Architects, within a supply-side dominated industry, are in the best position to speak for the user and to defend the consumer through our understanding of what buildings are for.
• Architects know how to design. Our training has been devised to help turn clients' aspirations into reality.

These two propositions – provided we collectively are prepared to work to continue to make them correspond to reality – are the real power base of architects in a threatening world. They are aggressive propositions. They imply huge responsibilities. Whatever kind words John Warne (Marks 1, 2 and 3) speaks about the RIBA's conduct of its members' affairs in his report – and the even kinder compliments with which he endows the *Strategic Study* – the immediate commercial realities which face us are terrible and the task of creating a truly knowledge-based profession for an electronic future is enormous.

John Warne has told us nothing new. We know we have to fight for what we value. We know we have to know more about the users than they know about themselves. We know our designs must be based on superior knowledge as well as more vivid imagination. We know we have enemies. We know we sometimes fail and must have mechanisms to regulate our conduct which are more stringent than the law. We know we must continue to learn throughout our careers. It is helpful of John Warne to encourage the RIBA in what we are already striving to do. It would have been much more helpful if he had not recommended the removal of one of the few props which government has ever given us. But in the end, in the longer term, whatever the pain, it won't matter. Architecture transcends legislation and national boundaries. The word "architect" is not potent by accident. Its power comes from the continuing nature of architecture. What John Warne has really done is not so much open the floodgates as force us to redefine and to communicate what we mean by the profession of architecture, to give new meaning to the word "architect" that we love so much.

"The Three Voices of John Warne," *Architects' Journal*, 17 February 1993.

16 Keeping Faith With Our Professional Concerns (1993)

What I want to attempt this evening is not only to defend the architectural profession within the UK, which I have the honour for this brief period to represent, but more importantly to lay the foundations for the defence of professionalism itself.

Professionalism is an idea that many would argue is outmoded if not corrupt. I disagree. Professionalism is absolutely necessary for this and all other countries' economic survival as well as for sustaining our general quality of life into the twenty first century. To explain the full force of this argument I must describe the three rather different experiences that have stimulated me to make it.

The first is a sense of debt – my privilege in being part of a great international tradition of architectural endeavour. I was lucky enough – at the Architectural Association, at Berkeley, and at Princeton – to have been given what was probably one of the best architectural educations available in my time. But this experience is only a tiny fragment of a huge, international and developing whole. The RIBA validates courses in 36 architectural schools in the UK and over 40 abroad. We have in the UK the liveliest architectural journalism in the world, linking architects in continuing discourse. The Institute is gradually building up a network of Architecture Centres throughout the country. In London, where the density of architectural culture is comparable only to New York and Paris, the streets of the West End seem every evening to be full of people seeking architectural events, architectural ideas. Anyone, architect or not, who comes frequently to this building or to the Architectural Association or the Architecture Foundation for lectures and exhibitions or who visits one of the many Diploma shows of architectural schools or who has the luck to take part in the formal review of work in our schools (as I did last week at the University of Sheffield) will know what it is to be part of the continuous, critical and open-ended debate about what architecture was, what architecture means today and what architecture ought to become. Here is where Frank Lloyd Wright and Aalto lectured. This room is full of ghosts – Inigo Jones, Sir John Soane, Pugin, Butterfield, Morris, Lethaby are with us here tonight – but all rooms where architects gather are equally pregnant with the future.

The second experience is also personal but affects a wider audience. Architecture is not only interesting to architects; it is, in modern society and for modern business, an essential catalyst of change. Our open-ended debates are sometimes misunderstood as time-wasting, diversionary activities; our continuing self criticism is read as an extended apology. Wrong: architecture's perpetual critique of society is extraordinarily useful to society – especially in times of extraordinary change. I can illustrate this from my own field which, as some of you know, has been almost entirely office design. At the end of last century and at the beginning of this century the Chicago architects – Louis Sullivan and Frank Lloyd Wright (and their many colleagues) – created the cities of the twentieth century through their imaginative grasp of new forms of construction and more importantly of a new kind of brief: the necessity of housing a new office technology and new forms of administrative organization that were being invented by Frederick Taylor, Gilbreth and others. Today the universal dissemination of the new technology of information is forcing all organizations to redesign themselves and consequently their use of office space. Never has there been a livelier period in organization theory. What metaphors do such business gurus as Charles Handy and David Nadler, for example, use to describe the new forms of organization? Why, architecture, of course, the architecture of organizational structures that have to be redesigned to accommodate change.

To this metaphorical architecture there corresponds a real and novel architecture, the allocation of physical resources to house new organizational and social needs in an innovative way. Such a radical office architecture is being designed at this very moment. To understand its strategic importance to commerce it is essential to realize that this new architecture is not inert but catalytic. Without the messages with which the new office architecture is laden, organizational change cannot be managed. The old office fabric strangles change in a variety of horrible ways. Buildings can kill. The scope of this huge, essentially architectural task of creating a new environment for business involves the redesign and the reuse not only of buildings, but the redesign of time and space, and eventually of the whole urban landscape – making obsolete many existing buildings and certainly the stereotypical models of office location and office building so dear to the richly conservative, imaginatively impoverished, utterly supply-side dominated, property and construction industries.

This is merely my own experience. Other architects are continuing to apply their imagination to organizational, economic and societal renewal in the fields of health, tertiary, secondary and primary education, and housing. There is infinite scope for design in late twentieth-century Britain. Which brings me to my third and utterly contradictory experience: the systematic devaluation, marginalization and trivialization of design – in what is clearly a period of enormous imaginative opportunity – by government and the construction industry. It is obviously not enough for the UK to have the best architects in the world. The evidence of siege is all around us: continuous downward pressure on fees and on building costs that extend beyond the bounds of justifiable competitiveness and cost cutting into discrimination and persecution. Death by a thousand cuts.

The subtext to this pragmatic destructive pressure is that design is considered to be a dangerous, costly and easily expendable luxury. I must remind you of the continuing threat to abbreviate the funding of the academic part of our architectural course, based on the assumption that design training is inconveniently lengthy, that too many resources are consumed in labour-intensive and pedagogically-atypical project work in studios, that attempting to integrate diverse skills into holistic designs is pretentious (sounds expensive, that holism) and above all that "favouring" design training in this way can only perpetuate division and discord within the construction industry.

And then there is the Government's proposal that architects' registration should be altogether abolished since it is held to be self evident in the era of the Citizens' Charter that architects are self seekers like everyone else. Thus, since everyone is equally venal, it is in society's interest that the title of "architect" should no longer be protected but should be open to all. In short, the word "architect" and the substance and significance of design don't mean anything special and can be safely discounted. I have to admit that I am enormously grateful to the Government for the conjunction of these three attacks on the position of the architect in society. Had each attack come separately, the emptiness of the short-termist and deal-saturated philosophy on which all three are based would not have been so blatant. The factor common to all three is the opposite of what the government as guardian of consumer interests should really intend. It is nevertheless something that is believed in fervently and consistently by vocal parts of the construction industry: whatever happens, nothing should stand in the way of the supply-side getting its way.

BETWEEN SUPPLY AND DEMAND

Design does three wonderful things. It brings together consumer and supplier, supply and demand, treating each equally. It takes responsibility simultaneously for past, present and future. And it takes for granted the limitations of the resources available and, nevertheless, is prepared to invent the future.

Our predecessors, the founders of this Institute and their immediate predecessors, worked this all out in rather different circumstances 200 years ago. Margaret Richardson conveys what it was like to be a pupil in Sir John Soane's office at the very beginning of the nineteenth century. Already in 1788, in an age of rampant capitalism and of ruthless exploitation of the poor supplier by the rich client, Soane had defined the architect's duties: "to be the intermediate agent between the employer, whose honour and interest he is to study and the mechanic whose rights he is to defend". By "employer", of course, Soane meant what we call today the client; by "mechanic", the builder. Studying the client's interests (note the beautiful choice of words) connotes both ethical distance and an organized body of knowledge on the basis of which clear-headed judgement can be exercised. The intermediate position between client and builder of which Soane speaks does not connote a legal or mechanical neutrality but is totally consistent with that imaginative, future-inventing, restless drive towards a higher and longer-term purpose which is so characteristic of architectural thought.

Soane's pupils not only learned to design through drawing, copying and planning in the terms of their day but they learned, to satisfy Soane's own self-imposed standards, how to measure, in as meticulous and transparent a way as possible, builders' materials and clients' money. They also sat at their master's feet and learned what it was to share in intellectual discourse about what architecture had been and what architecture should be. All these terms and distinctions are relevant today. When Soane talked about the relation between employers and mechanics, he was really addressing the fundamental issue of the balance between those who deliver and those who consume, between what we now call supply and demand. He badly wanted justice for suppliers and so he defined the limits of the interests of the consumer. He knew that the power of each consumer, vital as it is, has to be controlled; just as consumerism itself, important as it is for the general good, can be taken to excess. There are many other constituencies: the historic building stock, social justice today and the sustainability of this endangered planet tomorrow.

Some things have changed since Soane's day: it is quite clear, for example, that the balance of power in the modern British construction industry has substantially shifted in favour of the supply-side to the detriment of demand. Clients and users are relatively far more in need of protection today. How else can one explain, for example, the growth of litigation, the rise of claims departments, or the banal and inefficient design-and-build sheds that disgrace the industrial landscapes of both the UK and US? Or tracts of new, badly-landscaped, mean-spirited homes? Or the meretricious design of most superstores? These are alleged by their perpetrators to be what the customer wants. I simply don't believe it. Or the blind and spectacular supply-led excess of much office development of the 1980 where "devil take the hindmost" seems to have been the only rule? It didn't even work. How wrong can you get? What supply-side thinking in construction and property has in common is profound and ill-concealed contempt for clients and users who "never know what they want" and "always change their mind".

We must do better than this. We could do worse than reinterpret Soane in the systems language of today.

To architects today, measurement must mean far more than straight accounting. It is the duty of developing and using systematic and consistent measures of building performance through time in terms of changing patterns of user demand. Measurement means feedback and, as Tom Markus used to say, feed forward. Economics is the base. The supply-side – that is, construction and property – need to know not just what buildings cost but what wealth they can generate in use. The interests of the demand-side – the users – must be measurable in terms of the use capacity and the occupancy costs of all the buildings occupied. Users need us to invent and apply these measurements so that they can best manage design to achieve their continually changing goals. To architects today, discourse must mean continual willingness to debate as well being infinitely open to criticism. It means empirical tests as well as scholarly debate – not only about ends and means, not only about our own work now but where it stands in the context of the future and also of history. This is why it is necessary to ask continually what insights and methodologies other developing disciplines can contribute to architecture.

Soane was right: only with such professional and intellectual disciplines in place, only with an ongoing and inspiring professional educational programme, and only with an institutionalized and collective professional conscience is there any hope of keeping architects honest enough to straddle the San Andreas fault which divides construction industry from users, supply from demand.

I do not want to argue that architects from Mr Pecksniff onwards have always lived up to the Soaneian ideal nor that Soane's ideas do not need reinterpretation in a late twentieth-century context. My objectives are to test their fundamental soundness and to learn from comparing them to other parallel professional programmes.

Certainly there is something badly wrong. From puzzlement to open contempt is the narrow spectrum of client opinion which many architects and most of the construction industry attract. There is constant bickering within the construction and property industries and much failure to perform. Some of this is our own fault. An architectural vice is exclusivism – the tendency to be far too aware of the barriers that separate us from clients, from fellow professionals and from construction. Exclusivism, which the architects of the early nineteenth century had to rely on because of their urgent need to distance themselves from graft, has far worse effects than snobbery and self interest – exclusivism cumulatively diminishes the development of knowledge. For professional that is death.

The opposite of intellectual and political isolation is achieved by redefining our professional boundaries in terms of knowledge. Knowledge is our only real source of power, our only real lever to achieve change. The three chief propositions I want to make this evening are, first, that there is such a thing as specifically architectural knowledge which is quite different from other forms of knowledge; secondly, the development, application and transmittal of this special kind of knowledge are what this Institute, the RIBA, exists for; and, thirdly, the possession of this knowledge gives architects both an intellectual duty and a practical imperative. These are to throw our weight equally into the development of user and client understanding just as vigorously as into the long-delayed and much-longed-for improvement of the construction and property industries' ability to deliver what clients really need.

You will not be surprised to hear that my test of what is architectural knowledge is whatever is common to the user (defined in the widest and most longitudinal sense) and to design (defined again in the rich but precise sense I described above). No user information that does not relate to a physical design decision is relevant. Nothing about the material out of which architecture may be made is relevant unless it relates to the intentions of the users.

I hasten to add that this is far from a functionalist definition, because the ideas of user and design embrace all human knowledge and all human values – provided they relate to buildings and to users' intentions. The first value of the definition is that it insists on purpose. Architectural knowledge is incomprehensible beyond the world of action. The second is that the definition insists on values. Architectural knowledge is incomprehensible without taking into account the past, the future and the moral significance of what we do each day. I warned

you earlier that in this room this evening, jostling your elbows, are
Pugin and Ruskin, Morris and Lethaby.

THE RIBA AS CUSTODIAN

The corollary of my propositions is that it is only through bodies like
the RIBA that this special kind of knowledge can flourish. The RIBA is
typical of those voluntary collectives of practitioners invented in the
last century that are inextricably involved in action and yet committed
to the sharing, the development and the transmission into the future of
knowledge. This knowledge is open-ended, action-orientated, value-
laden, project and precedent-based, ethical, and, as my old, lamented
master at Berkeley, Horst Rittel, taught me to say, deontic – that is,
concerned with what ought to be. Professional institutions need the
universities and their complementary kind of knowledge to keep them
thinking – but this is not enough. Similarly we need the kind of
knowledge that exists in commerce to keep us trading – but this, too, is
far from being sufficient. The history and the sociology of the
professions are well worth revisiting. When our forebears hammered
out in the early nineteenth century the idea of professionalism –
expressed, for example, so eloquently in the Charter of this Institute –
they may not have seen themselves as epistemologists, but intellectually
and morally they had moved far beyond self interest.

Ironies are everywhere. Two months ago in Beijing, Richard
MacCormac and myself had the interesting task of explaining – to the
Vice Minister in charge of architects in the Ministry of Construction –
the RIBA's autonomous constitution and well-honed ways of
determining and validating the architectural curriculum. It seemed to
us that these Chinese architects wish for nothing so much as to be able
to free themselves from the practical and ideological restrictions of
being tied to a centralist government. They wish to found a free
profession with its own mission and in charge of its own educational
programme. Why, they asked, is your government so keen to
abbreviate your excellent architectural training that we are eager to
emulate? Why does your government want to abolish the registration
that seems to us to distinguish architects and to foster their difficult
collective task?

The RIBA is not withdrawing behind the barriers of exclusivism.
Rather the opposite: having reaffirmed our position, thanks to the
government's misguided stimulus, you in the construction and property
industries will see us more and more coming out and mingling with

your businesses – keeping you alive, speaking for the consumer and reminding you of what your own varieties of professionalism mean. I think you will find that we have a lot of extremely valuable information to give you about clients and users – how to work for them and not against their interests. Not everything we say will make buildings cheaper and easier to build – users matter too – but architects have much to contribute in developing badly-needed, more rational building products and better ways of building. Equally, clients and users will find us continuing to take an increasingly active interest in their affairs – continuing into the private sector what has been a long and honourable tradition of architecturally-inspired user studies in the public sector. Don't forget that even in the last decade architects have taken a notable role in establishing facilities management, a demand-side profession if ever there was one, in the US and here in the UK.

But I hope everyone will understand why we architects wince when it is proposed to us that education throughout the construction industry should be conducted in a meaningless mélange of undifferentiated courses. We have built up our full-time educational programme over 150 years. We believe that the logic of architecture leads inevitably and rightly to differentiated skills. I hope you will all understand how absurd it is to shrink the difficult process of design teaching because it is alleged to be élitist or, even worse, because architecture appears to bureaucrats to be expensive and inconvenient to teach.

I hope clients and government will see the folly of using the wrong forms of procurement to cut fees to the quick; that architects themselves will realize that design is their greatest financial asset and resist the temptation to buy busy work for their offices on the basis of devalued imagination. Knowledge and judgement, as the lawyers have always found, are worth paying for. To the extent that architectural knowledge collectively adds value to society, it is power. The stupidity and treachery of individual, petty surrenders will become increasingly apparent as the catalytic, wealth-generating capacity of architectural knowledge is made more and more systematic and overt.

I hope that the essential idea of registration – whatever form it takes – will be preserved by government, not as a bastion of privilege, but as a marker of excellence to guide consumers in an intelligent market. Our colleagues in the European Community (and I can add, by affirmation in the International Union of Architects) are with us on this. They, too, believe that there is more to architecture, as I have tried to argue this evening, than a series of deals.

I am proud and lucky to follow Richard MacCormac who has raised the profile of the Institute, culturally in Portland Place, in community planning exercises almost everywhere, and by his own excellence as an architect and an intellectual. The three things I particularly want to do are complementary. First, I want to make architectural knowledge generally far more accessible in schools and local communities throughout all our regions. Secondly, I want to develop architectural knowledge (design and the user) through working systematically with many, many clients, sector by sector, helping them to explore the future, so that they can articulate what manner of buildings they will need by the year 2000. I want to bring clients in by the bus load to work with architects to use architectural knowledge to build the future. Thirdly, I want to work with the Construction Industry Council and with all other bodies in the construction industry to use architectural knowledge to help them deliver the new and revitalized buildings that this society needs, not only efficiently but well, not only for now but for the future.

That's all. Except that I hope that when I hand over to the next president of the RIBA the ghosts of the architects and the architectural intellectuals that haunt this room this evening and even more our great library upstairs and our drawings collection, that these ghosts – Inigo Jones, Soane, Pugin, Ruskin, Butterfield, Morris, Lethaby, Sullivan and Wright and all the others – will not think that, whatever rough jargon I use, I shall have betrayed the great tradition of this Institute, our collective and ongoing love of architectural knowledge.

Delivered by Frank Duffy as inaugural address as President of RIBA, July 1993.

17 Liberalizing Professional Services (1994)

In this OECD conference about the liberalization of professional services – which I am delighted to be invited to attend – I speak with three quite different voices. First, with extreme diffidence, as President of the Architects' Council of Europe (ACE) which represents approximately 300 000 architects to the European Parliament and the European Commission. Secondly, with rather more confidence, as the democratically-elected President of the Royal Institute of British Architects which represents about 30 000 British architects – 75 per cent of those architects registered in the UK plus 5000 architects practising outside the UK, in the US, in Europe, in India, in Australia, in South Africa and other places, who still choose, by reason of education, affection or work experience, to cling to the membership of the RIBA, one of the two architectural organizations which, worldwide, have achieved so far any international recognition for consistent quality. Thirdly, with sharp self interest as the founder chairman and major shareholder of one of the handful of architectural practices which have achieved some measure of international success – although in commercial terms, and especially in comparison to the performance internationally of the six major accountancy practices, an infinitesimally tiny proportion, measured in annual fee income, of all architectural practices. More of these economic factors later.

Temperamentally, politically and culturally I am in favour of the liberalization of professional services worldwide. I am also compelled by my ethical beliefs and by the pressure of my everyday experience to reveal what may not be immediately obvious to civil servants or to our colleagues in other great professions.

For the vast majority of the members of ACE, for an equivalent proportion of the members of my own national Institute, the RIBA and even for well over half of my own practice measured by annual fee income, income from international services ranges from the infinitesimal to the minuscule to the trivial. Day by day, project by project, what exactly is the problem? Why should architects send representatives to this international conference today and tomorrow when their exact, empirical experience, everyday, is almost entirely national, regional, local?

Let me sketch the statistical background. Robert Gutman's review of the realities of architectural practice in the United States revealed in 1989 that, while there are perhaps 90 000 members of the AIA, the American Institute of Architects (itself comprising a minority of registered US architects), the distribution of these architects and their practices is something like this:

- 25 000 practices
- 12 500 are "one man or less"
- only 250 US practices employ more than 50 registered architects
- 12 practices in the US aggregate approximately 30 per cent of the income of the entire profession. (See Chapter 12.)

A more violently-skewed distribution of results could hardly be imagined. Nevertheless, a similar profile of economic performance would undoubtedly be obtained were such a survey to be conducted in Greece, in Australia or in Ethiopia.

These statistics are not accidental. They relate to the underlying reality of the distribution of architectural services in an economic context in which there is consistently a huge divergence – for reasons that are structural, due to differences in culture, in peer group approbation, in regulation and in inclination – between the most and the least ambitious of members of our vast architectural international community.

When globalization is the topic of discussion, regionalization and localization of the delivery of professional services are the inevitable, inescapable concomitants.

THE ACE EXPERIENCE

Europe is different from the rest of the world. Europe is uniquely the cockpit of massive, profound, internally-generated pressure for change. During 1994 I had the privilege of observing part of the process of the crystallization of the interest of architects within the European Union in response to huge external pressures from a globalizing construction industry and from international user driven demand. The consequences of this special perspective have not been as elegant, as straightforward nor as wealth-generating as I should have wished.

From a British perspective – saturated by years of Thatcherism and by the vicious consequences of severe economic recession (from 1989 to 1994) – there seems to us to be a huge spectrum of architectural opinion within the European Union ranging from the dazzlingly centralized and uncomfortably cosy system of the Spanish Colleglos to the deregulated but extremely culturally and artistically effective, but almost invisible, system of the Danes. What is astonishing to us in the UK is that equivalent levels of world-class architectural excellence seem to have been achieved under totally different regimes of architectural politics. Puzzling as these differences and similarities certainly are, at least from a British perspective, the rest of Europe seems to be very limited in the forms of practice that are available to architects and yet simultaneously over-privileged in terms of the levels of immunity from contractual conflict. Thus the emphasis upon the responsibility of the proud, autonomous, "liberal" professional seems anachronistic – a concept that hardly survives in our much more commercial, cynical, litigious Anglo Saxon environment. Four litmus tests are:

- protection of function for architects – taken for granted in Spain and Germany, illegal in the UK
- protection of title of architects – not accepted in Ireland and Denmark (where the standard of urban design and architecture is the highest in Europe), taken for granted in Germany, Spain and France, and only surviving after a fierce political battle in the UK
- ability for architects to form capital under normal commercial rules of limited liability – strong in the UK in theory, weak everywhere else in Europe
- direct employment of architects within the construction industry – taken for granted in Japan to the extent of being the predominant mode of employment, rare practically everywhere else.

PARADOXES AND PECULIARITIES

Oddities abound. In theory, post-Thatcher Britain is for architects the most liberal, open and deregulated economy in the world. As a consequence a dozen or more North American architectural practices flourished in the UK in the last decade. And yet hardly any German or French, and certainly no Spanish or Italian practices, have been able to establish footholds there. Is this a matter of language, business relations, artistic sympathy or free trade? Nobody knows. A trend towards success for more liberal or maybe simply better capitalized professional structures can be seen in the relative success of British architectural practices in continental Europe via a well developed and – until today – welcoming architectural competition system.

A great fact, however, remains at the heart of the culture and site-specific nature of architectural service – there is still no such thing as a truly global architectural practice. Some big US practices – SOM, HOK – come close to achieving this status but they depend very much on the international activities of US clients. What international success has been achieved by architects is relatively rare and is related either to the highest levels of international artistic and intellectual culture or to following historic patterns of international trade – politically imperial in the case of the UK, economically imperial in the case of the US.

INTERNATIONAL PROFESSIONAL STRUCTURES

Whatever internationalization of the professional structure of architecture has taken place has been the result of either cultural or commercial forces. The background to international trade in architectural services is – it must be stressed again – the overwhelmingly predominant local and regional nature of the delivery of architectural services. And by local architects I really mean local – working within 100km of their practice. I believe this to be largely a factor of the underlying, widely-distributed pattern of demand for architectural services. However, architectural culture through the medium of internationally-read magazines and a close network of inter-university links is relatively easily exported.

New architectural styles flash almost instantly from continent to continent – almost without benefit of commercial relations or rewards. Such cultural networks are real, vital and informal and very hard to map. Formal international architectural professional structures exist for three major reasons.

First, because of politically inspired, cross-cultural international unions of national architectural institutions. The classic example is the International Union of Architects (UIA), the product of post-Second World War idealism which now seems largely to exist to keep architects in the Third World in touch with those in the First World.

Second, as a result of sharply-focused groupings of architectural institutions within such entities as the European Union. The classic example is the body which I have the honour to represent, the Architects' Council of Europe, which represents the interests of practically all the architects within the European Union to the European Parliament and the European Commission. Another similar body is the Commonwealth Association of Architects (CAA). International groupings of architectural institutions can be expected to develop within NAFTA and SE Asia.

Thirdly, such structures exist as international extensions of the individual membership of national architectural institutions. The 5000 international members of my own Institute, the Royal Institute of British Architects, come into this category. Such international membership is partly a legacy of the past, partly the result of international programmes of accreditation of architectural qualifications (in which the RIBA has historically been very active) and partly due to the pressure on national institutions to expand through increasing membership (RIBA, AIA).

LIBERALIZATION AND PROFESSIONALISM

The question which OECD is currently addressing is the extent to which professional structures, whether national or international, inhibit free trade in professional services.

Architects are not free from protectionist tendencies. However, many aspects of architectural practice which may appear exclusivist are, in fact, profoundly functional.

State registration (protection of function or title or both) which is so widespread in the European Union could be interpreted as a device to exclude competition. Registration of architects, however, has generally been adopted with the consumerist objective of protecting the public from poor design and low quality construction. In practice, registration is often linked to the administration of building and planning regulations. Registration is based on the architect's education which is notoriously long. Why? The science and art of architecture, particularly design skills, are hard to teach, difficult to learn. Fixed fee scales, which are common in Europe, should not be construed as a conspiracy against the public interest but as a remarkably effective contract with the public to keep design costs constant in order to encourage disinterested advice and upwards only commitment by architects to design quality.

Such arguments are not simple nor are they non-controversial. The US has been notorious for widespread abuse of state registration to protect local and even national interests. The record of the European Union is much better, with an ongoing commitment to harmonize educational standards throughout the EU in order to encourage free access of architects from one part of Europe to another. "International" competitions are widespread. Public projects are advertised throughout the EU and architects from all countries are free to offer their services without constraint. Harmonization of regulations, of professional indemnity, of building standards are the bread and butter of the day-to-day work of the Architects' Council of Europe. An enormous amount of progress towards free trade in architecture in Europe has been achieved without reduction in architectural standards. Many would argue that harmonization has meant an overall increase in architectural standards in the EU.

THE STRANGE CASE OF THE UK

By European architectural standards, the UK represents an extreme of liberalized practice – mandatory fee scales are illegal, architects may be protected by limited liability, the concept of the autonomous "liberal professional" is weak, competition from other providers of design and construction services is strong, architects are protected only by title and not by function. Recently, in a spasm of latter-day Thatcherism, attempts have been made by the British Government to abbreviate the funding of architectural education and, more fundamentally to abandon registration altogether.

The question is whether this rough form of liberalization of a great profession is a model for the OECD as a whole.

The answer has to be emphatically, "No". However, in the course of reaching this conclusion some useful experience has been gained and some excellent fundamental thinking done about the real nature of professionalism. The RIBA conducted a vigorous campaign against de-registration, winning widespread support from Members of Parliament in both main parties who were concerned about protecting the quality of their constituents' lives. Significantly, the crucial point in the campaign was when the main British consumer organization came out in support of registration – in the public interest. They felt that the term "architect", with its collateral implications of high standards of education and practice, is in itself a most useful marker for protecting consumers from the rapacious and unreliable construction industry. So much for practice. At the intellectual level, the threat of de-registration has forced the RIBA to think hard about the nature of professionalism.

THE TRUE NATURE OF PROFESSIONALISM

Short-term consumerism cannot justify professional privilege – the special contract which society is prepared to make with doctors, lawyers, architects to ensure high and consistent standards of service. Nor are historical arguments of long-held status – and certainly not claims by professionals based on self interest.

The fundamental justification for the peculiar position of the professions in society has to be based on knowledge. The voluntary association of highly-trained men and women who are willing to develop their skills in the context of action and who are prepared to act ethically and to share their knowledge open endedly for the common good is the only way in which certain kinds of knowledge can be developed. The universities cannot rival this way of accumulating knowledge because they are at best one step removed from action, nor can commerce, bound as it is by cruder, more competitive rules of behaviour (paradoxically for free marketeers) which by professional standards in relation to sharing knowledge are ultimately more restrictive. To put the proposition even more strongly: professions such as architecture can be justified in modern society if and only if they can demonstrate continually to their clients and to all users that the bodies of knowledge they exist to foster (in the case of architecture the relation between design and the user) can be developed better in no other way. This is the ultimate form of intellectual – not commercial – competition which justifies professional status, professional privilege. I believe the professions actually fulfil this promise – not completely, but adequately – today. They could do better.

Any legal or regulatory mechanisms, any bilateral arrangements, which inhibit this dynamic, open-ended, action-orientated, knowledge-based, future-seeking pursuit of excellence are dangerous. The professions must be willing to accept criticism and be prepared to reject sub-optimal forms of statutory protection which, in effect, are minimalist and contradict fundamental professional objectives. Knowledge ultimately is everything; knowledge is the final arbiter.

This presentation has taken an enormous leap from a simple calculus of whether the removal of trade barriers will affect the cumulative commercial success of the architectural profession. I have not been able to attempt to discuss the position of architects within the construction industry – itself a huge topic. I have shown that the practice of architecture tends to be very local but the ideals of architecture are universal. What I have attempted to do on behalf of the Architects' Council of Europe is to demonstrate that professions such as architecture exist to defend the public interest and that they can only do that through the autonomous, open-ended pursuit of action-orientated excellence in their own particular fields of expertise – which we call professional knowledge. I believe that there is an inevitable conflict between short-term views of public interest (selfishness, market research) and longer-term views (ethics, real user research) – that to defend the long view is ultimately in the public interest and that therefore the idea of professionalism in architecture, and in other fields, is entirely justifiable and must be strongly supported by OECD.

All this explains why I, as President of the Architects' Council of Europe, President of the Royal Institute of British Architects and Chairman of DEGW, an international architectural practice, am delighted to be able to be here today justifying the profession of architecture on behalf of my 300 000 colleagues in the European Union. Our argument transcends self interest.

ACE presidential programme for 1994, published in the *RIBA Journal,* January 1994.

18 The Way Forward (1995)

The two years of my presidency of the RIBA have been good for architecture, in terms of growing public appreciation, but far from good enough for architects, if we use any ordinary measure of relative economic success. Here in the UK, and even more abroad, there is abundant evidence of a rekindling at the very highest levels of British architectural skill and, more importantly, of a new appreciation by an increasingly discriminating public – and even by some politicians – of the pleasures and benefits that everyone can derive from the widespread application and development of architectural imagination. There is also plenty of evidence of a contrary phenomenon: widespread economic underperformance by architects and frequent personal demoralization and sense of failure.

Being president gives one a special sense of the shape of the profession – 30 000 architects of various ages and conditions flying, through space and time, collectively exhibiting at any one moment skills, habits and attitudes, some going back to the 1920s, others stretching forward into the second decade of the twenty-first century.

If I may generalize, despite this complexity, to attempt to explain an immense social phenomenon, the architectural profession in the UK is still suffering from its post-war success. The profession was traumatized by the sudden end in the 1970s of its post-war prominence as the sole begetter of the built fabric of the Welfare State. An alternative *raison d'etre,* a new myth for architects to explain themselves to themselves and to society at large in the vastly different social, political, economic and cultural climate of Britain in the last two decades, has not yet been fully forged, despite the formidable national and international success of the best British architects. I believe it has been this 20-year failure of confidence, this freezing of our collective imaginative faculty – not helped recently by an appalling, five-year recession – that explains why architects have been so slow to change our ways of thinking and working in response to a totally different and in many ways much more challenging environment.

The converse of this severe analysis is more cheerful. Clearly the fundamental problem is not lack of talent, nor intelligence, nor design quality. Moreover, should architects succeed in redefining their proper role in modern society – as I confidently believe many are doing already – then the leverage, as the Americans would say, of architectural imagination properly applied to solving contemporary societal and economic problems would be terrific. Knowledge is power and it is the architect's genius as well as duty to exercise imaginative power to help ordinary as well as extraordinary people make the best use of their physical surroundings.

It is exactly this task of redefinition and, in fact, of reinvention of the role of the architect in modern society that the RIBA Strategic Study set out to accomplish.

The first two phases of the RIBA's four-year study of architectural practice in the UK, our *Strategic Study of the Profession,* were full of harsh lessons for architects. The first phase (1991–2) was designed as a *tour d'horizon* of contemporary practice. It turned out to be a severe critique of certain unintended consequences of the managerial revolution in architectural practice that stemmed from the RIBA's seminal 1962 study, *The Architect and his Office.* Models of good practice that had been established with great effort and good will in the 1960s turned out to have been subverted in the totally different conditions of the late 1980s and 1990s. Under the fierce pressure of market-based competition in post-Thatcherite Britain, in which (to the horror of our architect colleagues in the rest of the European Union) it had become illegal for British architects to "collude" against the public interest by offering fixed fee scales. Some, if not many, architects, desperate to survive, had become accustomed to giving away, or at least spectacularly discounting, a major part of their intellectual property – conceptual design ideas – to buy the busy work of detailing, working drawings and contract administration which they imagined would be enough to pay the bills and keep their practices busy.

A more foolish bargain could hardly be imagined. Dr Faustus dealt more successfully with Mephistopheles when he traded his immortal soul for an illusion. We had discovered that architects were devaluing their most precious, most hard won, asset: design imagination.

To compound what must be the worst marketing error of the century, architects were also learning fast that it is in detailing, in the preparation of drawings and in contract administration that architects are most vulnerable to automation and to cheaper, less competent and far less scrupulous competitors.

Phase 2 of the RIBA Strategic Study (1993) concentrated on discovering what the best contemporary clients think about architects and also on discovering the secrets which had made it possible for certain architectural practices to succeed even during the recession.

From our studies of what clients think of architects the RIBA has learned that clients really do like and value design ideas – the intellectual property which our weaker architects are increasingly tempted to give away – but also that they very much dislike the ways in which architects tend to deliver what they have designed. This is partly because clients find it difficult to disassociate the architect's contribution from that of the rest of the construction industry and partly because architects, by the inherently enthusiastic nature of our calling, often succeed in raising clients' expectations without always having the power or the managerial control to provide all that we have appeared to promise.

Worst of all, in the RIBA's detailed studies of the performance of the most "successful" architectural practices, we found that the cleverest, the most able architects did not feel impelled to measure systematically the application of their design skill to what happened subsequently to their clients' operations. In other words, "success" is being measured all too often, even by our best architects, by internal – one is tempted to say by introverted – architectural criteria.

Such are the findings, which some architects found so depressing, of the first two phases of the RIBA Strategic Study. Instead of being depressed, the RIBA's Steering Group drew the obvious practical conclusion and made very sure that the third phase of our work (1994–5) would be marked by building on our collective strengths, by being willing to rethink together what it is that architects should be trying to achieve in modern society. This was done with the optimism characteristic of that great gift that comes from our long architectural training – the belief that, given a problem clearly stated, we architects can somehow design a way to solve it. Surely, we thought, architects can regroup our scattered and sometimes tattered forces by making sure that we can justify our special contribution to society through using design to win the hearts and minds and, above all, the imagination of our clients.

Wider matters than the fate of the architectural profession hang currently in the balance. The RIBA's Strategic Study is about architects and their future but we do not intend collectively to make the mistake that we have already accused certain individual architects of making – that is, of being too introverted, too self referential, too protective. In the course of 1994–5, substantial thought is being given in the UK to the future of the entire construction industry through the *Latham Report* under Sir Michael Latham, and with the work of the consequent Latham Working Parties in which the RIBA is taking such a vigorous part. Our main contributions to this debate are to:

- agree that to be successful, architecture and the construction industry must be interdependent
- insist that the contribution of architectural design must not be devalued by our colleagues. Design transcends styling. Architectural design affects the performance of everyone in the construction industry. It is no less than the intelligent and directed use of physical resources to achieve what users, clients, society really need – as opposed to what they may demand – now and into the future
- attack any bias towards supply-side thinking – that is, the tendency, common enough among architects but even worse elsewhere in the construction industry, of preferring, as an industry, to deliver to our clients what we like delivering rather than what we ought to be delivering
- remind the industry not to allow itself to be bullied by the big players: there are many small clients and many small suppliers whose interests also need to be respected
- ensure that every detail of the reform of contract procedures and of the processes of construction should take these values into account.

What we are arguing is, in effect, not that architects have any historic rights or residual importance in the construction industry independent of the interests of the users, clients, society whom we exist to serve. Nor, conversely, is our case that the construction industry would prosper better if architects were to abdicate their identity and become indistinguishable within a kind of alphabet soup of integrated skills and common education. Rather, the RIBA is finding the Latham review a marvellous opportunity to assist our rethinking of what is the unique, the characteristic, the value adding contribution of architects to the construction industry. We believe that the future prosperity of the construction industry, in this country and abroad, will depend not only on architects becoming more closely integrated with the skills, interests and concerns of our colleagues but also on a much more precise and realistic calculation of our own specific contribution to shared success.

WHAT IS SPECIAL ABOUT ARCHITECTURE AND ARCHITECTS?

Vitally important to the RIBA's thinking on the future of architectural practice has been a programme, parallel to the Strategic Study, of even more fundamental work on the redefinition of what professionalism in the late twentieth century should really mean to architects. This rethinking was partly stimulated by the government's unsuccessful attack in the early 1990s on the principle of funding the full five years of the full-time architectural course. Implicit in this official attempt to abbreviate the funding of students was an underlying critique of such a long and unusual course with such a strong emphasis on design and project work. We were being asked what was it that could justify such an inconveniently different and inherently expensive form of training.

The RIBA's official response was in the form of two documents, *Less Means Worse* (1990) and the *Burton Report* (1992). The reports, taken together, while not uncritical of the current state of architectural education, provided what was needed at the time: a robust defence of a particular educational programme which is now recognized by HEFCE (as it always has been internationally) as an exemplary programme of professional education, very well run and well regulated by the profession and the universities, working together.

However, the Government's attack stimulated a more fundamental response – a response that was also necessary to make intellectual sense of the growing importance for architects of continuing professional development (CPD: made mandatory by the RIBA in 1993) – which means, in essence, that an architectural education is never complete and that all architects have the obligation not only to develop their own skills continually but to do so in co-operation with their colleagues throughout the construction industry. This response has been nothing less than the redefinition of architectural knowledge.

The only way for architects to measure quality is through the systematic and collective use of architectural knowledge. Each individual architect interprets emerging user needs and tries to respond to them with imaginative, innovative design solutions. Architects acting together have chosen to organize themselves voluntarily in the UK, largely within the professional body which calls itself the RIBA. Why? For a very good reason. We have, in effect, invented in the RIBA a powerful, shared learning device in order to develop our common skills more effectively than each of us would be able to achieve separately as singleton architects. We use the RIBA to pass on this shared knowledge and executive skill to subsequent generations of architects. This is far from being a selfish or protectionist argument. Quite the opposite: it is an open-ended, generous, expansionist, confident policy. We believe there is no better way of developing architectural knowledge – including all the skills and methodologies by which this knowledge is applied to our clients' myriads of practical problems – than through the voluntary association of architects who have willingly agreed to pool their knowledge and to pass on their skills. The test which a sceptical consumer of architectural services would use to check this proposition is obvious: could a better way be found of achieving the same end? So far no more successful formula has been found anywhere for testing, extending, transmitting, broadcasting for the public good our particular body of knowledge and skills. Should such a way be found, we architects would be ethically bound to abandon our present professional structure in the interest of developing architectural knowledge and architectural skills further and faster. To make this argument fully operational in the competitive and consumerist environment of today it is absolutely necessary for architects to define and present architectural knowledge in a way that commands the interest and the respect of the general public as well as of our colleagues in the construction industry. Our title, our mode of remuneration, our ways of working, our relations with clients, our utility in the construction industry, our educational programme all depend upon this. The challenge is that the benefits to the general quality of life to be derived from the skilful application of architectural imagination are not widely enough understood. Nor does architectural knowledge fit comfortably within the neat categories of conventional academic structures. Architectural knowledge does not flourish when skills are divorced from ideas, when practice is separated from theory but when all are brought together in the context of action. Architectural knowledge is usually challenging, sometimes uncomfortable, always open ended, inherently value laden.

The easiest way to define architectural knowledge is to observe what architects do and how they think. Architects, compared to most disciplines and certainly to every other discipline in the construction industry, distinguish themselves by deploying two extremely powerful and characteristic ways of thinking: they invent and they use their skills to relate what they invent to the aspirations of those who use buildings. Design invention, a wonderful but unfortunately all too rare commodity, is obtained only at the cost of a long, highly disciplined, project-based training. User understanding is equally important as the critical bridge between what users, clients, society demand and what the resources of construction can supply. It is the combination in action of these two special ways of thinking, in all their myriad of infinitely complex applications and ramifications, that ultimately add up to what we mean by architectural knowledge.

THE RIBA'S ACTION PLAN

The objective of the whole Strategic Study is the redefinition, the reinvention of the role of the architect in modern society. The core of this redesign of architecture, the invention of a new myth, is the axiom that whatever influence an individual architect may have in any particular situation depends ultimately upon architects' collective ability to advance architectural knowledge. If we ask how the profession of architecture in this information-hungry, knowledge-based, last decade of the twentieth century can set about reforming itself, then the answer has to be through architects collectively being empowered to release the potential of architectural knowledge.

In order to change the RIBA to make it achieve this objective, we have already set about the three parallel tasks of:

• making sure that the RIBA accelerates the development of architectural knowledge through finding the most effective ways of ensuring that architects are continually communicating with and learning from clients, in as systematic a way as possible, about what architectural design can do to anticipate and satisfy the emerging needs of users, clients, society
• redesigning the organizational structure and the information technology of the RIBA so that we encourage and reward networking among members in order to help them acquire, develop and share specific facets of that highly practical and extremely valuable commodity, architectural knowledge
• making sure that the RIBA's educational programme for architects, both in schools and in practice, is as effective an instrument as possible for developing, diffusing and transmitting that body of knowledge.

"Communicating with and learning from clients" – architects must focus their attention upon the strategic advantage, for themselves and for the profession as a whole, of being in the pole position of articulating the emerging needs of clients. The RIBA has set about this in the most direct possible way by organizing a series of sectoral studies (organized regionally through 20 focus group discussions involving over 200 clients). These were designed to explore in some detail the emerging needs of seven types of client:

• higher education
• retail, housing
• health
• offices
• primary, secondary and further education
• sport and the arts.

The overriding objective of each series of focus groups in each of these seven sectors has been to determine the kinds of buildings and the overall stock of space likely to be most in demand in the year 2005.

In order to achieve the rapidest possible diffusion of the key findings to the widest possible RIBA audience, the results of each of the seven sectoral studies were published in the *RIBA Journal* as soon as they were completed. The whole series is now reprinted, giving in aggregate an unprecedentedly wide and comprehensive sketch of the future building needs of this country.

Another vitally important objective of the sectoral studies is to establish ongoing relations between client groups and specialist networks of architects. This objective is well on its way to being achieved since the value of an ongoing relationship became quickly clear to clients as well as to architects. The RIBA is now organizing Client Interest Groups and corresponding architect networks on a permanent basis.

"Networking among members" – the structure of the RIBA has, until very recently, been based first upon the technology of paper, secondly upon the workings of committees, and thirdly upon the geography of the regions. Information technology has a tremendous amount to offer to supplement these three ways of carrying out our business. Networks of members are now being established to help them share information about such specific areas of architectural expertise as the conservation of older buildings or the skills involved in practising in, for example, the sectors of housing or health. Such networks will stimulate and validate the work of our specialized committees and will aid Council in the creation and diffusion of RIBA policy. Networks will supplement and enrich the existing strong pattern of branch and regional membership – creating another dimension of Institute membership.

"Educational programme for architects" – it is critical to make sure that all 38 UK schools of architecture, all of whose courses the RIBA validates, are informed of the profound implications of the findings of the Strategic Study for educating future architects. This process has begun with a series of day-long visits to eight of these schools in the spring of 1995 designed to encourage a friendly and open-ended dialogue about how architectural education – and architectural research – should develop.

In parallel an extensive programme of CPD events has been held throughout the regions – four seminars in each of seven regions and more to come – to make sure that the same messages are communicated to practising architects. The purpose is to develop the new skills architects need to deliver to clients the full range of services that the Strategic Study has discovered to be so important to clients. This is the first time that the RIBA has assembled for members from central resources, through the CPD programme, the high quality programme of seminars that they now need. A summary of the same information is being disseminated through the *Architects' Journal.*

This vigorous and ongoing activity of "re-designing" the architectural profession, in a period of accelerating societal change, is based upon a theory. That theory is a development of the classical idea of professionalism which was hammered out for British architects almost 200 years ago by such founders of the Institute as Sir John Soane. The classical idea of professionalism in architecture argued that the autonomy of architects depended upon the neutrality that Soane thought necessary, in a violently competitive and often corrupt early nineteenth-century world, to hold the ring between client and contractor. The new idea of professionalism argues that neutrality – or rather dispassionate professional judgement – depends in our own increasingly complex world not just on personal ethics but upon the dynamic development of knowledge. To Soane's wise and long-lasting but somewhat static formulation has been added a new, additional and urgent professional responsibility: to justify architectural autonomy continually through demonstrating a superior body of architectural knowledge deployed in the service of society through a measurably superior battery of skills.

What this means for the RIBA is very clear.

If the new idea of professionalism is inherently based on the quality of our collective knowledge base, then the RIBA's most important task must be to develop architects' knowledge and architects' skills. However, it is equally clear that the architectural profession's knowledge base is unstable and shifting, needing continuous maintenance and development to remain credible. Hence the importance of research as well as of teaching. Hence the vital necessity of linking practice and education. Hence the criticality of CPD as a way of keeping all architects as up-to-date as possible. Hence – as architectural knowledge rapidly increases – the inevitability of specialization in architectural education, in research and above all in practice. Without specialization, increasingly complex user demands cannot properly be addressed.

The RIBA is a learning as well as a teaching organization. Our influence depends not upon the careful maintenance of our professional boundaries but on our ability to apply design imagination and design skills to anticipating and satisfying user needs projected into the future. Alliances with other disciplines are even more vitally necessary. Our colleagues' insights and their own areas of special knowledge in the construction industry and elsewhere are needed to advance our architectural programme. Architects must cross more boundaries – lose the fear of being marginalized. Our power to advise clients on how best to use building procurement and the construction process is multiplied by the extent to which we can understand and foresee what ought to be done to meet clients' needs. Our field of action is not simply new buildings but the design and the management of the entire building stock. Our confidence must not just be based upon what we know about the past but on our confident ability to help our clients predict their futures.

Architects, more capable of helping users, clients and society through design, will become, even more, an invaluable and integrating force within a reformed construction industry. Everyone – colleagues, users, clients, society – will benefit. Given these conditions, architects can be confident of a future that will be equally good for architecture and for architects.

Delivered by Frank Duffy as a valedictory address on termination of his presidency of the RIBA, 27 June 1995, and also to introduce the publication of the final phases, 3 and 4, of the *Strategic Study of the Profession*.

Afterword

One of the most striking consequences of the extraordinary current revolution in office work is that it is no longer sensible – or even possible – for clients, or indeed for architects working on their behalf, to make decisions about the design of their physical working environment independently of decisions about the future use of information technology or about the reshaping of organizational structures. Dealing with one matter at a time is certain to guarantee sub-optimal results in the other two. All three factors have become so systematically and operationally related that they are inextricable.

The same kind of integrating logic is essential to comprehend the three levels of discussion that make up this book and to understand why these papers, incomplete and inadequate as each one of them is, have been brought together in this way. Once upon a time, in a far more stable world, it would have been considered quite normal to discuss the development of such a specialized and particular area of professional activity as my own field of office design separately from the changes that were currently taking place in the general practice of architecture. Similarly both of these discussions would almost certainly have been disconnected from any analysis of the way in which the architectural profession as a whole was being affected by major shifts in the political and regulatory environment. Such serial detachment is no longer possible. Today the issues that architects face at all three levels are obviously and intimately connected. Professional structures, professional practice and professional focus have become simply three ways of talking about the same thing – the consequences of irresistible and unstoppable change. The practical objective at each level is how best to deploy the rapidly growing body of professional knowledge in new ways for the maximum benefit of society, clients and users – as well, of course, as for the maximum impact on the development of architecture itself.

In office design the systemic approach to organization theory is a reaction against mechanistic, divisive and ultimately inhuman ways of thinking about business operations and business culture that is the legacy of Frederick Taylor and his many followers who had such a profound impact at the turn of the century on the design of offices –

and on so many other aspects of modern life. Scientific management exalted division in order to rule, supervision in order to control, synchrony in order to discipline, hierarchy in order to master. All these values instantly found their way into the design of millions of square feet of corporate offices and shaped the character of practically every city centre in the modern world. It is only after two decades of pouring powerful new information technology into every corner of every office everywhere and after another decade of lively speculation and continuous experiment in "re-engineering" office organizations themselves that it has occurred to architects that the physical infrastructure of the office building might have to change to accommodate and even stimulate new ways of working. Such is the inertia of the divided world we have inherited.

But dividing problems into detached components in order to make it easier to address each one of them separately has been one of the characteristic features of twentieth century intellectual life. It has thus been legitimate to speak of the management and marketing of architectural practice without any detailed understanding of the new kinds of services that clients are beginning to want. An almost universal habit in architectural schools has been to teach design without any reference to practice and, with precisely reciprocal indifference, to teach courses on "professional practice" without once drawing attention to changing priorities in design. Similarly, what little debate there has been at the level of restructuring the profession of architecture has been carried out by architects themselves in response to external political pressures without any serious examination of how architectural practice is changing. Nor has there been much interest in whether any light can be thrown on the question by studying changes in other professions, or by examining the reality of the changing role of the architect within the construction industry or, once again, of investigating why clients – users – have changed their expectations of what architects can provide.

Children of a pragmatic century, toying with the puzzle piece by piece, many architects have lost the big picture. The result is that many debates about the future of architecture have been fragmented, self referential, introverted, diminished by supply-side thinking. Gathering these papers into this book is an attempt to reverse this reductionist process by reintroducing ideas into the debate, by trying to explore how things hangs together, by daring to essay at least one or two hypotheses to elucidate the dynamics that are changing late twentieth-century architecture.

Why should this particular body of writing be free, or at least relatively free, of the general malaise? If excuses are needed, there are three. The first has been the stimulus of a career spent in office design – a field that has grown so rapidly, in such a non-traditional way, in so many different cultures, and with such vigorous and articulate users, that the main lesson about the closeness and urgency of the connection between architecture and corporate values, for good or ill, has been impossible to avoid. The second was the good fortune to have been let loose as a graduate student at Berkeley and Princeton in the late 1960s with good teachers, enough confidence in my design skills and with enough time on my hands to raid the human disciplines surrounding architecture – especially sociology, psychology, anthropology, history, industrial engineering, operational research – for ideas and methods that could illuminate the interest I already had in the relationship of office design to changes in society. However, it is the third excuse that is the most cogent, if also the most accidental and unlikely.

This is the fact that I was caught up in the micro-politics of the architectural profession, as president elect and then as president of the RIBA, in the first half of the 1990s, at a time of significant action and extremely rapid change. In this position, in a period during which the profession had come under severe external attack, I was forced back far more than I anticipated on my own specialized professional experience in DEGW and on my scattered and half-forgotten intellectual formation to try to construct an adequately robust defence for my profession. No doubt the job could have been done better but the result for me, and for my colleagues at the RIBA, was to emphasize the lesson that in order to defend architecture for the future, the reforming of architectural expertise, architectural practice, and the architectural profession are all profoundly interconnected and are best undertaken together by architects working collectively within a common intellectual programme.

The context, in addition to being in the midst of the longest and deepest recession for architects that anyone could remember, was three attacks, all from government, on the architectural profession. Threats to fees, education and registration galvanized the profession into eventually succesful action and created a model of what can be achieved against great odds by a relatively small but well-organized professional body. Design is growing in strategic importance as it comes to terms with information technology and organization theory in such fields as office design. Cases, comparisons, quantification, feed back have suddenly become very important indeed in a time of rapid change. In exactly the same way, as architecture becomes more knowledge based, practice is now in a position to take advantage of the greater influence that can be won through the application of systematically collected information about buildings and their use. Equally the profession will have to reorganize itself to take advantage of the new responsibilities that such power will bring.

The symptoms of these changes are evident. Architectural expertise, for example through the influence of CAD and through new electronic information sources, is becoming more accessible, much more manipulable and cumulatively far more powerful. The impact on architectural practice is already great – for example, in my own experience, a new emphasis on developing specialized skills both at a practice and a personal level; a new interest in analysing and classifying the sectoral needs of clients; new ways of measuring building performance in terms not only of energy and occupancy costs but also in relation to general business and social goals; new ways of communicating with ever more demanding users that are leading to new briefing techniques, often involving computer simulation; a new emphasis on feedback and continuous service. The economics of architectural practice have been shaken up both by new technology and by new forms of competition. New, more flexible kinds of management style are replacing the paternalism and the bureaucracy of previous eras of architectural practice. These changes have a lot to do with the ways in which the technology of practice is being revolutionized. Technology, organizational structure and the physical environment are as intimately correlated in architectural practice as anywhere else. Nothing will remain the same. Everything is subject to change.

At the level of the whole architectural profession, despite much destruction and personal anguish, the troubles of the last decade have also had good consequences. Both the AIA and the RIBA have always seen themselves as deeply involved in the dissemination of information to their members. What is new, as communication becomes more electronic, is that professional networks are now becoming both two-way and decentralized so that membership of a professional institute is taking on an entirely new meaning.

Most important are the initiatives that are being taken by the RIBA to open up architecture systematically to clients and users to gain more knowledge about buildings and their use for everyone's benefit. The function of such professional institutes in building up and disseminating the body of action-based and value-laden knowledge that constitutes professionalism is becoming increasingly obvious. This is still best done, as in the nineteenth century, on an open-ended and voluntary basis. Equally well founded but refreshingly regenerated is a growing awareness of the tremendous importance and value in modern society of cultural leadership – demonstrated in the growth of architecture centres in London and in many other cities. Also strongly revived in the RIBA is an urgent sense of the responsibility for transmitting this growing body of knowledge to succeeding generations of architects.

Not surprisingly, it is impossible to maintain old-fashioned professional discriminations within such an open-ended and ambitious programme of developing architectural knowledge. Collaboration across disciplines is inevitably becoming much more important. Least possible of all is continuing to draw national boundaries round these expanding intellectual, artistic and commercial activities. The globalization of the architectural professional is under way.

What all this demonstrates is that one of the most powerful instruments for developing, applying and transmitting knowledge ever invented, the professional institute, has an enormous amount of potential and is likely to have a much more central place in the society of the twenty first century. The price will be the rewiring of all conventional professional procedures. Architecture is a fine example and is reforming fast and at every level. The idea of a knowledge-based architectural profession will be catalytic in an increasingly knowledge-based society.

Francis Duffy, London, November 1997

Appendix: key documents
1962 – 1994

The Architect and his Office (1962)
RIBA Plan of Work (1963)
Less Means Worse (1990)
A Research Policy for the Architectural Profession (1991)
The Burton Report (1992)
RIBA Strategic Study of the Profession: Phase 1 (1992)
The Latham Report (1994)

The Architect and his Office (1962)

Presented to the Council of the Royal Institute on 6 February 1962. Based on a survey team set up in the autumn of 1960 to study problems of organization, staffing, quality of service and productivity in a sample of architects' offices. Financed by a grant from the Leverhulme Trust.

William Holford, President. Members, Michael Austin-Smith, Andrew Derbyshire, Denis Howard, Janet Madge and Joan Milne.

SCOPE AND QUESTIONS ASKED

- **Architectural education**
  What sort of work needs to be done in architects' office and what proportion of kinds of staff, professional and non-professional, does this argue?
- **Fees and salaries**
  To what extent is the present scale of fees remunerative and what, if any, changes are desirable and practicable?
  Is it possible to lay down any broad levels of comparable responsibility common to a number of offices and if so, indicate the range of salaries paid at each level?
- **Management and technical competence**
  How can the efficiency of the architect be raised through better management of the office and the job; and how far is efficiency inhibited by factors beyond his control?

"We have confined the survey to the functions of the architect as designer of buildings, and have not looked in detail at his broader responsibilities in other fields such as town planning or research.

"In presenting the factual information asked for, we have taken advantage of our possibly unique experience in visiting nearly 70 architects' office of different kinds to add our own interpretation of the data in the light of the quality of service being offered to the client and the community."

MAIN CONCLUSIONS

Education and training
Architectural education should be diversified in order to bring technical design skills back into the profession. Architects who choose to specialize in the application of these skills ("architechnologists") should not be debarred from membership of the RIBA.

At the same time, closer relations should be established between architects and engineers in order to reach a better understanding of what the architect requires and how the best use can be made of the consultants' services.

The education and training of architects should be planned as an integrated whole, a seven-year period in which the stage or stages of practical training should be co-ordinated with the school syllabus to ensure that both aspects are complementary and together cover the necessary ground.

The profession should recognize that practical training of students in the office is an essential investment for the continuity of practice. There should be close co-operation between the office and the school, to ensure that the necessary standards are maintained throughout the training period, and that the experiences gained in each are integrated.

Technicians are needed in architects' offices in order to raise productivity and standards of services. They should be given some form of organized training for work concerned mainly with technical administration and the preparation of production information. The technician should not be concerned with design, and his training should exclude this aspect.

The existing National Certificate course in Building, with modifications, could provide a suitable medium for training technicians, as their work will have much in common with that being done by technicians in other parts of the building industry. It would be beneficial to the whole industry if they were to some extent interchangeable.

Technicians, as non-professionals, should not be admitted into a class of membership of the RIBA, but there should be an institute for technicians sponsored by the RIBA to ensure the maintenance of standards of education and training.

Fees and earnings

There should be an increase in the Scale for small jobs, through a more gradual reduction in the percentage charged at the lower end of the Scale as the size of job increases.

The possibility of a uniform higher percentage charge for custom-built private houses should be considered.

Consideration of reductions at the upper end of the Scale for large simple jobs should be linked with the possibility of charging more for complex jobs.

The RIBA should collect regular information on a standard basis about the movement of costs and productivity of offices over the next few years, as a check on the adequacy of the Scale of Fees. This information should also be widely disseminated to encourage offices to increase their productivity.

No recommendations for a differential fee scale by type of building can be offered, because the evidence was not sufficient to establish a basis that would genuinely reflect the variations in design costs that occur. A possible alternative would be to have a negotiable element in the scale to provide for higher fees for more complex work, and this should be looked at.

Research should be carried out into the time taken at various stages of the design process to provide the basis for a more rational fee scale, as well as providing aids to the planning and programming of work.

The RIBA should exercise greater control over the standard of service given by its Members, in return for the protection given them by the Scale of Fees.

Local authority architects' departments should exchange information with each other about costs and productivity achieved. They should establish their own basis of comparison rather than making unrealistic cost comparisons with other types of practice.

The possibility of local authority Chief Architects being allowed to run their departments within a given budget, without being held to parity in staffing with other departments of the authority should be explored.

It has been possible to establish four main levels of responsibility, apart from that of principal, within the architect's office. The report gives information about the range of salaries paid at each level of responsibility, analysed by age and type of office. Salary information on a similar basis should be collected and published at regular intervals.

The level of salaries and responsibilities of senior architects in the larger offices should be examined in relation to different form of work organization to ensure that more satisfactory career prospects are available. This might help to solve present staff shortages and to attract new entrants of high quality into the profession. The relative shortage of senior posts for both principals and assistants in local authority offices when compared with private offices should be one aspect of this study.

Management

The RIBA Management Handbook should be published as soon as possible.

The RIBA Management Advisory Service should be set up as soon as possible.

Immediate steps should be taken to widen the scope of the school curricula and the Professional Practice syllabus to include management theory and practice. More systematic use should be made of the practical training period, emphasizing office and job management problems and techniques.

There should be more refresher courses available for practising architects. These should cover management, technical and design subjects.

Uniform methods of costing, overheads analysis and budgetary control should be developed and spread throughout the profession.

Architects should be encouraged to obtain from their accountants, in addition to auditing services, the wider range of services which accountants can provide, such as assistance in the interpretation of accounting information, advice on matters of financial policy.

A study of the purpose and use of drawings should be put in hand, (a) to clarify the architect's own design processes, distinguishing "constructional design" drawings from "production" drawings, and (b) to see how far these compare in efficiency with other methods of communicating information to the other members of the building team.

The methods of working which are used by the centralized and dispersed types of office organization should be investigated, with a view to evolving a way of working which combines the advantages of each and avoids their defects.

The RIBA should gather and disseminate information and experience on user requirements for different building types. Greater attention should be paid by practising architects and by Schools of Architecture to the application of work study techniques to problems of this kind.

The profession should promote and encourage the application of standardization and industrialization to building in such a way that the architect's position is strengthened rather than weakened; and to that end the RIBA should disseminate information on the design implications of dimensional co-ordination and on the economics of standardization.

The possible advantages of group practice and various forms of consortia should be studied as a means of (a) strengthening the technical resources of the individual office and (b) achieving a more rational distribution of the work load among offices. This would make it possible to combine individual jobs into a building programme of sufficient size to enable the economic advantages of industrialization to be realized.

Ways should be sought of reducing fluctuations in work load which lower the output and efficiency of the individual office. These should include (a) an objective examination of existing methods of allocating jobs and (b) a review of the RIBA Code of Conduct with a view to liberalizing the "professional" attitude towards getting work.

A study should be made of all forms of placing contracts, for there is evidence to suggest that traditional forms of competitive tendering lead to increased building costs, introduce delays, inhibit technical development and prevent the application of good management procedures to the building process.

Effective action on all these points depends on joint work by all members of the building team. Architects, no matter in which field they are employed, should act in concert as one profession. Whenever possible they should bring the related professions on the design side into their deliberations, and should strengthen contact with the manufacturing and constructional sides of the industry.

RIBA Plan of Work (1963)

The *RIBA Plan of Work* was originally published in 1963 to provide a model procedure for methodical working by the design team. Procedures are set out as a sequence of diagrams – outline plan of work, stages A to M (inception, feasibility, outline proposals, scheme design, detail design, production information, bills of quantities, tender action, project planning, operations on site, completion, feedback); detailed procedures for the design team, stages A to H; and outline of post-contract activities, stages J to L.

When the 1963 mode was being developed, certain assumptions were made:

- that it applied to a building costing around £300 000 (in the region of £2 million at 1997 prices)
- that the architect would be responsible for leading the design team
- that the architect had been appointed early in the project
- that because of the complexity of this type of project, the sequence of stages, A to M set out in the first diagram, would have to be followed.

Each stage has the objective of launching the next, with the following cycle of work entailed:

- stating objectives and assimilating relevant facts
- assessing resources required and establishing appropriate job administration procedures
- planning the work and setting timetables
- carrying out work
- making proposals
- making decisions
- setting out objectives for the next stage.

Plan of Work simply offers an outline method of working. It will need to be amplified as appropriate for each office and for each new project, and to be modified to suit larger or smaller jobs, or for non-traditional methods of procurement.

It represents a logical sequence of actions to be taken so that good and timely decisions can be made and so that progress is not held up and abortive work is not undertaken. All the decisions set out or implied in the Plan have to be taken. Where the nature of the project, the design solution, the method of construction, the client organization and the design team are all familiar, it may only be necessary to check that the procedures cover all that has to be decided. Progress then may be greatly accelerated.

Where consultants other than the architect, quantity surveyor, and the various engineers designated in the diagrams are required, they must be introduced at the indicated stages.

In most traditional procurement projects, contractors will not be appointed until after the normal tendering procedure. Where for good reasons they can be appointed early in the design stage, there are opportunities for:

- forward planning and organization of the building operation before the completion of contract documents
- development of good communication and understanding between designer and contractor.

The model therefore includes a function for the contractor who is appointed early, so as to indicate the nature and timing of the contribution they can make.

Inevitably some circumstances will demand a degree of departure from the model Plan. For example, the architect may not be appointed as early as desirable. Their first task then will be to see that any omissions on the part of the client up to the time of appointment are rectified, and that the client is well informed and in a position to provide the necessary information as required, make sound decisions and understand the likely consequences if they fail to deal properly with any of these matters.

Thereafter the architect has two distinct functions:

- a management function – to ensure that the project as a whole is well run, and to co-ordinate the design process
- a design function – to contribute particular architectural skills.

Under the architect's management function, the main responsibilities are:

- to foresee, as far as practicable, any problems likely to arise and take steps to enable them to be resolved
- to take actions necessary to deal with unplanned eventualities
- to ensure that information is available, that appropriate professional skills are available and that everyone understands their responsibilities
- to ensure that lines of communication are clear and effective
- to ensure that optimum decisions are reached at the right times.

As part of the management function, the architect must adapt the Plan to suit the existing administrative procedures of the client, of their own office, and of the other members of the design team. They can graft on to it additional procedures such as submission of progress reports, job costing and claims for fees.

The design actions are listed in the diagrams. The key issue is for each member of the team to realize that their contribution is only part of the whole, and that the best possible result will depend upon good teamwork throughout. To achieve this, it is always desirable for the full design team to be appointed at the outset and to follow through the entire design process.

Less Means Worse (1990)

On 2 May 1990, the Secretary of State wrote to the President of the RIBA advising him that the Department of Education and Science (DES) had asked the Higher Education Funding Councils (HEFC) to consider the desirability of reducing their funding for courses in architecture to a maximum of four years. The RIBA was surprised that the Secretary of State had found any evidence of substance to support a *prima facie* case for reduced funding. This is the summary of the RIBA position on the future funding of architectural education and on the length and structure of courses.

The Institute considers that there is a stronger justification than ever before for public funding of the five academic years of initial education and training in architecture. Its view is based on nine principal factors.

1   Education for architectural design, developing a synthesis of aesthetic, economic, managerial, social, spatial and technical skills, starts in higher education – it has no substantial source in primary and secondary education.

2   The syllabus for architecture in the UK, developed by the RIBA, matches that laid down in the EC Architects Directive, which was originally drafted by the UK delegation and supported in all the negotiations over the 1960s to 1980s by the UK government.

3   All reports confirm increasing applications to architecture courses, the high calibre of recruits, the higher and faster growing proportion of women on these courses (greater than any other construction industry course), the progressive nature of the architectural education and training process, and an employment rate for architecture graduates among the highest of any discipline in higher education.

4   There is a need to strengthen and expand the content of the course, both in traditional and innovative areas including those promoted by the Government, such as EC-related topics, energy efficiency and other green issues, health and safety, and management.

5   The RIBA Visiting Board has consistently urged schools of architecture to make links with related disciplines in the same academic institutions and the Institute has been promoting interdisciplinary studies and dual qualifications.

6   The public's growing concern with architecture and the built environment and its support for architects' response to the green agenda indicate a need for more education and training in architecture, not less, and certainly no less funding.

7   The UK profession's pattern of education and training is admired throughout the world. It is increasingly imitated, and the success of UK architects overseas continues to grow. It is not good sense to damage these achievements by a major reduction of investment in education and training.

8   The RIBA has led the way in Continuing Professional Development (CPD) and open learning, in fulfilment of government policy, winning seedcorn funds from both PICKUP and the Training Agency. This increasingly successful strategy is integrated with the present five years of funded initial education.

9   The architectural profession is a creative and dynamic part of the small business sector upon which the health of the economy depends, but shares the problems of that sector, particularly in relation to undertaking the necessary formal aspects of initial education.

These factors are elaborated in the RIBA's detailed position paper responding to the Department of Education and Science's consultation document which was sent to the RIBA on 7 August 1990. In that document two fundamental issues are raised which beg a number of questions arising from the RIBA's arguments in its detailed response. The first is the academic issue: "whether it is reasonable for architectural students to be supported for more than four years from the higher education budget, having regard to the nature of the studies involved." The second issue raised in the DES document, which is practice related, concerns "the effectiveness of the present architectural curriculum in preparing its students for the realities of contemporary practice."

ACADEMIC ARGUMENT

The academic charge is answered in three parts.

• Architectural education is constantly under review through the RIBA's system of validation and the regular school inspections of the RIBA Visiting Board. The syllabus has been progressively enlarged. There has been an increasing demand for a more environmentally responsible solution to building problems and for greater emphasis on rehabilitation and conservation. The need for more efficient procurement and delivery of buildings and for greater management skills all require a substantial input of taught knowledge if the competence of the profession is to keep pace with the needs of society through the 1990s and into the next century.

Does the Secretary of State accept that a reduction of one year in funded full-time education will reduce the possibility of broadening and deepening the curriculum for initial education?

• Architectural education has at present no direct connection with or access to secondary education. The burden of new knowledge and reorientation of attitudes required during initial architectural education is formidable. Government-led changes in the curriculum at secondary level are now enabling potential students to take a wider mixture of subjects at both GCSE and A/AS-level or their equivalents. Government is also encouraging wider participation in higher education. Faced with this changing situation and the need to broaden curricula, several vice chancellors are now recommending the lengthening of courses in higher education in order to maintain standards. Yet the DES is considering a reduction in funded course lengths for architecture. This flies in the face of worldwide opinion about architectural education and runs counter to growing UK opinion.

Does the Secretary of State understand that a reduction in funded length of the architecture course will exacerbate the problems of the transition from secondary education and of wider access?

• In the opinion of the RIBA the existing educational process in architecture has been misunderstood and undervalued by the Government's advisers, but the profession's clients understand and value the product. The nature of architectural education is unique: it is centred on the iterative process of designing, onto which is grafted an unsurpassed variety of specialist knowledge. It offers an educational discipline which provides the basis for a variety of careers in architecture, the built environment, the construction industry and beyond, in the UK and overseas. The majority of countries regard five years as the normal minimum basic period of formal architectural education.

Does the Secretary of State appreciate the significance of the five-year educational continuum and its interwoven practical training as the mainstream of professional formation in the UK?

PRACTICE

The practice-related issue is answered in five parts.

• For a decade, the RIBA has been addressing the current issues in education and training as well as the question of the relationship between initial and continuing education. The strategy is now to shift the balance from initial to a combination of initial and continuing education, leading to life-long learning. The RIBA had moved by the 1970s from a pattern of five years of academic education plus one of practical training to five plus two, with one usually in mid-course. The Institute now believes that the right education and training mixture for entry to the profession in future will require at least three practical training years with a minimum of two years occurring after the end of the academic phase of five years. In addition, after 1992 participation in the Institute's Continuing Professional Development system will be obligatory for all members of the RIBA. During the 1980s great strides have been made by the RIBA in the creation of a CPD service and the development of open learning, with considerable and growing investment by architects. These activities have also directly fulfilled government policy, with the RIBA among the earliest successful bidders for PICKUP and Training Agency funding.
• Extended practical training and obligatory CPD are part of the RIBA's considered response to the preparation of students for the changing challenges and realities of contemporary practice. The profession is, therefore, responding positively, with considerable thought and resources. However, the profession will only be able to offer a limited number of students a full education, alongside structured practical training and CPD in offices. It is often overlooked that, apart from their key role in the public sector, the majority of architects constitute an especially creative and dynamic element of the small business sector upon which the health of the economy depends. They carry out projects for clients, but in employment terms they are largely self-employed. They share the problems of small business, particularly in the extent to which education and training can be supported. There are nearly 7000 practices in the UK. Only 800 employ more than five architects and have at least one partner with more than five years' experience, and at least one partner aged less than 60. These are the broad considerations which the RIBA sees as applicable to DES's proposition that a portion of initial education can be carried out within practice.

Is the Secretary of State prepared to accept that the present careful balance between education, training and CPD offers the most cost effective and appropriate structure to serve the needs of student, architects and society in relation to the realities of contemporary practice?
• The RIBA's educational strategy is in line with government thinking about access and competence. The Institute welcomes the changes in the secondary educational curriculum. It wishes to widen access, to encourage an enterprise culture – to which its courses are uniquely suited – to develop interdisciplinary education and to stimulate interprofessional qualification, within a climate of raising levels of competence and responding to the challenges of the EC and the worldwide market.

Does the Secretary of State recognize that shortening the course would cause an erosion of UK standards and a lessening of abilities to fulfil government-inspired objectives at a critical time for the nation?
• The UK profession has produced an education and training system for architecture over the last 30 years which is admired throughout the world; it is looked to as a model by such countries as those in the Commonwealth and as far afield as Chile, China, Hungary and Saudi Arabia. Within the EC, moves are now taking place to model the process for

professional formation in other member states upon the UK system.

Why does the Secretary of State now wish to reverse an international trend and undermine a model for education and training which is widely admired and followed?

• Architectural education is not over-funded. The responsibility placed upon architects by clients and society is today very considerable and, rightly, increasing. The rapidly growing range of skills which are necessary to meet this responsibility must be taught, effectively, and this will require certainly no less than a period of five full-time years or the equivalent. Anything less will result in a reduced knowledge base available to the industry, to society and to the UK in its overseas markets. It will lead to impaired building performance with financial consequences greater than the minimal savings achieved in the higher education budget.

What is the overall cost to public funding of architecture courses in relation to comparable disciplines or courses of similar length and what would be the level of saving represented by the alternative pattern which the DES is considering?

NORMAL PATTERN

In response to the question, What should comprise the normal pattern of professional education and training? the RIBA is in no doubt that the five-year full-time course with its integral, minimum period of structured practical training should be the mainstream provision not the preserve of "the exceptional minority" as implied by the DES.

The RIBA believes that in order to absorb the changes in secondary school education, to widen access, to broaden and deepen the syllabus, to provide the foundations for CPD and open learning, and to increase the range and competence of UK architects operating in the EC and overseas, the present pattern is needed and is justified.

The DES's alternative proposal takes little or no account of recent developments in education and training and is likely to cause a reduction in competence, in the quality of design, in reputation and achievement in overseas markets and in the ability of the profession to serve the nation and adequately to play its part in the wider environmental programme.

A Research Policy for the Architectural Profession (1991)

Recommendations made to RIBA Council by the RIBA Research Steering Group, 4 January 1991.

Of all branches of architectural enquiry, the one that has the highest priority for the effective conduct of architectural practice is the accumulation and maintenance of a systematic body of knowledge about how to make buildings which serve users better. This is because two essential features of architectural practice are firstly comprehending the needs of building users and then cleverly turning an imaginative grasp of these needs into buildable and pleasing design.

Consequently, the architectural profession's most effective contribution to a collaborative research endeavour within the construction industry will come from recognizing two things: that architects' core discipline is "design", and that their most effective means of adding value to design is through understanding and interpreting "user requirements".

By conventional academic standards, architectural research may not seem to be of major importance. Nevertheless, the architectural profession in the UK has benefited greatly from several categories of research work.

First, the performance of building construction, systems, and material: much of this work was carried out at BRS (later BRE) by multi-disciplinary teams. Second, building science, which has become an academic discipline in its own right, often separate from but allied to schools of architecture. Third, specialized environmental matters (such as lighting, acoustics, comfort, energy management), often studied by multidisciplinary teams, frequently but by no means exclusively within the orbit of schools of architecture. Fourth, architectural and cultural history: there has never been more activity that today in architectural history, both scholarly and popular. Fifth, the sociology of architecture: the RIBA itself has the distinction of conducting one of the best studies ever written of a profession: *The Architect and his Office* (1962). Sixth, but not finally, design theory and design method: fundamental work in both architecture and urbanism has been closely related to the development of Computer Aided Design (CAD).

However, the most memorable (and by academic standards the most unconventional) work of all was carried out not in universities but in government ministries since the 1940s and later to some extent in private architectural practice. This is the tradition of "development" work – that is, the systematic application of user-based research to architectural design, resulting in the preparation and testing of design guidance to meet emerging user needs in such building types as schools, housing, hospitals and universities.

The excitement and quality of the best of this work has been well captured by Andrew Saint in his account, *Towards a Social Architecture*, of architects' work on innovative British schools that linked educational policy through systematic observation with the testing and development of design ideas.

Neither public sector programmes nor their architectural consequences are in favour in the early 1990s. The habit of learning from experience in use has not always been carried through. Nevertheless, the same tradition of research is very much alive in the design of better contemporary commercial buildings – offices, business parks, and retailing. Some developers, realizing that changing patterns in user requirements imply novel design solutions, have resorted to very similar techniques of enquiry into user needs as were used in previous decades in the public sector.

The benefits of studying accumulating data – so characteristic of law and medicine (legal precedents, medical case histories, the statistical base of epidemiology) – have not been fully achievable in architecture, until now. Information technology is rapidly overcoming problems of data management in the study of the use of buildings over time. Feedback from users is becoming much more attainable. Moreover, concentrating on user needs and how they can be satisfied in building design, gives a new, and highly topical urgency to architectural research.

Properly viewed, architectural enquiry – because of its huge scope, its inherent, integrative and interdisciplinary nature, its long time dimension, and its human and political urgency – should be recognized as being at the frontiers of knowledge: the kind of intellectual problem that can only be confronted in the late twentieth century. This view is particularly timely – not just for architects themselves but for the whole of society – given the emerging importance and vulnerability of the environment, the increasing sophistication of clients, the potential of information technology, and the growing power of the consumer.

Many key issues in society are now directly related to the use of architectural resources. It is hardly an accident that the green debate about regional, national and global priorities is so highly interesting and attractive to the architectural imagination. It is not by chance that those who procure space and buildings for client organizations are currently in the process of professionalizing themselves as facilities managers. Nor is it an accident that so much emphasis is currently being placed by architects on opening up the design process to the user.

Vitally important policy decisions, all of a complex and integrative nature, have to be made. On none is enough data available. The priorities on which decisions will be based are not clearly articulated. The interests of the individuals and groups involved are neither stable nor clear. And yet on each issue, action by architects on behalf of society, clients and individual users, is urgently necessary.

POST-OCCUPANCY EVALUATION

Perhaps the most significant development in architectural research over the last 20 years has been the rise, particularly in the US, of post-occupancy evaluation (POE) – the systematic study of building in use to provide architects with information about the performance of their designs and building owners and users with guidelines to achieve the best out of what they already have.

The least implemented section of the excellent and much-used *RIBA Model Plan of Work* of 1963 was the far-sighted but, at that time, over-optimistic Work Stage M: "feedback". The first reason that learning from feedback was not institutionalized was that no operational distinction was made between the evaluation of process, technique and utility. The evaluation of techniques of building procurement, such as forms of contract and project management, was not clearly distinguished from the appraisal of how well buildings satisfied client requirements. The second reason was that no fee basis was established for what seemed an inherently costly procedure.

The perspective has changed. If architects focus on their principal responsibilities to their clients and users, the twin uncertainties about who benefits, and who pays, vanish; it is the consumer who has the motivation to ensure that the supplier performs, rather than vice versa. This argument is considerably reinforced by the increasing understanding of the importance to the consumer of occupancy costs, and their very real relation to capital expenditure.

Post-occupancy evaluation is in the consumer's interest. It is equally the key to the popular, universal, and practical application of architectural research and to the development of such consumerist techniques as building appraisal.

RESEARCH-BASED PRACTICE AND EDUCATION

The RIBA's Research Steering Group has identified post-occupancy evaluation of buildings as central to these concerns and as a powerful means of continuing to master and apply the art and science of building for the benefit of the consumer. Post-occupancy evaluation should be interpreted widely to encompass the main topics brought out in debate in the six workshops, particularly in such matters as:

- briefing
- post-occupational evaluation
- academic/practice links through, for example, practice-based research
- specialization in architectural practice
- the potential of information technology to use data more effectively.

It must not, however, be employed to the exclusion of other matters of concern to designers, users, contractors and manufacturers.

Research, vigorous and forward-looking practice, and education, are the essential means by which the architectural profession will confront the challenging demands of building in the last years of this century and into the next. What is proposed here is a strategy to make architecture a research-based profession. It is the primary purpose of Research Policy of the RIBA is to strengthen the relationship between the designers and users of buildings in order to inform and inspire the architecture of the future.

RECOMMENDATIONS

Four key activities are necessary to achieve this strategy of creating and sustaining a truly research-based profession.

1 The RIBA will establish a combined Research and Marketing Committee and will include in its membership representatives of building owners and users, with the object of providing the Institute with advice and guidance on the kinds of research needed to meet the needs of the consumer. The terms of reference of the expanded committee will include, besides matters already dealt with by marketing, those matters of consequence raised in the course of the research steering group's work – in particular, encouraging briefing, post-contract building evaluation, academic-practice links, sharing research between practices, specialization within architecture, and exploiting the potential of information technology in handling data on building performance in use.

2 The RIBA will provide the resources for an Office of Consumer Affairs which will link the RIBA Research and Marketing Committee with the wider research community, advise on the building types most suitable for study; focus the attention of architects upon emerging issues and priorities as perceived by consumers; devise an appropriate

methodology to relate research to the aims of practice and education and above all demonstrate the RIBA's continuing commitment to users and clients. The terms of reference of the office and the best way of achieving its objectives to be established and agreed.

3   The RIBA will initiate an independently funded Architectural Research Trust which will administer the trust funds of the existing RIBA research awards, take all available steps to increase the funds available for architectural research, maintain a directory of relevant funding agencies and seek imaginatively to encourage and support research workers in the field or architectural design, especially but not exclusively on the recommendations of the Research and Marketing Committee and the RIBA Office of Consumer Affairs.

4   The RIBA will inaugurate annual Awards for Distinction in research to confer public distinction on researchers whose work has made a demonstrable contribution to the furtherance of architectural design or education especially, but not exclusively, on the recommendations of the three principal committees of the RIBA – education, practice and research and marketing.

The Burton Report (1992)

Richard Burton's Steering Group conducted its investigations into architectural education and training during 1991 and the early part of 1992 – the same period as the first phase of the RIBA Strategic Study of the Profession. Both reported in 1992.

Architecture creates bridges – between science and the arts, the client/consumer and the built form, resources/technology and ability to pay, certainty and uncertainty. The resolution of these in harmony is vested in the architect through design and design management with the other design professions. The role of education is to prepare the architectural student for this highly complex activity.

The RIBA Steering Group wishes to reaffirm the central role that architecture plays in defining and raising the quality of life for the community, in serving the public interest and in contributing to the nation's heritage. The relationship between the architect and the clients and users of buildings is at the core of the process by which quality, good design, appropriateness and value for money are achieved, especially with the greater awareness of interdependent environmental issues.

In pursuing this role, it is essential that architects continue to benefit from advanced education and training, increasingly with a research awareness. It is for this reason that the profession has committed itself to lifelong learning. Continuing professional development (CPD) – shared wherever possible with other disciplines and designing professions.

The profession – and hence its education and training – must continue to change. Failure to do so will risk its eventual marginalization and the diminution of the qualities and values identified above. In taking up the opportunity offered by the Secretary of State, the Steering Group sees the recommendations in this report as providing the basis for further improvement, which will ensure that the profession continues to be properly prepared.

The overall curriculum needed review and this we have done. The syllabus has also been reviewed and will continue to be so. Both these reviews will lead to greater relevance of the course to the contemporary requirements of clients, users and industry. They will be monitored by the professional validation system.

Our project-based learning system is a jewel which accepts and encourages responses to change and development of judgement. It is an iterative system, facilitating cross-disciplinary work. We agree it must be supplemented by further specialisms. We cannot risk not having the time for it.

In view of the profession's considerable financial contribution and society's increasing realization of the centrality of and demand for good architectural design and landscape and the potential risks which would flow from inadequacy in education, government funding should continue for the full period of five years and the profession must be prepared also to continue its funding at or above current levels.

Value for society's money is clearly being achieved with substantial financial help from the profession. Funding is not expensive at less than half the cost of other five-year courses. Some more investment is needed for equipment and research because of the increased demands of an advancing profession requiring a well-prepared student entering it.

The added value of the specialisms and alliances with schools in Europe and beyond is now very evident in our schools and they are responding to previous encouragement and demands from the profession: more is required. We need an even better-educated profession. The ability to speak and work in a foreign language has become highly desirable.

More thought is required in the institutions about cross-disciplinary working, particularly with the construction-related departments, but also exploiting the wide range of connections available with such disciplines as social science, design, business and art. The industry and profession should better structure the student's year out by introducing more cross-disciplinary experience opportunities. In this way, the mutual respect of each team member's contribution, the creative talents of others and a common understanding of the design process will be fostered. The year in practice should also be better structured and controlled with a better rapport between practices and schools.

A critical burden now falls on full and part-time staff. They must have time to carry out CPD, and HEIs should have a policy for this and implement it rigorously. A staff college concept is recommended.

The teachers are in many cases practitioners which is to be encouraged. It is disappointing that more women are not employed as teachers.

The talent and quality of our students is encouraging. They work hard. The entry numbers are increasing. This is welcomed. They should, however, be counselled that continuation to RIBA Part 2 will be based on high quality and suitability to the profession and that after a degree there are high-quality, useful and honourable directions for those who do not proceed further. We are interested by the proposal that the intermediate RIBA exemption (Part 1) might be given only after the requisite period of practical training to complement this process.

We have recommended that the Institute review its policy regarding membership.

Student hardship is an issue which must be faced and a survey of it is necessary.

Other professions are realizing the intrinsic value of our project-based, studio-centred learning system with peer-group review of results. In addition, imagination is being used to look at new ways of teaching more efficiently, using the potential of information technology and distance learning.

Research into architecture is essential to avoid problems and to innovate. It is at an unacceptably low level at present and it has an important future role in the teaching of students and in CPD. Further, in view of the centrality of the user and the complexity of the process and the risks, comprehensive feedback of information must be achieved.

Our system of education and training, and our supervision of it, are lauded internationally, with RIBA recognition of 39 schools abroad and the RIBA being consulted on education and training and validation in Chile, China, Columbia, Czechoslovakia, Hungary, Russia and Saudi Arabia, supported by the British Council. All these countries accept that a minimum of five years' academic work is essential: some have six years. The system is a precious asset not to be wasted and now needs encouragement to evolve.

With the RIBA committed to CPD, we see our initial educational system of a minimum of seven years' education and training as the start of a lifetime of further study and personal development. We appreciate that our recommendations together with CPD will place a considerable administrative burden on the RIBA Education Department, which will require resources to be able to respond to them, as will the British Architectural Library to support education and research.

This is a dense and complex subject meriting a serious approach. In our report there are aspects which should be taken into account by government, the profession, the industry and the institutions and their schools of architecture with their staff and student bodies. I hope then it will form a solid base for the education of a profession which will play an essential part in the future fabric of our nation and beyond.

RIBA Strategic Study of the Profession: Phase I (1992)

In July 1991, the RIBA Council committed the RIBA to funding the first phase of a study on the future of the British architectural profession. The objective was to lay the foundations of a new Institute strategy to help all architects – principals, assistants, employed in central or local government, consultants, teachers – to prepare themselves to practice architecture more effectively in a rapidly changing world. This is the introduction to a report of the results of that first phase of work, carried out under the direction of Dick Patterson, between September 1991 and April 1992, and published in May 1992 as *Strategic Study of the Profession – Phase I: Strategic Overview*.

The model that both stimulated and guided this study is the RIBA's own *The Architect and his Office* (1962), not only one of the best studies of a profession ever carried out anywhere in the world but a most effective and practical agent in the modernization of architectural practice in the UK. There is a direct link between the 1962 and 1992 studies in the person of Sir Andrew Derbyshire, who is both a member of today's Steering Group and was, with Mike Austin-Smith, one of the two principal authors of the previous study.

This long perspective allows us to compare today's situation with the problems that faced the authors of the *Architect and his Office* in the early 1960s, a period of massive social reconstruction and inevitable and largely unquestioned demand for architectural services. The problems of that time, unlike today, were mostly internal to the profession and were focused on difficulties of supply rather than those caused by demand. The critical task for over-worked and underorganized architects was to get their own house in order quickly to meet society's self-evident needs as quickly as possible. The fruits of that reforming endeavour are typified by the RIBA's great *Plan of Work*, which is still the backbone of conventional British architectural practice.

The architectural profession's problems today are no less intractable but far less private. Client expectations are changing. The balance of work between public and private sector has shifted fundamentally. Consumers are more articulate. Many clients, especially in the private sector, have become far more sophisticated in their management of the design and building procurement process. Buildings have become more complex. Information technology has entered – and some would argue is taking over – both the studio and the drawing office. The architect's relationship with the construction industry, never easy, is less and less predictable. While British architecture is admired everywhere, international and often unfavourable comparisons of professional performance and fee levels are commonplace. Competition is everywhere, as much from inside as from outside the profession, allegedly once so privileged, protected and self-interested.

In response, many architects have already changed their working practices radically. There is, compared with 30 years ago, much more diversity in architectural practice, from large, international, properly-capitalized public companies to idealistic individuals designing with minimal resources in and with the community. Architects today are employed in many different ways – even allowing for the decline of the public sector. Nevertheless, only 20 per cent of the profession's fee income in 1991 came from Other Services (as defined by Architect's Appointment), implying that such diversity as exists at the fringes of the profession may not apply to the central mass. Architectural discourse is richer, more diverse, more accessible and apparently much more interesting to a larger and larger public. Certainly, all over Europe and undeterred by the current recession in the UK, increasing numbers of students are entering the schools of architecture, attracted by what is clearly seen to be a challenging vocation. Collectively, however, architects are almost certainly less aware than they ought to be of the extent of impending change.

Nor will architects be left alone to discuss their future in peace. There is considerable and increasingly impatient criticism of architects by other members of the construction industry. Clients are by no means inclined to rely upon architectural advice as uncritically as they once did and many are seeking ways of procuring buildings in which the architect no longer plays a central role – if indeed any part at all. The abandoning by the RIBA a decade ago, under pressure from the the Monopolies and Mergers Commission, of mandatory fee scales and other apparatus of professional monopoly, has done nothing to assuage a growing anti-professional bias in government circles, and perhaps society in genera.l.

For these reasons the RIBA has commissioned the first phase of this study as a *tour d'horizon* to provide a well-reasoned and empirically sound basis for redirecting policy in its three major committees for the next decade.

• Practice. What forms of practice, what relation to other professions and to the construction industry, what modes of remuneration, what regulatory framework, what information bases and what technologies can be anticipated?

• Marketing. What competition will architects face, what are architects' strengths and weaknesses, what dangers are to be avoided, what new opportunities are opening up?

• Education. How are architectural values and ideas best transmitted to future generations, what relation should architectural education have to other disciplines in the construction industry, how best to educate architects, young and old, to cope with change?

It is intended that, after a period of dissemination and review of the findings of Phase I, within the RIBA and beyond, the *Strategic Study* will be furthered by a series of detailed investigations of particular issues and experiences.

CONDUCT OF PHASE I STUDY

Finance has been severely limited. It has not been possible to carry out in Phase I anything like the extensive field work that was one of the best characteristics of *The Architect and his Office*. In retrospect this may have been a blessing, because what has been possible is to complete an overview of what is, by any standards, an extremely complex situation in such a way that:

• many different points of view have been articulated
• major trends have been identified
• many recommendations for action have been collated
• next steps – particularly for dissemination and field work – have been proposed, all of which relate to the testing of the *Strategic Overview* of the future of the profession which is the main product of Phase I.

The main decision about method, given limited resources, was not to attempt field work in the first phase, but to illuminate as many of the enormous range of issues confronting architects in a period of rapid change. This has been done by seeking informed opinion from a wide variety of sources. The structuring of the results of this survey of divergent perspectives was the main task of Touche Ross Management Consultants, who also acted as a powerful check on what might otherwise have been a tendency towards architects talking about themselves to themselves in their own language. Their contribution has been invaluable.

Issue papers were therefore commissioned from 11 carefully selected authorities, roughly half of whom are architects, under three main headings – the market, or the clients' perspectives of architectural services; the environment, or how architects are perceived by their colleagues in the construction industry and particularly by their competitors; and, thirdly, the profession, or the issues as they are seen by architects themselves.

Each Issue Paper is about 6000 words in length and is written in a similar format consisting of a review of the relevant literature on the topic; a polemical but informed discussion of issues related to architectural practice; and finally recommendations for action for individual architects, for practices and, of course, for the RIBA.

The completed issue papers were reviewed and debated by all the authors at a full day workshop run by Touche Ross at the RIBA on Friday, 3 April 1992. Professor Robert Gutman also took part in this workshop. He is the author of *Architectural Practice: a Critical View*, a seminal study of the American profession, much referred to by many of the authors.

The study has benefited considerably from, and should be seen to complement, recent work on the future of the construction industry as a whole being carried out at the Department of Construction Management at Reading University, from the work of the NEDO Construction Industry Steering Group, from CIC initiatives, and from other contemporary academic and commercial sources in the UK and abroad. Close contact was maintained throughout Phase I with the work of the parallel RIBA Steering Group on the future of architectural education led by Richard Burton.

A series of seven contextual seminars on various aspects of change as perceived by representative of external interest groups was conducted in parallel with the planning and preparation of the issue papers. Approximately 100 people – clients and co-professionals as well as some architects – attended these discussions.

SETTING THE SCENE

What faces the architectural profession is unprecedented change. Yet architectural practice is already flexible enough to have become highly diverse, much more so than the twin ideals of equal and universal competence that underpin the Architects Registration Act would lead one to believe. More different forms of practice and more kinds of architectural career exist than may be assumed from a cursory reading of RIBA advice to members. To appreciate the full spectrum of the scale and the forms of architectural practice, some benchmarks are necessary.

• Number of architects. The number of registered architects in the UK has increased by approximately 50 per cent since the previous study of the profession – 20 911 in 1964, 32 004 in 1990.
• Architects' workload. In 1991 fee income totalled £1.4bn. The contract value of new commissions peaked at almost £15bn in the second quarter of 1989. In the current quarter, in deep recession, the level of new commissions has declined to about half that peak level (1985 prices).
• Architects historically have certified between 30–40 per cent of the contract value of building output and have been involved in about 75 per cent. In 1990, architects certified over 50 per cent of building output.
• In more detail, architects in 1990 certified about 75 per cent of a total of £16bn of new building work and about 25 per cent of £10bn of work to existing buildings.
• Architects' total overseas fee income in 1991 was £50m. The percentage of practices

doing overseas work has been about 9 per cent for the last five years.
- Number of practices. The number of private architectural practices in the UK has doubled approximately since the previous study – 3200 in 1968, 6500 in 1991.
- This aggregation, however, hides a very wide range of size of practice. Of the total of practices, 70 per cent employed 1–5 architectural staff; 15 per cent employed 6–10; 15 per cent employed 11 or more – a similar profile to 1968.
- The number of foreign architectural practices in London has more than doubled in the last five years to approximately 30 – not, on the face of it, a big number, but most are large practices and very well connected with an international clientele.
- The percentage of architects employed in the public sector declined from 39 per cent in 1964 to 22 per cent in 1991.
- Architects' earnings per head in 1991 averaged £23 500. In the same year, fee income per head is estimated to average £60 000. Such earnings compare unfavourably with those of other professions.
- There is evidence that architects are employed in more diverse ways than ever before – as developers, facilities managers, consultants, community architects, builders, product designers. This trend is not yet strongly reflected in the work of schools of architecture.

Most of these trends are replicated even more strongly in the United States.

These figures could be read as a record of considerable success. Our conclusion from the Phase 1 data is rather the opposite: at once pessimistic and more ambitious. British architects, despite considerable residual strength and certain new circumstances which are working in their favour, are not responding confidently or quickly enough to the changing environment. Even discounting the highly destructive – but presumably temporary – effects of the current recession. What may be drawn from this study and from the last two decades of architectural practice in the UK is, on the whole, a tale of limited success, of fumbled rather than seized opportunities.

PHASE 1 FINDINGS

The mass of data indicates that British architects are subject to irreversible change in three main ways.

- In the market. Clients are becoming much more professional in the way they procure both buildings and design services. This does not mean that they discount design – although they may not always comprehend fully what design can do for them – but they are increasingly unwilling to accept at face value the forms and terms of service that architects have been accustomed to offer in the last three decades since the publication of *The Architect and his Office*.
- In the commercial environment. While popular opinion in an increasingly wealthy and visually discriminating society tends to favour, at least in theory, what architects can offer, competition is increasing in practically every aspect of architectural services – particularly for the valued role of strategic adviser to the client and for all aspects of the management and control of the production process. Architects are said not to be so good at understanding either money or time. Many in the construction industry would prefer for their own operational reasons to split conceptual design from production design. Architects have tended to react by cutting fees (not necessarily costs) rather than enriching or widening their services
- In the profession. The shift of patronage from public to private sector has reduced the

influence of the profession and has eroded what was perhaps the strongest concentration of architects' managerial skills. Meanwhile, architects in private practice have been sluggish in taking advantage of advance in information technology, business and project management, and communication. Architecture education has generally been even slower than practice to recognize the implication of change particularly – despite some interesting experiments – in respect of relating to other disciplines.

Architects have reason to be confident – but only if they build on their real strengths rather than claiming the impossible or retreating into doing only what they find most comfortable.

The implications of the changes identified in this study are threatening and, if left unchecked, will certainly erode architects' influence, levels of employment, remuneration, vigour, ability to defend the user and their freedom to design. Within the construction industry architects have two great assets. First, they are still in the best position to speak for the user. In a supply-side dominated industry, architects are closest to being able to defend the consumer through understanding demand – that is, what buildings are for. Secondly, architects know how to design – that is to say, their training has been devised to help clients turn aspirations into reality.

There are many situations, both in well-organized larger practices and in a great many small practices, in which the architect is well placed to act as "the leader of the building team". However, for architects to claim such leadership as a matter of right is neither self evident, nor unique, nor universal, and is certainly capable of attracting the strongest chance of rebuttal

How can architects redefine their role in order to establish a strong, dependable and unique position for their profession? The distinctive skill of architects lies in their ability to provide design solutions which satisfy the needs of both clients and users. Delivering both the functional and aesthetic benefits of design, architects have a critical central role in the building process, as the leaders of the design team.

These considerations have led Touche Ross to make three strategic recommendations.

• Architects must consolidate their central role as designers by focusing on understanding and meeting client and user requirements.
• Architects must strengthen their ability to deliver design services.
• Architects must be prepared to provide a wider range of design and management-based services.

OPPORTUNITIES

The Steering Group considers that these strategic recommendations – and all their detailed consequences – provide an excellent basis for prioritizing and restructuring the work of the RIBA for the next decade. The architectural profession is tremendously well-endowed both by its great traditions and by the quality of new entrants. It is essential that these assets are cultivated and exploited rather than wasted. The underlying lesson from the Phase I study is that architects should concentrate on their real ability to satisfy clients' requirements and anticipate society's aspirations. Architects should be positive about the future – not sigh for imagined glories of the past.

Such an attitude will lead inevitably to relinquishing certain cherished but obsolete beliefs, and to identifying obvious opportunities for applying architectural imagination in the service of clients and society in a changing world.

Rethinking the plan of work

Huge opportunities for the application of architectural skills remain untapped.

The chief reason for architects' relative failure to embrace new services paradoxically stems directly from the enormous success of the predecessor to this study, *The Architect and His Office*. This excellent piece of work did much to reform architectural practices and led directly to the rationalization of architectural practice particularly through the *Plan of Work*. Each stage of the architect's work "from inception to completion" was isolated and described in a beautifully clear and unambiguous way which has been and still is of enormous help both to architects and to their clients.

Excess of virtue leads to vice – and *The Plan of Work* is no exception. If the chief virtue of the *The Plan of Work* is the step-by-step rationalization of the architect's standard method of work, its greatest vice lies in normalization – in the apparent minimizing of the importance of alternative ways of doing things. What are inevitably – and unforgivably – called Other Services are thus constantly construed by client and architect as non-essential. This unconscious habit of diminishing the significance of "non-normal" services is ironically best encapsulated in the very document which has been for thee decades, in various forms, the chief presentation of architectural services to potential clients – the so-called "Blue Book", *The Architect's Appointment*.

Architects must be more comprehensive, flexible and imaginative in their offer of services to clients.

Reversing the habit of exclusion

A certain rigidity leading to the exclusion of whatever is unusual, novel, non-central lies very deep in the British architectural psyche. Taking a long historical perspective, British architects have consistently tended to exclude from their canon of "normality" whatever activity doesn't seem to fit – aspects of surveying, many management and engineering skills, cost estimating, landscaping, town planning, building science, the competences of building technicians, interior design. The list is very long. Meanwhile, antipathy and mistrust between architects and constructors have grown. The habit of such puritanical exclusivity seems to be peculiar to architects: other professional bodies have dealt with growing specialization either by developing a federal structure (like the surveyors) or by elaborating systems of advanced qualification (as in medicine).

The exclusivist habit must be reversed. A rich mix of old as well as new skills must be on offer to clients.

New fee structure

The Plan of Work has been the basis of the architects' fee structure from the very beginning – each stage representing a precise fraction of the total "mandatory" (and, of course, latterly "recommended") percentage fee scale. While this is an excellent convention which has worked on the whole very well for architects for a very long time, the system is becoming counter-productive.

• It is a very British system, reflecting the long Arts and Crafts tradition of architects claiming prolonged responsibility right through the design and construction process – a claim which is by no means universal. Hence fee percentages seem high – and uncompetitive – compared to those customary in France and the United States, for example, where the architect's involvement in detailed design and on site is abbreviated.

- It is a rigid system which is increasingly having to be modified on an ad hoc basis as more and more clients adopt non-traditional forms of building procurement and as architects become used to working within such frameworks as "design and build".
- It provides little or no guidance for charging fees for "non-normal" services, which may be far more normal and a greater source of income for architects than is customarily recognized.
- It is increasingly detached from a realistic, management accounting basis for charging architects' fees – that is, on the real cost of hours actually expended on different activities on typical jobs of various kinds. Such information is now very well understood by the larger and better organized practices, especially those that are highly computerized, but is not yet widely disseminated.
- Fee structures must be more realistic in terms both of value added and of time expended at each stage.

Revaluing design

The main argument against the total correlation between stages in the *Plan of Work* and fee scales is that a totally unintended and very destructive consequence has been the tacit devaluation of design.

Design is not well understood. Although modern society (largely because of television) increasingly values visual things – and thus plays into architects' hands – the non-linear and iterative process by which design is achieved needs explaining to clients and to the construction industry. Design is seen by many – even by architects' friends – as an optional extra rather than the basis of all successful building. For architects, design is much more fundamental – very much like the best kind of management: the skilled and cost sensitive allocation of physical resources, despite uncertainty, inadequate information and shifting goals, to solve immediate as well as longer-term accommodation problems of users, clients and society at large. This deliberately wide definition of design is intended to embrace both high culture and deep practicality – from the superlative excellences of "named" architects to far less visible (in the short term) contributions of strategic planning – as well as many humbler architectural contributions which cumulatively make the world a more livable and better place. Design is by no means the exclusive preserve of architects but architects, by virtue of their long and difficult training, are in an excellent position to apply knowledge and judgement to hard and controversial decisions which have, more often than not, long-term consequences.

Design is the core of the architect's contribution to the construction industry and to society. Fee scales as they exist in the UK at present, even though they may sometimes be front loaded, subsidize the precious but elusive design contribution of the architect by an implicit guarantee of further fee earning throughout the whole construction process. This is an increasingly dangerous trade-off especially as the very clarity of The Plan of Work encourages competitors to bid to take over the architect's role – not all at once, but stage by stage. Design, in the full sense as described above, must be defended and promoted as it is the architect's greatest contribution to client, to society and to the construction industry.

Briefing

Very closely related to design is the briefing process. The architectural imagination cannot easily be separated from the determination of client requirements. Individual architects, despite the profession's great and continuing tradition of user research and brief writing, have not always been successful in articulating and defending client interests, especially at the very early stages of projects. At worst, the priority of the unimaginative architect has been to secure a single, one-off, conventional project rather than to provide for the client over time a comprehensive, unbiased and open-ended service. Such a policy is unethical because it betrays the client's interest. It is also bad business. Architects, individually and collectively, must defend – and be seen to defend – user interests so that they continue to be the gateway of the client to the construction industry.

Specialization

Good briefing is based on knowledge not only of what individual clients want but more and more on the systematic compilation of comparative information about similar clients and similar building types. This very special form of knowledge – design rooted in use and user orientated – is the data base of architecture, the profession's most valuable possession.

Building up this knowledge base is not easy nor is it cheap. Inevitably, increasing dependence upon the intellectual capital of hard-won information implies more specialization in architectural practice – first for large practices and eventually for all. Nobody can claim to know everything. Sharing information between practices – developing the excellent British tradition of publishing technical information, particularly in the context of CPD – is the best way of disseminating and simultaneously building up the collective knowledge base upon which all architects will increasingly become dependent. The highest priority must be given by the RIBA on behalf of the profession to fostering and sharing user-based, design-orientated research.

Building economics

Perhaps the worst mistake made by the British architectural profession in this century has been to tolerate the delegation of responsibility for estimating building costs. Strategic advice to clients depends upon a grasp of "building economics" – that is, relating building costs to clients' financial planning. To claim to advise clients on their interests without reference to costs is a fantasy – and a particularly easily exploded one. Design without costs is meaningless.

Fortunately information technology, as in so many other matters, is coming to the rescue because, like architecture itself, it is an integrating force and has the potential to bring cost data back where it belongs – in the designer's consciousness. How this revolution in professional practice can be best achieved is another matter. Possibilities include more interdisciplinary practices, the urgent extension of commonality with other construction professionals in the education and training of architects, better training and simulation in the schools, CPD, professional alliances. Whatever route is chose, and there are many, the recovery, development and use of sophisticated cost information in the practice of design is essential.

Architects must command building economics in order to give sound advice to clients and to use the construction process for the clients' benefit.

Significance of the existing building stock

New buildings, especially in an old country, are a fraction of the total building stock. For many clients the real design problem is how to make best use of a changing stock of space through time. Architects have always been deeply involved in urban design. They have been conspicuously successful in turning their attention to the conservation, repair and rehabilitation of the fabric of existing buildings. An even greater opportunity lies in extending these hard-won technical skills to planning and replanning the use of cities and of the entire existing building stock. To do this effectively depends on knowledge of occupancy costs as well as an intimate and ongoing understanding of the developing and changing needs of user organizations. These are natural applications of architectural skill and imagination.

Architects must become the custodians of the entire building stock by turning their attention to all aspects of designing space to meet changing client needs.

Mastering the procurement process

The decline of public sector architecture has eroded a considerable body of well-developed managerial skills once taken for granted as peculiarly architectural – the management of the procurement of both design and other building resources. Selecting the architect is usually the biggest single architectural decision – and architects have always had all the skills necessary to manage this process to best effect.

There is no reason why in the new, more commercial procurement environment, architects should not play an even more important role in the connecting of architectural skills and building resources to different sorts of user. Architects are the obvious source of advice to clients on the procurement of architecture and building services.

NEXT STEPS

Design is the core architectural skill: creating new buildings on green field sites is an important way in which clients' problems can be solved by design, but by no means the only way. For architects, design means something wider: the skilled and cost-sensitive allocation of physical resources, despite uncertainty, inadequate information and shifting goals, to solve immediate as well as longer-term accommodation problems of users, clients and society at large.

Given this comprehensive definition and understanding of design, it is worth repeating the RIBA's consultants three main recommendations.

• Architects must consolidate their central role as designers by focusing on understanding and meeting client and user requirements.
• Architects must strengthen their ability to deliver design services.
• Architects must be prepared to provide a wider range of design and management-based services.

Architects should be more catholic and imaginative in their offer of services to clients. To do this does not mean abandoning well-tested ways of working. The Plan of Work is working perfectly well in many situations especially for smaller and more traditional practices. Nevertheless, its simple, linear logic now needs to be complemented by a much wider range of design-based and user-orientated services which are increasingly appropriate to clients in all their burgeoning variety and complexity.

To help clients solve strategic problems in the use and reuse of buildings, architects should not hesitate to be inventive in using whatever tools come to hand. Equally, architects have every incentive to involve themselves deeply – if it is in the clients' interest – in every aspect of development and building. Inventing and perfecting new building components and processing are perfectly suited to the application of architectural imagination.

The three main recommendations – not to mention the myriad of detailed recommendations made by the authorities consulted and the speculations made by the Steering Group – will affect all architects. All forms of architectural practice will be affected by them over the next decade. Architectural education in the schools and CPD will be revolutionized. However change – already quickly assimilated in some quarters – will not happen overnight. Nor will it occur everywhere in the same way in all types of practices nor at the same rate. Architecture in the UK is, after all, a very large and diverse profession, geographically and economically very wide spread.

What the Steering Group proposes is that Phase 2 of the Strategic Study should be a period of testing the recommendations against informed opinion – of architects, of clients and of our colleagues and co-professionals in the construction industry. Such fundamental recommendations must, over the next six months, be disseminated, debated and validated through a series of presentations to:

- Council
- key committees, particularly Practice, Marketing and Education
- the Corporate Plan Committee
- branches and regions
- clients
- representatives from throughout the construction industry.

Dissemination should be done in such a way that implications of Phase I for both large and small practices is explored and:

- feedback is systematically collected
- priorities for detailed fieldwork and further investigation in subsequent phases are identified
- realistic plans for action for various kinds of practice are developed and shared.

The essence and justification of all professions is the development, sharing and passing on of certain kinds of high-level, judgemental knowledge for the collective good. Architectural knowledge, like all other kinds of professional knowledge, is largely derived from action and experience. Architectural knowledge is distinguished by relating to design and to user requirements. Such knowledge belongs to practice and cannot be substituted by the different kinds of knowledge which belong properly to the world of commerce and to the universities, important allies as they both are. It should come as no surprise to those who know the RIBA that it will be in an open, shared, democratic and essentially professional way that the future of architectural practice in the UK will be determined.

The Latham Report (1994)

The 1994 Latham Report on procurement and contractual arrangements in the UK construction industry was not a government review but a report commissioned jointly by the government and the industry, with the participation of clients. Chaired by Sir Michael Latham, it anatomized the industry and made 30 key points, summarized below, but its chief plea was for a holistic view of the industry, for collective responsibility expressed through modified contracts and agreed codes of practice. Its sub-title was apt: Constructing the Team.

1. Simon Report (1944), Emmerson Report (1962) and Banwell Report (1964) widely welcomed, widely ignored. Action is imperative.
2. Clients are key: the government must commit itself to being a best practice client.
3. The state of the wider economy remains crucial to the industry. Some difficulties are inherent to the industry – others are contingent on current economics.
4. The CIC should issue a guide to briefing for clients. The DoE should publish a simply worded Construction Strategy Code of Practice.
5. The process plant industry should be consulted by the DoE and be part of the Construction Clients' Forum.
6. A checklist of design responsibilities should be prepared.
7. Use of Co-ordinated Project Information should be a contractual requirement.
8. Design responsibilities in building services engineering should be clearly defined.
9. A set of basic principles is required on which modern contracts can be based. A complete standard family of interlocking contract documents for clients should be produced. The New Engineering Contract (NEC) fulfils many of these principles and requirements but changes to it are desirable and the matrix is not yet complete.
10. The structures of the JCT and the CCSJC need substantial change.
11. Public and private sector clients should begin to use the NEC, and phase out bespoke documents.
12. There should be a register of consultants kept by the DoE for public sector work.
13. A DoE-led task force should endorse one of the several quality and price assessment mechanisms available for choosing consultants.
14. Roles and duties of Project Managers require definition.
15. A list of contractors and subcontractors should be maintained by the DoE.
16. Tender lists should be rationalized. Advice should be given on partnering arrangements.
17. Tenders should be evaluated on quality as well as price.
18. A joint Code of Practice should be drawn up for the Selection of Subcontractors.
19. Proposals on the CITB (Construction Industry Training Board) need to be examined.
20. The industry should implement previously formulated recommendations to improve its public image. It should also address the issue of equal opportunities.
21. The CIC is the body best placed to co-ordinate the implementation of previously published recommendations on professional training.
22. Existing research initiatives should be co-ordinated and should involve clients. A new research initiative should be launched, funded by insurance premiums.

23. More evidence is needed of the effects of BS 5750 within the industry.

24. A productivity target of 30 per cent real cost reduction by the year 2000 should be launched.

25. A Construction Contracts Bill should be introduced to give statutory backing to the newly amended Standard Forms, including the NEC. Some specific, unfair clauses should be outlawed.

26. Adjudication should be the normal method of dispute resolution.

27. Mandatory trust funds for payment should be established for construction work governed by formal conditions of contract. The British Eagle judgement should be reversed.

28. The Construction Contracts Bill should implement the majority recommendations of the working party on construction liability law.

29. BUILD insurance should become compulsory for new commercial, industrial and retail building work, subject to a de minimis provision.

30. An Implementation Forum should monitor progress and consider whether a new Development Agency should be created to drive productivity improvements and encourage teamwork. Priorities and timescales for action are suggested.

Latham laid down 13 principles on which a modern contract should be based – and which the New Engineering Contract (NEC) attempts to address.

Specific duty
All parties to deal fairly with each other

Firm duties of teamwork
Shared financial motivation to be fair and to co-operate
General presumption: achieve win-win solutions

Interrelated contracts
Clarity of roles and duties
Suitable for all types of projects, any procurement route, all disciplines

The contract
Easily comprehensible language with comprehensive guidance notes

Role clarity
Separate the roles of the supervisor, designer, project manager, adjudicator: project manager clearly defined as the client's representative

Risk allocation
Choice of allocation of risks appropriate to each project and allocated to the party best able to manage, estimate and carry the risk

Control of change
Avoid changes to preplanned works information
Where variations occur they should be priced in advance with provision for independent adjudication

Payment methods
Express provision for assessing interim payments by methods other than the monthly valuation, by using milestones, activity schedules or payment schedules, the objective being

to phase out monthly measurement or remeasurement based on work progress

Payment time
Clearly set out the period within which interim payments must be made to all participants in the process, failing which they have an automatic right to compensation
Payment of interest at a sufficiently heavy rate to deter slow payment

Trust funds
Providing for secure trust fund routes of payment

Dispute resolution
Take all possible steps to avoid conflict on site but provide for speedy dispute resolution by predetermined impartial adjudicator/ referee/ expert if required

Performance
Provide incentives for exceptional performance
Provide penalties for non-performance

Advance payments
Make provision where appropriate for advance mobilization payments
Advanced mobilization payments to contractors and subcontractors including for off-site fabricated materials provided by part of the construction team

The Construction Industry Board (CIB) was set up to implement the Latham Report, and is supported by the Department of the Environment, Transport and the Regions.

Bibliography

Alexander, C., Hirshen, S., Ishikawa, S., Coffin, C., Angel, S., 1969, *Houses Generated by Patterns,* Center for Environmental Structure, Berkeley, California.

Alford, L. P., 1924, *Management's Handbook* (especially section 7, "Office management", J. Barnaby), The Ronald Press, New York.

Argyle, M., 1967, *The Psychology of Interpersonal Behaviour.* Penguin, Baltimore.

Alsleben, K., 1964, *Neue Technik der Mobiliarordnung im Büroraum.* London and Germany, Quickborn and Verlag Schnelle.

Bairdain, E. F., 1966, "A Human Factors Analysis of Workspace Accommodations for Programmers", George W., Fotis and Associates.

Banham, R., 1969, *The Architecture of the Well-Tempered Environment,* Architectural Press, London.

Barker, R. G., Wright, H. F., 1955, *The Midwest and its Children,* Harper and Row, New York.

Black, F., 1972, "Office building—needs of small firms", *Building,* 8, 87-97.

Broady, M., 1968, *Planning for People,* (especially chapter 7, "The social context of urban planning"), Bedford Square Press, London.

Broady, M., 1966, "Social Theory in Architectural Design", *Arena,* Architectural Association Journal.

Brown, J. A. C., 1964, *The Social Psychology of Industry,* Penguin, Harmondsworth.

Building Research Station, 1966, National Building Studies Research Paper 41, "Modern offices: a user survey", F. J. Langdon, HMSO.

Bums, T., 1967, "The comparative study of organizations", in *Methods of Organizational Research,* Vroom, V.H., ed. University of Pittsburgh Press, Pittsburgh.

Burns, T., Stalker, G. M., 1961, *The Management of Innovation,* Social Science Paperbacks in association with Tavistock Publications, London.

Canter, D., 1966–1967, "The measurement of appropriateness in buildings", *Bartlett Society Transactions,* 6, 41–60.

Canter, D., 1968, "Clerical performance and office size: an example of psychological research in architecture", *Architects' Journal,* 147 (17), 881-888.

Case, D. F., 1967, "The influence of architecture on patterns of social life", unpublished junior paper, Department of Sociology, Princeton University, NJ.

Cave, C., Duffy, F., 1973, "The organization's demands on the scenery", *Architects' Journal,* 158 (42), 933–935.

Churchill, W. S., 1924, from an address to the Architectural Association at the annual distribution of prizes in 1924. Reprinted *Architectural Association Quarterly,* 5 (1), 44–46.

Clark, P., 1972, *Organizational Design,* Tavistock Press, London.

Craik, K. H., 1968, "The Comprehension of the Everyday Physical Environment", *Journal of American Institute of Planners.*

Davis, G., Becker. F., Sims, W. and Duffy, F., 1985, *Orbit-2.*

Dickens, C., 1848, *Dombey and Son.* London, Chapman and Hall, Vol. I p. 207.

Dickson, P. G. M., 1960, *The Sun Insurance Office, 1710–1960,* Oxford University Press.

Duffy, F., 1992, *The Changing Workplace*, Phaidon.

Duffy, F., 1966, *Office Landscaping: a New Approach to Office Planning*, Anbar Publications, London.

Duffy, F., 1974, "Office design and organizations: 1 The theoretical basis" and "Office design and organizations : 2 The testing of a hypothetical model", *Environment and Planning B*, 6 June 1974 and 15 October 1974.

Duffy, F., 1973a, "The place and the process", *Architects' Journal*, 157 (18), 1063-1067.

Duffy, F., 1973b, "Scenery and change", *Architects' Journal*, 158 (39), 755-758.

Duffy, F., Cave, C., 1973, "The demands of the organisation on the shell", *Architects' Journal*, 158 (42), 929-931.

Duffy, F., Freedman, J., 1970, "Patterns and semiology", in *Emerging Methods in Environmental Design and Planning*, C.T. Moore ed., MIT Press, Cambridge, Mass.

Duffy, F., Chandor, M., 1983, *Orbit-1. The Orbit Study: Information Technology and Office Design*, London.

Emery, F. E. and Trist, E.L., 1960, "Socio-technical systems", in Churchman, C.W. and M. Verhuist, M. (eds.), *Management Sciences, Models and Techniques, Vol. 2*, Pergamon Press, Oxford.

Fayol, H., 1930, *Industrial and General Administration*, London.

Festinger, L., Schachter, S., and Back, K., 1963, *Social Pressures in Informal Groups*, Stanford U.P., Stanford, Calif.

Forrester, J.W., 1961, *Industrial Dynamics*. Cambridge, Massachusetts and London, England, Massachusetts Institute of Technology Press and John Wiley, chapter 8.

Fucigna, J.T., 1967, "The ergonomics of offices", *Ergonomics*, Vol. 10, No. 5.

Galloway, L., 1918, *Office Management: Its Principles and Practice*, The Ronald Press, New York.

Gibbon, E., 1950, *Autobiography*. Oxford University Press, p. 160.

Goffman, E., 1961, *Encounters*, Bobbs-Merrill, Indianopolis.

Goffman, E., 1963, *Behaviour in Public Places*, Free Press, New York.

Goffman, E., 1964, "On face work", in *Interpersonal Dynamics*, Bennis, W.C., Schein, E.H. eds., Dorsey, Homewood, Illinois.

Gilbreth, F. B., 1911, *Motion Study*. New York, Van Nostrand.

Gottschalk, O., 1965, *Flexible Verwaltungsbauten*. London and Germany, Quickborn and Verlag Schnelle.

Gottschalk, O., and Lorenzen, K. J., 1967, "The new shape of office buildings", *Kommunikation*, 111/1.

Gullahorn, J.T., 1960, "Distance and friendship in the gross interaction matrix", in *The Sociometry Reader*, Moreno, J. L., ed., Free Press, Glencoe, Illinois.

Gutman, R. (undated), "The social effects of the urban environment", Working Paper, School of Architecture and Urban Planning, Princeton University, Princeton, NJ, mimeo.

Gutman. R., 1988, *Architectural Practice: A Critical View*, Princeton Architectural Press.

Haire, M., ed., 1959, "Biological models and empirical histories of the growth of organizations", in *Modern Organization Theory*, John Wiley, New York.

Hall, E.T., 1966, *The Hidden Dimension*, Doubleday, New York.

Hayek, F.A., 1986, *The Road to Serfdom*, Routledge.

Herzberg, F., Mausner, B., Snyderman, B. B., 1959, *The Motivation to Work*, John Wiley, New York.

Homans, G. C., 1950, *The Human Group*, Harcourt, Brace and World, New York.

Homans, G. C., 1954, "The cash posters: a study of a group of working girls", *American Sociological Review*, 19, 724-733.

Hoos, I., 1961, *Automation in the Office*, Public Affairs Press, Washington.
 Industrial Fatigue Research Board, 1930, (later the Industrial Health Research Board),
  The Tenth Annual Report. HMSO, London.
Jacques, E., 1951, *The Changing Cultures of a Factory*, London: Tavistock/Routledge.
Joedicke, J., 1962, *Office Buildings.* Crosby Lockwood, London.
Joiner, D., 1971, "Social ritual and architectural space", *Architectural Research and
  Teaching*, 1 (3), 11-22.
Kent, R.T., 1911, in the introduction to *Motion Study* by F. B. Gilbreth (Van Nostrand,
New York), p.xiii.
King, A. D., ed., 1981, *Buildings and Society*, Routledge.
Klingende, F. D., 1935, *The Condition of Clerical Labour in London*, Martin Lawrence,
  London.
Kuper, L., 1951, "Social science research and the planning of urban neighbourhoods",
  Social Forces, 29, 237-243.
Langdon, F. J., 1965, "A study of annoyance caused by noise in automatic data
  processing offices", *Building Science*, 1, 69–78.
Langdon, F. J., 1966a, *Modem Offices: A User Survey*, National Building Studies, Research
  Paper 41 HMSO, London.
Langdon, F. J., 1966b, "The social and physical environment: a social scientist's view",
  Journal of the Royal Institute of British Architects, 73, 460–464.
Leffingwell, W. H., 1925, *Office Management: Principles and Practice*, A. W. Shaw,
  Chicago.
Lockwood, D., 1969, *The Black Coated Worker*, Unwin University Books, London.
Lorenzen, H. J., Jaeger, D., 1968, "The office landscape", *Contract Magazine*, April.
Manning, P., ed., 1965, *Office Design: A Study of Environment*, University of Liverpool Press,
  Liverpool.
Manning and Wells, B.W. P., 1965, "The psycho-social influence of building environment:
sociometric findings in large and small office spaces", *Building Science*, Vol. 1, 1965,
  pp. 153–165.
March, I., Steadman, P., 1971, *The Geometry of the Environment*, RIBA Publications,
  London, p.9.
Markus, T. A., 1967, "The function of windows – a reappraisal," *Building Science*, Vol. 2,
  June.
Mayo, E., 1933, *The Human Problems of an Industrial Civilization*, Macmillan, New York.
Mayo, E., 1945, *The Social Problems of an Industrial Civilization*, Harvard University Press,
Cambridge, Mass.
Mayo, E., 1960, *The Human Problems of an Industrial Civilization*, paperback edition
  (Viking Press, New York), p. 54.
McGregor, Douglas, 1980, *The Human Side of Enterprise*, McGraw Hill Book Co.,
  New York.
Merton, R. K., 1948, "The social psychology of housing", in *Current Trends in Social
  Psychology*, Dennis. W., ed., University of Pittsburgh Press, Pittsburgh.
Michelson, W., 1970, *Man and His Urban Environment: a Sociological Approach*, Addison-
  Wesley, Reading, Mass.
Mills, C.W., 1951, *White Collar*, Oxford University Press, New York.
Moreno, J. L., 1934, "Who shall survive? A new approach to the problem of human inter-
  relations", Nervous and Mental Disease Monograph Series No. 458. Washington.
Morgan, W.T.W., 1960, *The Growth and Functions of the General Office District in the
  West End of London*, Ph. D. Thesis, North Western University, Evanston, Illinois.
Parsons, T., 1951, *The Social System*, Free Press, Glencoe, Illinois.

Pugh, D. S., Hickson, D. J., Hinings, C. R., Macdonald, K. M., Turner, C., Lupton, T., 1963, "A conceptual scheme for organizational analysis", *Administrative Science Quarterly*, 8 (3), 289–315.

Rapoport, A., 1969, *House Form and Culture*, Prentice-Hall, Englewood Cliffs, NJ.

Rhee, H. E., 1968, *Office Automation in Social Perspective*, Oxford, Basil Blackwell.

Robinson, A., 1962, *Working in the City*, City of London.

Roethlisberger, F. J. and Dickson, W. J., 1939, *Management and the Worker*, Harvard University Press, Cambridge (Mass.).

Saint, A., 1987, *Towards a Social Architecture: the Role of School Building in Post-War England*, Yale University Press. New Haven and London.

Saphier, M., 1968, *Office Planning and Design*, McGraw-Hill, New York.

Schnelle, 1971, *Kommunikation*, Zeitschrift für Planungs und Organisationskybernetic, Verlag Schnelle, Quickborn, from Vol. 1 1965–Vol. Vii 1971.

Schulze, J. W., 1914, *The American Office: Its Organization, Management and Records*, The Ronald Press, New York.

Schulze, J. W., 1919, *Office Administration*, McGraw-Hill, New York.

Scott Myers, M., 1964, "Who are your motivated workers?", *Harvard Business Review*, 42 (1), 73–88.

Seers, D., 1950, *The Levelling of Incomes Since 1938*, Blackwell, Oxford.

Silverman, D., 1970, *The Theory of Organizations*, Heinemann, London.

Sommer, R., 1959, "Studies in personal space", *Sociometry*, Vol. 22, Sept.

Sommer, R., 1962, "The distance for comfortable conversation", *Sociometry*, 25, 111–116.

Sommer, R., 1965, "Further studies of small group ecology", *Sociometry*, 28, 337-348.

Sommer, R., 1969, *Personal Space*, Prentice-Hall, Englewood Cliffs, NJ.

Sullivan, L., 1947, "The tall building artistically considered", from *Kindergarten Chats*, Wittenborn Schulz, New York (originally published 1896).

Tannenbaum, A. S., 1966, *Social Psychology of the Work Organization*, Wadsworth, Belmont, California.

Tennant, W. L., 1966, "Developing Design Criteria for Research", paper given at the 20th National Conference on the Administration of Research, Miami Beach, Florida, 1966 (mimeographed).

Terry, G. R., 1958, *Office Management and Control*, Irwin, Homewood, Illinois.

Thompson, E. W., 1906, *Bookkeeping by Machinery* (private publication by the author, New York).

Trist, E. L., and Bamforth, K. W., 1951, "Some social and psychological consequences of the long-wall method of coal-getting", *Human Relations* 4: 3–38, 1951.

Trist, E. L., Higgin, G. W., Murray, H. E., Pollock, A. B., 1963, *Organizational Choice: the Loss, Rediscovery and Transformation of a Work Tradition*, Tavistock, London.

Urwick, L., 1951, *The Elements of Administration*, Pitman, London.

Wells, B. W. P., 1965a, "Subjective responses to the lighting installation in a modern office building and their design implications", *Building Science*, Vol. 1, pp. 57–58.

Wells, B. W. P., 1965b, "The psycho-social influence of building environment: sociometric findings in large and small office spaces," *Building Science*, Vol. 1, pp. 153–165.

Whitehead, B. and Eldars, M. Z., "Approach to the optimum layout of single-storey buildings", *Architects' Journal*, 1964, June 17 pp. 1373–1830.

Woodward, J., 1965, *Industrial Organizational Theory and Practice*, Oxford University Press, London.

Wotton, H., 1624, *Elements of Architecture*.

Index